Motor Launches in Action

H.M.S. *VINDICTIVE* LEAVING DOVER HARBOUR WITH ATTENDANT M.L.S,
TO COMMIT HER GLORIOUS *FELO DE SE* AT OSTEND, MAY 9, 1918.

Motor Launches in Action

The Royal Navy's Small Submarine Hunters
During the First World War

ILLUSTRATED

The Motor Launch Patrol

Gordon S. Maxwell

and

Cinderellas of the Fleet (Extract)

William Washburn Nutting

LEONAUR

Motor Launches in Action
The Royal Navy's Small Submarine Hunters During the First World War
The Motor Launch Patrol
Gordon S. Maxwell
and
Cinderellas of the Fleet (Extract)
by William Washburn Nutting

ILLUSTRATED

FIRST EDITION IN THIS FORM

First published under the titles
The Motor Launch Patrol
and
Cinderellas of the Fleet (Extract)

Leonaur is an imprint of Oakpast Ltd
Copyright in this form © 2023 Oakpast Ltd

ISBN: 978-1-916535-48-0 (hardcover)
ISBN: 978-1-916535-49-7 (softcover)

http://www.leonaur.com

Publisher's Notes

The views expressed in this book are not necessarily
those of the publisher.

Contents

To All
My Fellow Officers and Men
Who Served on
H.M. Motor Launch Patrol
And to the Ever-Living Memory
Of Those Who Died That We Might
Carry on

Foreword

By Vice-Admiral Sir Roger Keyes

The operations on the Belgian coast between March and November 1918 gave the officers and men of the Royal Naval Volunteer Reserve in the motor launches opportunities of winning distinction and honour.

That these opportunities were seized is fully borne out in the pages of the *London Gazette,* which record the daring self-sacrifice and devotion to duty displayed by these gallant seamen, and made a tale of glorious enterprise which will live in the history of our Service.

At the Zeebrugge-Ostend raid the duty of making smoke-screens and laying smoke-floats was imposed on a large fleet of motor launches. Without the services of these little vessels for this duty, and for inshore work generally, an attack of this nature could hardly have been considered.

The rescue of the crews of the blockships by the motor launches, which had been standing by under heavy fire of every calibre, was carried out in the gallant manner which distinguished the work of the crews of the motor launches generally throughout the action. The zest of these officers and men compels one's admiration, and their conduct in this operation confirms the opinion I expressed of them in my despatches on previous occasions.

In *The Motor Launch Patrol* the author has dealt not only with the operations on the Belgian Coast, but with these boats generally in an entertaining way, which, combined with the realistic drawings that illustrate it, should make this book valuable historically not only to the Royal Naval Volunteer Reserve, but also to a wider public to whom the doings of this section of the "New Navy" that came into being under war-time conditions should make a strong appeal.

Roger Keyes

A Quebec Nocturne.
M.L.s awaiting shipment to England.

Prologue: The Building of the Ships

By Henry R. Sutphen

It was in February 1915 that we had our initial negotiations with the British Naval Authorities. A well-known English shipbuilder and ordnance expert was in New York, presumably on secret business of the Admiralty, and I met him one afternoon at his hotel. Naturally, the menace of the German submarine warfare came into discussion; we both agreed that the danger was a real one, and that steps should be taken to meet it.

I suggested the use of a number of small speedy motor launches for use in attacking and destroying submarines. My idea was to have a mosquito fleet big enough thoroughly to patrol the waters of Great Britain, each of them carrying a quick-firing gun. I said that my preference was for a type about 80 feet in length with a speed of some 19 knots. He asked how many units of this class we could build in a year, and I told him that I could guarantee fifty. He said he would think the matter over, and we parted.

Well, I had to think things over myself, and pretty carefully, too. Our yard, in addition to its smaller work, had been turning out perhaps half a dozen boats a year of the general dimensions that would meet the requirements. Now, very possibly, I might be called upon to build, say, eight times that number, and many factors had to be taken into account. Needless to say, I had no idea at the time of the truly tremendous task that lay before me. As I looked at it there was just one answer to the problem, and that was complete standardisation.

A few days later I had another interview, and was told that the British Government was ready to give us a contract for fifty vessels, the whole lot to be delivered in one year's time. Then arose the delicate question of how the job could be pushed through without embarrassing our own government, then maintaining its position of strict neutrality. Obviously, Canada offered a convenient field of operation,

11

and we went up to Montreal to investigate. We met and talked with several men in the shipbuilding line, but we could not seem to find any plant that would meet our requirements.

Then we heard of a small repair yard at Quebec, and we went over to see it. It looked pretty rough and badly appointed, and the grey, sullen surface of the river, filled with drifting ice, presented a most forbidding spectacle. But the owners of the yard showed a willingness to co-operate in every way; moreover, they assured us that the big spring tides would be of distinct advantage in the launching of the boats. And conditions in the labour market were satisfactory. The upshot of the business was that we took an option on the property, one more forward step.

On April 9, 1915, the contract for the fifty M.L.s—75-footers—was signed, and we went to work so diligently that by the first of May the master, or pattern boat, was in the frame at the Elco shipbuilding yard at Bayonne, New Jersey. It seemed to us like a big undertaking, but the real business had not even started.

The *Lusitania* sailed on her last voyage on May I, 1915, and a week later her torpedoing by a German U-boat was reported. My English friend was sailing that same day from New York, and he intimated to me when he received the news that he intended to advise the Admiralty to increase the number of "chasers" if I thought I could take a bigger order. I told him that I would guarantee to build a boat a day for so long a period as the Admiralty might care to name.

After we reached England, we shortly received a cablegram ordering 500 additional "Sutphens," our code word for submarine chasers: in other words, we were asked to build 550 of these boats and deliver them in complete running order by November 15, 1916. Taking out Sundays, this would give us an actual working schedule of 501 days. This meant pretty close figuring, but I was sure we could manage it.

On July 9, 1915, the new contract was signed, the 500 new boats to be 80-footers. Of course, we would now need to increase our Canadian assembling facilities, and we therefore leased a yard in Montreal and materially enlarged our original one at Quebec.

Once again, I must emphasise that the touchstone of our success was scientific standardisation. Our chief designer, Mr Irwin Chase, was quick to recognise this essential, as also were my other associates, Mr Thomas S. Hanson, general manager of the Bayonne plant, Mr E. B. Conrad, the purchasing engineer, and Mr Charles Lamont, the chief boat constructor. Of Mr Eugene A. Riotte of the Standard Motor

Construction Company, with whose engines the whole of the M.L.s were fitted, the same maybe said, and the whole success of our enterprise was dependent upon their brains and loyalty.

There is no room in this chapter to go into the details of materials used in the building of these boats, but it can be readily imagined how vast a task it was to work everything out on this hitherto unheard-of scale, when every mistake would be magnified five hundred and fifty times. There were stories of their own in all this work, and many an obstacle to be overcome before things ran smoothly. For instance, the foundries that ordinarily handled our orders for bronze castings for the quadrants and rudders could not turn out the quantity now required in the time, but the Tiffany studios, who had never before turned out any metal work save that of an ornamental and artistic nature, managed to do the job in the time, and do it well.

The bending of the frames, and indeed all of the fabrication work, was done at our Bayonne yard, the two Canadian plants being used only for assembling. Everything fabricated in Bayonne had to be absolutely correct in every detail; and the big pieces, such as the decking and keel frames, had to be kept within the railway clearances on both American and Canadian lines.

The men who put the boats together at Montreal and Quebec were ordinary woodworkers, with hardly a boat-builder among them; moreover, only three *per cent*, could speak English. And yet, under the direction of our experts from Bayonne, they did the final work of assembling with the greatest possible ease and despatch.

Every business enterprise has its moments of romance, and we got our thrills in the assembling work at the Canadian yards. In the first place, climatic conditions were not favourable. The average snowfall around Quebec runs from fifteen to eighteen feet, with temperature going as low as forty degrees below zero. We had to erect suitable buildings to protect our workmen against the biting winds, the snow, and the rain.

According to the terms of our contract, we were to make all deliveries at the launching slips in the St Lawrence River, and the Admiralty wanted as many boats as they could get before the close of navigation in late November. We gave them the first fifty, and then came the ice and stopped us. The Admiralty overseers suggested that boats might be shifted by rail and sent to Halifax, an open port, and tried out there during the winter months. We agreed to this, provided that the railway could handle the complete boat. Thereupon we constructed a skeleton model of an M.L. It looked very much like some extinct prehistoric monster, a mastodon or a "terrible lizard," and I have no doubt that more than one rural Canadian gentleman, after watching the train pass in the early twilight, was forthwith constrained to cut John Barleycorn's acquaintance. Talk of "seeing things by night"!

This fearsome "trial horse" was mounted on a lumber car and sent over the thousand-mile stretch of railway between Quebec and Halifax. In all, eighty-four boats were sent over the rail routes, shipments being discontinued in later February 1916.

The routine once established was vigorously maintained, each department concerning itself solely with keeping up its particular end. There were the draughtsman; the men who looked after the purchasing and ordering of material and supplies; the constructors at the Bayonne yard, intent upon keeping up their daily allotment of fabrication work; the railway "tracers," who followed up the car shipments through to destination; the erectors at the assembly yards; the launching organisation; the trial crews, who tested out the finished boats and remedied any slight defects that might appear; and finally, the British Government overseers keen to watch every step of the long process.

Once the boats were launched there were innumerable difficulties to be met and overcome. With the spring floods the great river was filled with driftwood, much of it waterlogged and, therefore, invisible. The testing of the engines was made with great care. Each boat was fitted with two 220 horse-power standard engines, which had to come up to certain definite standards in a special and rigorous trial.

After the trial the British overseers took formal delivery, then the M.L. was towed away to the storage basins. These had to be made large enough to accommodate a goodly number of boats, otherwise there might have been delay in loading the transports. Each ship carried four M.L.s, and in all a fleet of 130 transports was required to take over the 550 boats and the vast quantity of spares and standardised parts to England. Everyone arrived safely.

The Britisher always maintains his constitutional right to grumble, and at first there were many complaints of the cramped accommodation furnished for the two officers and eight men of the crew. But this now is ancient history, and the M.L.s have so distinctly made good that the carpers have been completely silenced; in fact, the crew are proud of their diminutive craft and of the work they can do.

In addition to those mentioned as materially assisting me in the construction of the Elco submarine chasers, I cannot close this chapter without reference to the loyal support, technical views, and administration services rendered by Mr P. L. Miller, the general manager of the Canadian Vickers Limited, Montreal, and Mr George Davie, general manager of the Davie Shipbuilding and Repairing Company Limited, of Quebec, both of whom rendered invaluable service in our great task. This task was really a challenge to us, and our answer was to build and equip 550 M.L.s in 488 days, an undertaking of which we naturally feel proud.

These, then, are the chief points of the early history of the motor launches with whose deeds in the war zone the author of this book has dealt in his vivid and spirited pages.

CHAPTER 1

Southampton

ON H.M.S. *HERMIONE*

"What time does the Salisbury train start, guard?"

"I'm sorry, madam, but I haven't the least idea."

"Then which platform is it?"

"I'm afraid I don't know that either, madam."

The elderly female who thus accosted me snorted "I think you're a very funny guard!"

"I think so too, madam, a very funny one."

"Now, no impudence, young man, or I shall report you," she retorted over her shoulder as she hurried off "I'll just ask the station master," she added, making for an admiral at full speed.

So, I can honestly say, by virtue of the above conversation, that my service career began at Waterloo. Lest, however, anyone should hesitate before putting me down as either a grand old veteran or a liar (or both!), I may add that I mean Waterloo Station, not the battlefield.

I was on my way to join the depot ship, and was wearing my uniform for the first time. My pride was rather hurt by this incident at the time, but on thinking this over, perhaps I ought to take it as a compliment that on my very first day I attained to something which seems inevitably associated with the career of every naval officer.

Since then, I have been asked on top of a 'bus to stop at Oxford Circus, and at the door of a tube lift have been solemnly handed a ticket by a lady (young), which I kept as a memento (the ticket, I mean, not the girl; unfortunately, there happened to be rather a crowd at the time, and I lost sight of her). Up to the present, however, I have not been asked what time the pictures start if I have been looking at the posters outside a "palace," though I live in hope.

Arrived at Southampton, I not unnaturally expected to find a ship of some sort, having been ordered by the Admiralty to report on H.M.S. *Resourceful*, but, like many others, I was doomed to disappointment. She had been burned out a month or so before, I found, and her relief had not yet arrived. It was quite dark when I got to the docks, which did not help matters, and after numerous inquiries managed to find a room in the basement of the Naval Transport Office which represented the ship. From there I was sent to the officer of the watch.

Those who have done duty at the "Bug Hut" will not need to be told where this was, but for the uninitiated I may mention that while there was no ship a shed was used as a watch-house, and it was to this that I had to find my way in the darkness. This was the first time I had ever been there in my life, and considering that there are about five hundred sheds in Southampton Docks, you can imagine the task. However, after a little wandering I met a policeman, who put me on the right tack.

On the subsequent hunt for a hotel, I need not dwell; everyone within a reasonable radius of the docks seemed to be full up; but I found a resting-place at last till 6 a.m. the next day. It was a miserable drizzling winter's morning when I turned out, and the drill-shed where we had to parade was, of course, at the very far end of the docks, where groups of men arrived in wet and muddy batches. I suppose everyone has felt the strangeness of their first parade, but everyone has not had such miserable conditions to damp their ardour. Real work, though, did not begin till later, and all we did before breakfast was to answer roll-call and be marched to the main dockyard gate and dismissed.

The feeling that was uppermost in the minds of nearly all during this training period was that it was like going to school over again, more especially noticeable at the navigation course which was held at an institute in the town in actual class-rooms. This, combined with a sense of utter ignorance during the first week of the various subjects, was, I think, felt by all. I know I felt the latter very strongly, and on comparing notes, in confidence, with several others, they confessed to the same state of mind. We were quite relieved to find that we were not the only ones who experienced this. For the first two weeks, before we began to think about the boats, our daily programme was:

7 a.m. Early morning parade and drill.
9.10 " Divisions.
Three-pounder gun—lecture and drill.
Maxim-gun.

Semaphore signalling.

2 p.m. Navigation and seamanship.

4 " Divisions.

5 " Morse signalling.

6 " Dismiss.

The first two weeks were certainly the worst, and after this time things began to get a bit easier and the corners of ignorance to be rubbed off a little. Remember that most of us had never seen, or at any rate examined, a naval gun before, and when the instructor held up a part of the mechanism of the three-pounder with the remark "This, gentlemen, is the 'ammer complete, but it ain't all 'ere," you will agree that there was certainly an air of mystery about things, till subsequent questioning and explanation elicited the fact that the "hammer complete" was the name of the part which held the firing-pin, but the particular one on this occasion happened to be a little faulty.

Maxim-guns at first tied us up in as much of a knot as we tied the cartridge belting—in all sorts of extraordinary and unexpected jambs. Semaphore we found, when we had once learned the alphabet, to be simply a matter of practice, and the same may be said of Morse (with a lamp, not flags) to a certain extent, although the latter is far harder to learn and far easier to forget. We worked hard; we had to, for we had to cram in a few weeks what *pukka* naval officers take a few years to learn.

At the end of the third week came the boat work, where some of us were more at home and did not feel such hopeless amateurs, though others—— But no, I will not give anyone away, even anonymously. I am speaking now of the days when M.L.s were merely rumours; we had heard of them, and that was all. We were then known as the R.N. Motor Boat Reserve. The boats we had to work on then were of all shapes and sizes, and our duties were varied: duty boats, patrol, emergency (which usually meant hanging about doing nothing"), and pilot boats. The last-named work was by far the best, from our point of view, and everyone, I think, looks back with pleasure on the days when they were attached to the pilot cutter *Jessica* and the merry parties aboard that trim, comfortable little craft. The pilots were good fellows and made us welcome. I was always sorry when that twenty-four-hour duty was over.

Minor excitements in our life were many, such as engine troubles, occasional sojourns on mudbanks, watching over-enthusiastic navigators ram the dolphins or climb No. 37 steps in a motorboat. We all

Breaking Dawn. H.M.S. *Hermione*, parent ship of the M.L.s at Southampton

remember "the hero of 37 steps," surely? The chief excitement during this time, though, was the arrival of H.M.S. *Hermione*, the old cruiser which was to be our "mother" ship in future. We had all heard rumours regarding her arrival, of course, but nothing definite was known, amongst us at least; some even held her to be a myth which would never materialise, and I remember how we first heard real information about her. A motor-boat dashed in from patrol with the news that she was on her way and had been actually seen—something after the fashion of the merchant ship Macaulay tells us first brought the news of the approach of the Spanish Armada.

It was about the chilly close of a cold winter's day,
There came a gallant motor-boat full speed from Calshot Bay;
Her crew hath seen Hermione beyond the Isle of Wight,
'Ere dawn Southampton Water too would view the goodly sight.

We were not exactly playing bowls at the time, nor did any beacon fires blaze forth from the top of the Hartley Institute and so on across Hampshire; the only beacons were our Morse lamps which flashed the news across the shed (we were in the middle of a Morse class), to be indifferently read by those at the other end. Sure enough, the next morning she was lying off the docks waiting to berth.

She was a good old ship, but had been out of commission for some time, I believe, or used as a prison ship, or something of that sort, and the men dubbed her the "Vermy one," and not without living reason, till she was fumigated and burnished up, for when she arrived, she was certainly not quite as immaculate as she might have been. The disposal of the officers' cabins during the first few days of muddle, before things got straightened out a bit, was of the nature of a game of general post. Only those on boat duty were supposed to sleep on board, which meant about ten spare cabins to about twenty men.

If you found a vacant one you commandeered it at once and asked no questions; but the chances were that if you went to it the next night you would find that another had nine points of the law against you, so all you did was to annex the nearest vacant one, regardless of any prior claim. This sort of thing came to be the unwritten law among us and was taken in a sporting spirit. The "overs" slept (or didn't) on the seats in the gun-room.

Getting the mail on the *Hermione* had an excitement of its own. At post-time the steward would put the letters in the gun-room, an apartment holding about twenty at the most with any degree of comfort. Into this immediately crowded some eighty men, all trying to get at the letter-rack at once; it was like a glorified rugger-scrum. Things naturally got a little better later on, but the first week on the *Hermione* was certainly a unique experience.

It was inevitable that the R.N.M.B.R. should have a nickname, and we soon got it—Harry Tate's Navy—though I am uncertain if this arose through our inexperience in those times or from the heterogeneous nature of a little fleet attached to the training centre. Perhaps it was both. Some people used to get annoyed at this name, I don't know why, for I think I heard it used more among ourselves than anywhere; though anyone who uses this name in a disparaging sense only shows his ignorance, for at various naval bases scattered round the coast there was a lot of real hard work done by these little motor-boats, forerunners of the M.L.

Some well-known author, Pliny, I think, has said that he would not trust anyone who was incapable of laughing at himself. We laughed at ourselves often then, I can tell you. Possibly this was why the Powers That Be trusted us with better boats later. It was this laughter, I think, that helped us along in those early days.

Chapter 2

"Pompey"

1

In the mind of a naval man the word "Pompey" does not conjure up visions of Imperial Rome, for it is merely the name by which Portsmouth is known in the service, though the derivation of this example of nomenclature seems lost in the mists of the past.

"Pompey" is more truly the sailor's home than any port in the world, for to this south-coast town we all were bound to come sooner or later, and generally a good many times, especially in the early days of M.L.s. Wherever we may have been, north, south, east, or west, it seemed inevitable that just as we got used to our patrol we got the well-known form from the Admiralty calling us back to Portsmouth, to roam once again in the wilds of the dockyard.

These sort of things we got used to, and of our life in the dock-yard I shall speak in another place; just now I want you to think of an R.N.V.R. officer's first arrival in Portsmouth.

Your form tells you that you are attached to H.M.S. *Victory*, but of course this is purely nominal, and in reality it is the last place you go to (unless you visit it privately on your own account); you see it, and that is all. You are told to report at the Royal Naval Barracks, and in the innocence of your heart you imagine that when you arrive here, after a long and tedious journey, your wanderings are over. By no means, they are only beginning. The hall porter, one of the most important men in the barracks, is very polite, but he knows nothing whatever about you; his mind is a complete blank as to your past or future history. He suggests that you try the Gunnery Office, and points it out to you across the road.

Leaving your luggage in the hall, you set out for the Gunnery Office, and, after going to about six wrong rooms, you find it. Here they are very busy, and, after being passed from Writer to Writer, you at last find one who suggests that you should visit the Flag Captain's Office in the dockyard, as they (the Gunnery Office) have no instructions whatever regarding you. There is no help for it, and you set out again, after listening to complete and intricate instructions from the writer as to how to reach your new destination, every bit of which you forget the moment you leave the office. It is fairly easy to find the dockyard—even a German spy would have no difficulty in doing that; but once in it your real troubles begin.

Vainly you try and recall the directions, but you might as well try and remember a passage from Xenophon for all the good it is to you, for Portsmouth dockyard, however well you may subsequently get to know it, is a bewildering place to find your way in at the first visit. It is, of course, only in the natural order of things that fate should bid you enter by the gate the farthest away from your objective, and the policeman on duty clearly thinks you are mad to want to go this way to the flag captain's office; but he directs you, and you go on filled with new hope.

This soon dies, for you are hot, dirty, and tired, and you wander round locks, across caissons and by engineering shops, but not a sign of anything approaching a flag captain's office can you see. It is seldom any use asking a dockyard "matey" the way, for he won't know, and you must wait till you see someone in uniform to be put on the right road. Well, you do manage to find the place at last, but as you have been so long on your travels, and it is now late afternoon, you find that everyone in authority has gone, and the very junior writer who is still left to run this department of the war is, of course, in complete ignorance about you, but *thinks* the Mail Office *might* know something of you, and offers to show you where it is.

This offer you accept without enthusiasm, with horrible visions of again tramping the dirty and obstacle-ridden pathways of the dockyard. But you are agreeably surprised this time to find it is in the same building. Here you certainly do get a little light, for you find that instructions have been received for any letters for you to be sent to H.M.S. *Redoubtable*. Though letting a glimmer into the darkness, it also raises new conjectures in your mind as to why you are being put on a battleship. Have they made a mistake or mixed you up with another man?

Still, though you have found out this much, you have no real instructions, nor have you yet reported to anyone in authority. The

Writer at the Mail Office is sympathetic but not helpful, and can only suggest that you return to the barracks, as he has no orders at all to send you to the ship. This seems the only thing to be done, and after more weary walking you come to a gateway. You have not the least idea if this is anywhere near the barracks, but it will lead you out of the dockyard, and for the moment that is all you care about. It happens that you have come out of the main gate by the Hard, which is the farthest gate of all away from where you want to go, but after wandering up several small and very dirty back streets you arrive at the place you are seeking.

This time a different hall porter is on duty, to whom you relate your troubles. He remembers to have seen a list somewhere or other concerning the destination of R. N.V.R. officers (in *this* world, I mean, of course; on the other point the naval authorities do not commit themselves), and after much burrowing among papers, he discovers it in an odd corner. This confirms what you heard—you are on the *Redoubtable*. You now get him to ring up for a taxi and collect your traps and set off, and after what seems an interminable drive through the dockyard (they invariably take newly arrived officers the longest way round) you arrive at the *Asia* Pontoon. Here you have a restful half-hour waiting for the duty boat (for as yet you are ignorant of the telephone hut nearby, the only hope of those who miss the last boat), and eventually you get on board utterly fagged out but glad to have a deck over your head at last.

Dinner is of course over, but you are thankful for some cold meat, bread, and cheese, with a cup of coffee a steward manages to procure for you. You find several men whom you were with at Southampton on board, and on comparing notes you find they have all had more or less the same difficulties you have had in getting here. But you are there now, and it is with a feeling of contentment that you sit and smoke in the wardroom and talk of the various jobs you have been on since you were on the *Hermione* together. One by one men slip off to their cabins, and soon you follow their example, tired out and glad to turn in to dream of what is in store for you in your new course.

2

Our first course—we were known as K class—was a week on H.M.S. *Vernon*, lying in Portsmouth harbour, one of the old "wooden walls" now used, with some other old ships, as a torpedo school. Here we studied explosives, at first by means of lectures, illustrated with diagrams, and learned all the mysteries of depth-charges, lance-bombs, detonators, and indicator nets, all devices for strafing the *Untersee-booten*, and later by going out to Great Horsea Island and seeing practical experiments in land and under-water explosives. This certainly woke us up as much as the lectures lulled us; I don't think I have ever had a greater struggle to keep awake than at some of those afternoon lectures on the *Vernon*. There seemed to be some sort of soporific about the old timbers of the class-cabin, for I was not the only one who fought this fight on those hot June days; in fact, one or two surrendered against overwhelming odds.

The lecturer certainly did his best to keep us awake, for he would sometimes take a piece of T. N.T. and hold it before our blinking eyes and tell us that there was enough there to blow up the Houses of Parliament. This would arouse faint interest in our breasts, but when he dropped this, banned it with a hammer, or set it on fire with a match, we stirred ourselves at once, wondering at the chances of waking up in another world. But then he would go on to explain the proper application for the operation mentioned, and tell us that under certain conditions you could build a house of T.N.T. A handy sort of shelter during an air raid, I should imagine.

The *Vernon* is a fine old ship and most interesting to be on, as, besides its age and construction, it contains many pictures and books of interest in the smoking-room, as well as various relics. It is a hospitable ship too, and lunch in the old messroom—a fine low-ceilinged timbered place the breadth of the ship and capable of seating about three hundred—is a most pleasant function.

At the end of the week, we sat for our exam: not without fear, some of us, that we should not do very brilliantly on account of our divided attention at the lectures. The paper, however, was a fairly easy one, at least to K class! It is perhaps hardly necessary to mention that this famous class was by far the smartest that ever took the "Pompey" course, in spite of what you may hear from envious rivals. We all discoursed learnedly on explosives for a couple of hours, drew weird and wonderful diagrams, and gave in our papers, and went out trusting to luck.

3

The engineering course was held on H.M.S. *Fisgard*, and it was here that fate led us for the next week. The *Fisgard* is really four ships, but (except one) nothing like as old as the *Vernon*, and quite uninteresting—that is to anyone other than an enthusiastic engineer. Very few of us (if any) enjoyed this week on the *Fisgard*; it is a miserable, dirty place and a complete contrast to the *Vernon*. At the latter we were comfortable, and at the former very far from it—nothing but oil and noise. Here was no pleasant mess or smoking-room for the midday rest; in fact, to be quite frank, there was rather an uncomfortable feeling about that we were not wanted. Perhaps we were not. So instead of lunching aboard we made our way by the long narrow wooden bridge to the shore, where at Hardway village we found a little inn. A scratch lunch, with a piano which cheered us up. Back again to more lectures and demonstrations, the latter consisting of all crowding round an engine and those in front seeing it stripped.

Then at the end of the week came the exam. When he saw the paper, a certain officer—who shall be as nameless as shameless—saw that to state all he knew about the questions before him would not take very long, and, having still enough decent feeling left in him (in spite of subsequent acts) to realise that idleness is a vice to be fought against, rather than sin by sitting still or pretending to answer questions (which would have caused him to commit the sin of deception), this exemplary young man worked hard during the exam., though not at engineering.

Before I say how he was occupied during this time, it will be necessary to mention that it was given out during this course (merely as "frightfulness," it transpired later on) that if any officer failed in his engineering exam., his seniority would be put forward by two months. Seniority, it may be explained for the benefit of the lay reader, is dated from the time of the commission being granted, and all promotions are governed by this date as a basis. Now as this unfortunate officer gazed at his scanty answers this fact came back to him with horrible vividness, and he pictured the months and months he seemed fated to be losing. Then an idea occurred to him: this might possibly be the making of his naval career instead of his undoing.

Every soldier, we are told, carries a field-marshal's baton in his haversack, and I suppose, on the same reasoning, every sailor carries an admiral's broom, marlinespike, or whatever the naval equivalent is, in his kit-bag. This might be one way of winning it. So, he composed some verses entitled "*How to Become an Admiral*," and these he pinned to his answers and sent them in with the paper. (The verses referred to in this chapter are contained in *The Rhymes of a Motor Launch*.) It was a sporting chance. If the examiner had a sense of humour he would take it in good part, if he had not, the author of the lines would be badly strafed.

Up to the time of writing the admiral's commission is still on its way; but the sequel came the next day, when the sub was sent for and told that the commander who corrected the papers wanted to see him. With fear and trembling the wretched sub went into the office, expecting at least instant dismissal from the service for his crime. What followed can best be described in dialogue:

The Brass Hat (*sitting at a desk with the offending verses in front of him*): "Did you write these?"

The Sub (*gloomily*): "Yes, sir."

The Brass Hat (*sternly*): "In the examination time?"

The Sub (*hopelessly*): "Yes, sir."

The Brass Hat (*still more sternly*): "And you pinned them to your paper?"

The Sub (*expecting nothing short of being told he was to be shot at dawn*): "Yes, sir."

The Brass Hat (*smiling*): "Then would you mind signing them for me." I should like to keep them."

The Sub (*bursting into tears of mingled relief and remorse*): "Yes, sir."

4

The fond aunt who, when she heard that her nephew had been appointed to H.M.S. *Excellent*, wrote to him saying she hoped he would not be sea-sick this terrible weather and that the ship would not be wrecked during any of the winter gales, had rather a shock when she heard that her dear nephew was safely living in comfort at the officers' quarters, brick-built and on dry land. This was true, nevertheless, and today it seems almost redundant to say that though H.M.S. *Excellent* is certainly surrounded by water, this is the only resemblance it has to a ship, for it is really Whale Island, the most famous gunnery school in the world. It was this place that was to be the scene of our labours for the next week.

There is something in the air of Whale Island that is quite different from the rest of Portsmouth. To begin with, the discipline is doubly strict, and a splendid thing, too, for a week on Whale Island will give you more sense of belonging to the Navy than a month anywhere else. There is no walking, or very little, on Whale Island, it is all marching, and as soon as a party, either officers or men, is landed in the morning it is formed up into fours and marched off to the large drill-shed. Here prayers are read, and after this the various classes march off to their respective stations for the day to the music of the band.

Our course here was very thorough and consisted of thirteen-pounder gun drill, rifle and revolver instruction and firing, range-finding, and miniature moving-target firing. For rifle and revolver instruction, which we did first, we remained in the drill-shed for stripping, and then marched to the revolver range for firing. The noise here was indescribable, as it was a long shed with a corrugated iron roof which echoed like a thunder-clap to the crack of the Scot-Webly revolver or the still more noisy automatic pistol. The rifle-range was on the mainland near, to which we were marched. It nearly always rained when we went to this range, which made lying on your stomach on wet stones a particularly cheerful occupation.

Our main business at Whale Island, however, was connected with the thirteen-pounder. The chief part of this took place at the West Battery, where we were marched through the main doorway with its lion and the famous Whale Island motto. *Si vis pacem, para bellum* (If you wish for peace, prepare for war). Here we took our coats off, literally as well as metaphorically, for it was the middle of a hot June, and worked like Trojans at gun drill and stripping, especially drill. Few of us will forget quickly those strenuous days at "Whaley," and how we worked at that gun. It was a most interesting course, though, and one we should have all been sorry to miss.

On some days we marched to the North Battery and had practice at moving targets. These were ships in miniature and ingeniously moved to represent the action of the sea, and while the gun-layer and the trainer got "on" the little ship through the telescopic sights the former fired, the shot coming from the sub-calibre aiming tube on the top of the large gun, and the position of the hits (or misses) was registered on a target. We also had practice in night-sighting, which took place in a darkened shed, the little ship being illuminated by a miniature searchlight worked from behind the gun by a man whose duty it was to keep the object in sight as it moved.

Another ingenious device was a gun which, when fired, marked your shot on a card with a pencil so that you could tell what part of the ship you had hit, or by how much you had missed; but I think the smartest of all was the range-finding machine. Here you "fired" at a little moving ship down a long tube by means of touching buttons for different ranges, when pieces of cotton wool bobbed up and showed you the exact position in which your shot would have gone, short or over. At a direct hit, of course, the ship fell over as the pad of wool came up right underneath it.

But all roads at Whale Island, for us at least, seemed to lead to the West Battery, and here we spent most of our time in those hot hours of summer at very strenuous three-pounder drill. When the G.I. yelled out "On the beam—a submarine—two thousand—ten right!" we set our range and deflection with feverish haste and trained our gun at a harmless flower-bed or the clock tower, and proceeded to pour round after round of imaginary shells into it with horrible vindictiveness. The only casualty was when the loader dropped a dummy (full weight) shell on to the toe of the breach-worker, when the latter would consign the former to the place to which we were supposed to be blowing the enemy, and dance about the gun like Charlie Chaplin going round a corner. On the whole, I think we all enjoyed our time at Whale Island (except for a few minutes if you happened to be the unfortunate individual mentioned above), and they are as hospitable as the *Vernon* as regards the mess. There is a very good library at Whale Island, and whoever chose the volumes certainly showed a catholic taste in literature.

From the island there can be seen (when the tide is up) what I think is the finest view in Portsmouth. This we used to see framed by the large open windows of the West Battery. As a foreground there is the large expanse of water washing the walls of the ancient ruin of Porchester Castle, a most venerable pile, in the middle distance, and as a background there is Portsdown Hill. On a sunny morning this view wants a lot of beating in any part of England, and to an imaginative mind conjures up endless visions of Saxon, Roman, and mediaeval times.

It is perhaps fitting that the best view of Porchester ruins can be obtained from here, for it played, indirectly, an important part in the Island's history. The last time the castle was ever used was to lodge French prisoners in at the time of the Napoleonic wars. These men were set to work to build the docks, or to improve the existing ones, and the soil thus excavated was dumped on a sandbank in the harbour, and so, literally, from the womb of Mother Earth was Whale Island born.

But to come back to the gun. After a week we had an exam, in drill and stripping. Now it is an extraordinary thing, but it seems to be an immutable law of human nature in a test of this kind, that you always know the question or portion of the drill that the man on either side of you gets, but you always forget the part you get yourself. This happened to nearly every one; when it was not our turn we burned with

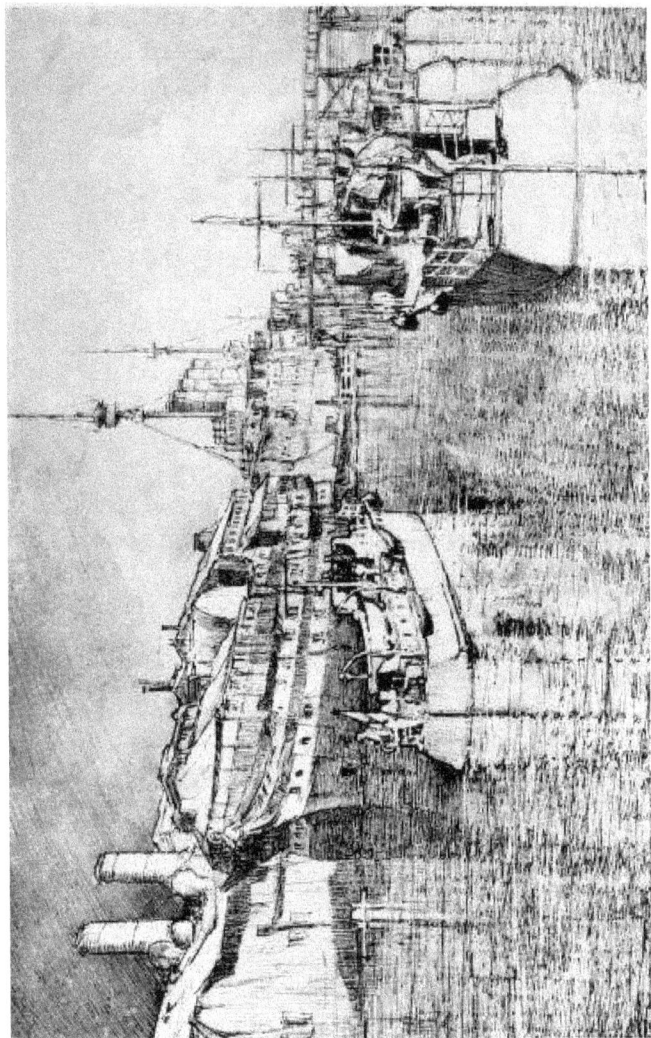

A Century of Progress M.L.s off H.M.S. Fisgard, at Portsmouth

eagerness, but this enthusiasm seemed to fade when we were called upon. Though it is painful to have to own it, truth compels me to say that at this first exam. "K"class did not cover itself with glory, though in justice to it it is only fair to say that on inquiry we found the other classes were no better, some even worse.

The result of the exam, was not made known the same day, and, though most of us guessed it, we had no official notification till two days had passed. Then we found that only three had scraped through— more by luck than anything else.

This meant another week at Whale Island. Knowing the discipline there, we wondered what was in store for us when we went back as "naughty boys." To make this illusion more complete, we were to be confined to the ship during the coming week in the evenings. Just like being "gated" at school. This idea was to "allow" time for extra study and drill, though how the authorities imagined we were going to do this without a gun I'm not quite clear, for there was no thirteen-pounder on the *Redoubtable* as far as we knew. Perhaps they meant us to use the wardroom sofa and supply the deficiencies with our imaginations. The "side" of the three who (by pure luck) had passed out was terrible: they tried all sorts of "frightfulness" in the way of stories of the gruelling we were going to get during the next week, and shed crocodile tears over the state we should be in by the end of the time. They were also most lavish in offering us entertainment in the way of dinners ashore and theatres during the evenings of the ensuing week.

The same shameless sub who had committed the sacrilege of writing verses in his engineering exam, paper, and who was one of the victims in the present instance, was again driven to verse (almost as bad as being driven to drink, according to some people), and voice the prevailing opinions in another classic epic called "*Wail Island*" to immortalise this tragedy in British naval annals.

Up to the time of writing, however, the Admiralty charts still bear the old name; the authorities are very slow to move in some things.

I will not dwell too much on the week that followed. We felt that in our hands lay the honour of "K"class, and set our teeth accordingly. Never, I think, has the West Battery witnessed anything more stirring. We worked, if not from dewy morn to eve, at least something very like it. The greatest trial we had was one evening when some unfeeling people were playing cricket just outside the window! Then came the fresh exam; but we were ready for the ordeal, and when the results came out all the world knew that "K" class had "made good."

The next two weeks were spent at the R.N. Barracks in seamanship and signalling. The former included rules of the road, lights, buoys, anchors and chains, and bends and hitches (known to humourists as hens and bitches). The signalling was chiefly semaphore, with lectures on flag hoists. Two weeks of good hard work, with nothing special to write about, however, but extremely useful to us.

During the whole of the course we attended twice a week at the Navigation School in the dockyard for classes. This, again, does not call for much description, but one regrettable incident cannot be passed over without comment. Before I relate this, another word of explanation will be necessary. It happened that on several occasions the instructor, when giving us examples of tides to work out, chose that at Singapore as an instance. This occurred so frequently that it became a byword that whenever a man could not answer a question, whether it was on tides or courses, as long as he managed to drag in something about the tide at Singapore it would be all right. Of course, it was about the last place on earth (or sea) an M.L. would be likely to go, but it was comforting for us to feel that if we had completely lost our bearings and were fast drifting on to a lee shore in the Hebrides, we at least knew what the tide was doing at Singapore about this time; it was likely to be so helpful.

The navigation exam, was in two parts on separate days. The first paper was on tides and the second on chart work, and it was at the former that the regrettable incident previously mentioned occurred. The shameless sub was, I am sorry to say, again the villain of the piece. He finished his paper fairly early. He had done moderately well— enough to pass, it transpired subsequently—but all the time he had difficulty in trying not to think of a special tide and comparing his answers with it. This, combined with a certain drowsiness, for it was a very hot evening, and the same praiseworthy wish to keep from the sin of sloth he had felt on a previous occasion, were responsible for the writing of some verses, "*The Tide at Singapore,*" which he again sent in with his paper.

It says much for the sense of humour and the sporting instincts of the examiners on these two occasions that the sub was not badly strafed, but he was not; perhaps that special Providence which we are told looks after children, fools, and drunkards, included him under one of these heads. I will not commit myself as to stating which of the last two is most likely to be true.

★★★★★★★★★★★★★★★★★★

Our course was now ended, and "K" class was told that all it had to do now was to wait for their M.L.s. Simple souls, they imagined they would soon be at sea, and that all would be plain sailing till they got there. Their innocence was touching, as the next few pages will show.

7

Commissioning an M.L. begins with a sort of game of hide-and-seek. You learn to which number you are appointed from the Flag Captain's Office. That is the first move. The second is reminiscent of the famous recipe for jugged hare—"First catch your hare,"—only in this case it is "First find your ship." No one seems to know exactly where it is (or the one who *has* definite information is at lunch, or something like that). All you are told is that it *may* be at any of the following places scattered over Portsmouth:—

The Pocket,
Lock B,
The Tidal Basin,
On a Transport,
At Floating Dock Jetty,
At Camper and Nicholson's Yard,
At Crampton's Yard,
At Vosper's Yard,
At Bevis's Yard.

This meant either coming back again when the lunching gentleman had returned (though he would probably be at tea by then) or going on a lengthy tour of inspection. Well, I will not go into details of how you find it—it would be too tedious; but, with the help of other rovers who had seen or heard of your boat, you do at last.

Wherever you found it, it always came to Lock B eventually, its last resting-place before the actual commissioning. Lock B is a large lock and capable of holding some thirty M.L.s or so, if closely packed, as it generally was at the time of which I am writing. The method employed in getting an M.L. out of Lock B seemed to be worked on the principle of the man who went into a post-office and asked for a halfpenny stamp, and when the girl produced a sheet of them pointed to one in the middle and said, "I think I'll take that one, please."

It invariably seemed to be the M.L. in the very middle that was wanted, which meant much shoving and warping and more language than either. I have heard enough strong language in Lock B which, if compressed, would run an M.L. for a year. In fact, someone suggested that owing to the danger to our moral characters on these occasions a special verse of the well-known hymn should be written, "For those in peril in Lock B." However, you eventually did manage to wriggle out, and a tug towed you to Fort Blockhouse for petrol and then back to the Tidal Basin.

Here the real commissioning begins, which is merely placing on board everything that a sea-going ship needs and a lot more that she doesn't. I use the word "placing," although the general appearance of the foredeck after a couple of hours is as if a giant grapnel had made a collection from various departments of dockyard stores and then dumped the whole lot pell-mell on to the deck of an M.L. It is perhaps unnecessary to add that you sign enough forms during this time to paper a suite of rooms. As the day wears on you wear out and sign anything that is brought to you in a dazed sort of way. For all I know, I may have signed a contract agreeing to keep all my crew in beer and baccy for the rest of their natural lives, though up to the present none has shown any signs of being aware of it.

This sort of thing goes on for about two days, and by the end of the third most of the various articles have been stowed away or apportioned to their proper places on board. So, in a sentence I dismiss what were, perhaps, the most strenuous days in all the history of our M.L.

The next thing is, where are you going? Everyone's nightmare at this time is Scapa Flow, but you are kept in ignorance of your new base until just before you sail. Of course, there is always the sense of rumour to help you, and this sense is very strong just now, though seldom (if ever) correct. Then we all know "the man who has seen lists" and says he knows exactly where each M.L. is going. He is, naturally, the least reliable source of all.

However, conjecture is useless; the only way is to wait for your sailing orders. This came at last, and we set off in "flotillas" of anything from two to ten boats for all bases scattered round the British Isles.

CHAPTER 3

The Tradition of Portsmouth

The average Englishman is a far more sentimental being than he will own, especially if he is a thinking man. But even a thoughtless man will at times be suddenly moved. If detected while displaying any sign of this emotion he will feel like a guilty schoolboy, and often go to the other extreme in his conversation to prove that he really doesn't care a jot for the sentimental side of life, and will call anyone a fool who does. He has, quite rightly, a horror of maudlin sentiment, and rather than come within the shadow of this he will pose as a gross materialist and vote all sentiment fit only for gushing schoolgirls. All the same, in nine cases out of ten he is a sentimentalist at heart.

After all, what is sentiment? Isn't it something which really governs the world under different names? We may call it patriotism, honour, tradition, or half a dozen other things, but even to a moderately analytical mind it all comes back to the same point.

Let us call it tradition, then, and in Portsmouth the sense of tradition is as strong as anywhere in the world. As R.N.V.R. officers in training for the M.L.s, I think we all felt it—that we had the whole glorious tradition (or sentiment) of the British Navy behind us, with its time-honoured customs. Why do we salute the quarter-deck when going on a ship? There is no longer a crucifix before us as in Elizabethan days, but though this has long disappeared we still keep up the custom, except that we salute instead of crossing ourselves. Why does a ship carry a long pendant at the masthead like a ribbon?

Simply in memory of Blake's whip, known to most through the medium of a song. Why, on certain occasions, do we drink a silent toast to the memory of Nelson? Why do sailors still wear a black scarf in perpetual mourning for him, and have three white stripes round their collars to commemorate his three great battles? In fact, why do sailors wear the broad collar at all save as a sentimental survival of the days when it was necessary to protect the cloth from the tarred pigtail? Why do we salute when a funeral passes? Purely sentiment, after all; and at Portsmouth it is impossible to escape from it.

It is partly the mingling of ancient and modern that brings this sense of tradition home to us here. We feel it when we go from a modern battleship on to the *Vernon*, one of the old "wooden walls"; and when on the *Excellent* we feel it in the strictness of the discipline there. The figure-heads scattered about the dockyard are constant reminders, and the naval museum, small but intensely interesting, contains relics that make a man's imagination run away with him.

To go on quoting cases is needless, they are everywhere; but the one great instance I have kept to the last, for it is the supreme one. I mean the *Victory*; surely the last word in naval tradition. You feel its influence as soon as you go on board, and realise that you are on the most famous ship in the world and one that has made history. When you go up to the quarter-deck and stand on the spot where Nelson fell, shot from the masthead of the *Redoutable*, mental pictures crowd fast upon you; you see the great little man, maimed and scarred in England's wars, standing calm amidst the turmoil directing the action. You see him in full uniform with all his medals, a conspicuous figure for enemy sharpshooters, for he would never disguise himself in any way for his own safety.

Around him the scene is almost indescribable: all the bloody horrors of battle; yelling men with tarred pig-tails, half-naked and begrimed with powder, rush past him on their various duties; the dead and dying are at his very feet, and over all a pall of smoke is hanging, broken here and there by bursts of flame from the muzzles of the guns. The noise is awful: shouts and groans from men and roar of guns below, with the sharp crack of muskets from the mastheads, the rending crash as solid shot tears its way between decks with red death in its train.

On both sides are enemy ships, and broadside after broadside is poured into them by the English gunners, for in the heat of the fight the *Victory* is engaged on both beams and her guns are never silent, as soon as they can be loaded or the dead men replaced, a fresh hail of iron and lead is crashing into the foe. And amidst all this The Little Admiral stands, taking in more with his one eye than most men would with six.

When the action is at its hottest the great tragedy comes. Nelson is seen to clutch his breast and stagger; one of his officers dashes forward and catches him in his arms as he falls, but the crimson stain on the Admiral's breast has told its fatal tale. Gently and reverently, strong arms take him up and bear him to the cockpit. As he passes the steersman Nelson gives an order to the man; dying as he is, the welfare of his vessel is never out of Nelson's mind; life is dear, but his ship is dearer.

Down in the cockpit the scene is even worse than on deck, and one word only can describe it—hell. It is below the water-line and but dimly lit with candles. Here, in this confined space, are some hundred and fifty wounded men; curses and groans rend the air, and shrieks of strong men in agony rise above the general clamour. Surgeons are busy binding up wounds and amputating limbs; no anaesthetics are known, and men must bear it as best they can. The limb off, it is hastily placed in a drawer of sawdust for the time, and the stump is smeared with boiling pitch to prevent the patient bleeding to death, then a rough binding put round, and the surgeon passes on to the next case. The smell of blood is sickening in this close atmosphere, and a more awful spot in this world could scarcely be imagined.

It is to this place, then, that the stricken admiral is borne, and they lay him in one corner on a mattress and prop him up with pillows. The best surgeons are hastily summoned, who cut away his uniform, and do their best to dress the wound through which the life-blood is fast ebbing. But all is in vain, and the hero is beyond human aid, and knows it himself. He bids those around him be of good cheer, and then, turning to his captain, he says, "Kiss me, Hardy." The tall sailor (he was six-foot-three) bends over the little recumbent body, and, with eyes filled with tears, kisses his leader on the brow as tenderly as a mother might kiss her child.

And so, in this awful inferno, the great soul of this little man passes to eternity, amidst the groans of the wounded and the roar of battle sounding dimly from above.

★★★★★★★★★★★★★★★★

The voice of the marine guide, with its mechanical intonation, came to me as from another world, for my mind had slipped back some hundred odd years, and I stood among the silent crowd around the dying hero, and, as if in a vision, the ghosts of the past became alive again, and I saw every detail of the great tragedy once enacted on this spot. So vivid was my dream that I could almost hear the cries of the stricken men. It was all terribly real. Slowly the vision faded, and I was back again in the present, leaning forward clutching the rail and staring at the corner of the cockpit, empty save for a few faded wreaths, at the painted words "Here Nelson died." The guide looked at me curiously, but he said nothing, as for a moment I stood to attention and saluted.

Then I turned away and left the cockpit without speaking—the tradition of Portsmouth is best felt in silence.

THE LONG NIGHT

CHAPTER 4

On Patrol

1: THE SERIOUS SIDE

There seems to be among some people an idea that life on patrol in the R.N.V.R. is a sort of glorified yachting holiday. The kind of people who think this are invariably those who know the least about it, and therefore, with the dogmatism of ignorance, say the most. I doubt if one of them could tell you offhand the difference between a binnacle and a barnacle, or a fairlead and a fairway; and they would have as much chance of success if they tried to box Carpentier as if they attempted to box the compass.

Of course, on the other hand, there are a few dear simple souls who imagine that we spend our lives with submarines popping up all around us like a school of porpoises, and that all we have to do is merely to round them up something after the fashion of a sheep-dog tending his flock. It would be difficult to say which opinion is the more incorrect. Nor are these erroneous ideas always confined to gossip; they find their way into print quite frequently. I remember reading one delightfully humorous—unconsciously so, of course—article in a newspaper on the work of the motor launch patrol, crammed with impossibilities; but the gem of them all was the statement that M.L.s always went out on patrol about twenty at a time, accompanied by a "mother" ship, usually a cruiser!

The latter, it went on to say, would remain in the centre of a seven-mile circle with the launches cruising round her, and (at the distance of seven miles) each M.L. kept in touch by *flag signals* with the "mother" ship the whole time! When it is considered that the size of the average M.L. flag is 32 inches by 23, it will be seen what eagle-eyed beings we are!—though I think a man with such a range of vision is wasted on an M.L; the sort of job *he* ought to have would be as assistant to the Recording Angel, when he could sit on a cloud "hard by heaven" with a pair of binoculars and a notebook, and watch the doings of mere mortals on the earth beneath.

For the benefit of those not acquainted with M.L.s, a few descriptive lines may not be out of place here of these little grey ships which patrolled out of almost every port in Great Britain and the Mediterranean. Eighty feet in length, with a twelve-foot beam, they are capable of a speed of over twenty knots, and carry two officers and eight men. Their shallow draught is a great asset, for not only does it render them more or less immune from a torpedo attack, but enables them to get to a certain point quickly by means of short-cuts which would be impossible for larger craft. For their size they are heavily armed; a gun is mounted forward, while aft are a couple of depth-charges, those unpleasant under-sea explosives, set for various depths, which make it very unhealthy for any submarine in the vicinity, even without a direct hit. Four smaller depth-charges are carried also. Then there are lance-bombs for close work, as well as the rifles and revolvers and a Lewis-gun.

Considering their size, the interior accommodation of these boats is very good; there is no waste space. Right aft are the officers' quarters, a sleeping cabin with two bunks, and a smaller cabin about as big as a fair-sized dining-table, which is dignified by the name of "ward-room." Next is the galley. The engine-room is amidships, with the chart-house just forward of it. The magazine comes after this, and this adjoins the fo'castle, where the crew sleep and have their being— rather a crowded being.

The seaworthiness of these boats is better than many people imagine, and on the whole they are fairly easy to handle, though in a high following sea an M.L. is apt to sheer badly, or to "take the bit between its teeth" at times and side-slip down a big wave. That, perhaps, is their worst fault. Of course, there are days when the sea is too high for patrol, for common-sense has to be used in the organisation of the work; but if it is too rough for an M.L. to keep the sea, it is usually too bad for a submarine to operate also. But M.L.s can stand, and have stood, some terrible weather, and to call them fair-weather boats is not a libel, it is merely a stupid lie.

It would be hypocrisy to deny that certain days of patrol work in the few summer months are pleasant—they are, with the spice of danger and adventure to save them from becoming too monotonous— but I think we earn this by the rough times we have in the winter months. Writing, as I am, just after going through a long and hard winter in the North Sea, I can speak as one who knows, and a glimpse of an average twenty-four hours on patrol may be interesting.

In the grey of a bleak winter's morning three M.L.s set out from an east-coast harbour "line ahead" (it would be more picturesque to say "stole silently out of harbour," but an M.L. is never silent, unless drifting). Once clear of home waters, the patrol leader runs up a signal to form line abreast; in this formation we proceed, with rails down and gun cleared away for instant action, depth-charges and lance-bombs set, and, if deemed necessary by the C.O., rifles and revolvers loaded; nothing is left to chance. There is a "certain liveliness in the North Sea" on this morning, quite a high sea is running, and soon the boat is feeling this, no boat sooner than an M.L., and before long she is "shipping it green."

Patrol may be a bit monotonous at times, but it can never be called dry work, anyhow in the winter. There are days when, however much you may wrap yourself up in oilskins, you will still get soaked, and your sea-boots act as involuntary foot-baths of ice-cold water. But this is a thing you have to grin (or curse) and bear on an M.L. on a rough day. Nor is the general wetness confined to the deck, as clothes and boots testify if not worn for a few days, and a calm day is as bad as a rough one for this form of dampness.

Towards midday the wind abates a little, but not so the cold, and oilskins give place to duffel coats—thick wool, yellowy-brown coats with hoods, and which, if worn with these up and baggy trousers of the same material, give the appearance of a ship manned by giant teddy-bears. Meals on an M.L. are "movable feasts," where the right hand never knows what the left hand may be doing, for while the latter is conveying food to the mouth the former is probably chasing the plate across the table or picking up a chop from the seat. No meal on patrol is ever dull.

So, the day wears on, varied by gun or rifle practice on certain days, and then begins by far the most nerve-racking part of patrol— the night work. Vigilance is always necessary, but this must be doubled during the hours of darkness. A look-out man must be stationed forward to warn the bridge of any object ahead, which may be a mine, a wreck, or a buoy, and recognition lights must be kept in readiness to be turned on in case of a challenge by another patrol boat. So, with engines running dead slow and every nerve alert, on through the blackness the M.L. prowls, with all lights extinguished save a couple or so in the engine-room, invisible from without, and the searchlight ready for instant use. Sometimes the engines are stopped, and we drift for an hour with the hydrophone out. This is an undersea telephone, and a man waits in the chart-house with the receivers to his ears for a submarine to "ring up."

A submarine will not attack a patrol boat if it can help it, and it is often more useful to keep one of the former under the water, locating its position with the hydrophone if it moves, than to drive it away or engage it; for fresh boats can be brought up by a scout, and, as a submarine can only stay a certain time under and must come up to charge its batteries, its chance is small in these circumstances. This is known as "sitting on a submarine." Naturally they get away sometimes, for the sea is a wide place, but they are at least rendered harmless while in the vicinity of a war channel.

A periscope is a very difficult thing to see. Even when you know it is there it is none too easy; but not so a floating mine. Its size renders this fairly simple to locate, except, of course, at night, when you may be on it before the look-out man can give the alarm. Sinking mines by rifle fire is interesting and exciting work; a specially heavy rifle or a Lewis-gun are used, and the mines make splendid targets. If a mine is more than usually obstinate the gun is employed as well. It is not only floating mines that have to be accounted for, but also those washed ashore, which have to be towed off the beach into deep water before they are sunk. These are not all German, some being our own which have broken away from the numerous minefields owing to bad weather.

Thus, night and day ceaseless, never-sleeping watch is kept round our coasts by these sea-wasps with their deadly stings, and when the history of the war is viewed down the perspective of time the public will realise better the strenuous, quiet, and effective work of R.N.V.R. men on these patrol boats.

The enemy is not the only foe an M.L. has to consider, for the elements have always to be contended within varying forms. Nor are rough seas and high winds the worst of these; fog is, perhaps, the bitterest enemy of the sailor. People talk glibly on shore in fine weather about "dead reckoning" in a fog, but a practical man knows about how much this is worth when you cannot see the bow of the boat from the bridge. You may know exactly how a certain buoy bears and make due allowance for tides, and even then, the chances of your picking it up a mile away are about one in a hundred.

A snowstorm at sea is hell, a frozen hell may be, but still hell. The driving snow, which more often than not is half sleet, lashes your face like a whip till it is all you can manage to see where you are going, and this with the boat pitching and rolling like an intoxicated joy-wheel trying to turn both ways at once. Such a state of affairs is bad enough in the daytime, but at night it is almost beyond description, and then kind-hearted folk, with unconscious irony, send cards and games "to relieve the monotony of our brave lads in the North Sea!"

If yachtsmen in peace-time had cruised about the sea in the darkness often without a single light afloat or ashore to guide them, and gone in and out of harbours under the same conditions, they would have been put down as lunatics; yet this is what they are doing nearly every night of their lives now; but it is wonderful how used you get to this sort of thing when you have *got* to do it. Coastal navigation at night, when normal times come again, will seem by contrast as easy as motoring down a well-lit street.

Naturally, there are some nights on patrol which live in the memory, and one of these I shall never forget. It had been a fairly quiet "stand by" day at Great Yarmouth Naval Base, and when we turned in about 11 p.m. we were congratulating ourselves that we should get a night in our bunks after all, a fact for which we were not sorry, for it was a raw, blustering night in November. However, we had reckoned without our host, in this case the Commodore's Office at Lowestoft, for, just allowing us time to get well asleep, a boy scout rushed down and awakened us with an urgent message to report at the Staff Office at once. There we found the duty officer in a state of great excitement, and others, hastily roused, in a state of semi-nudeness. They had just got a message through from Lowestoft to say that a German submarine had been reported eight miles due east of Yarmouth. On the arrival of the S.N.O., we got definite orders; the three available M.L.s were to proceed to sea at once, and search. Other craft would be sent to support us as soon as possible.

Blessing the Hun for his inopportune visit, we set out. It was the very devil of a night: half a gale blowing, a blinding rain in our faces, and as black as the Earl of Hell's riding boots. It was impossible to keep any formation. No lights were allowed, not even a stern light, and soon we were scattered, and for four solid hours we cruised and drifted. The weather seemed to get worse rather than better, and to use a hydrophone was out of the question on this account. It was not long before we lost all trace of the other two boats and they of us, and the supporting ships were equally conspicuous by their absence. The darkness seemed to shut us in like a curtain, and a submarine could easily have passed within fifty yards of us and we none the wiser. It became increasingly difficult to keep our exact bearings; we were turning and drifting continuously with a strong southerly set of the tide, but in spite of our search not a trace of anything could we find.

About 3 a.m. the weather got suddenly worse, and having lost the other M.L.s a couple of hours ago, and all hope of doing any good on our quest even before that, we decided to return to harbour. Now came the difficult part: what course were we to steer? There was nothing for it but to set an approximate one to where we imagined the harbour to be, and trust to luck. As we turned for home, we met the full force of the increasing gale. Great seas broke over us as we plunged our nose into the huge breakers. One gigantic wave was almost our undoing; it rose high above us as we dived blindly on, to settle on our deck with a thud that shook the boat from stem to stern. So great was the force of this wave that it broke one of the windows of the bridge-house, drenching all who huddled within in an ice-cold shower-bath. It was quite impossible to keep any sort of lookout forward; no man could have kept his feet in the raging seas that swept over us every moment. Nor was it much more comfortable now in the bridge-house, for though we tried to stop the gap by lashing an oilskin over the broken pane, the force of the water kept driving it inwards. The fact of the oilskin over the chief look-out place made little difference; we could not see even as far as the gun, anyhow.

So, we struggled on, tossed and buffeted about like a cork, one moment nose down with both propellers racing like windmills, and the next "sitting down" in the trough of the sea with our nose in the air.

Another huge mass of water plunged down on us, but the gallant little ship rose again, but crippled. The water that swept off our decks in sheets carried away our mooring rope, that was coiled on the after-deck, overboard, and this got entangled in the starboard propeller. This we did not know at the time; all we knew was that the starboard engine stopped suddenly and all the efforts of the engineers could not get it to start again. The chief reported that nothing was wrong with the engine, as far as he could ascertain, but its non-starting. Subsequently we discovered the cause of the trouble, but we could do nothing in this sea, even in daylight, to clear the propeller, and there was no help for it but to stick it and strive onwards as best we could with one engine.

For an hour we made our tortuous way shorewards to where we

imagined the harbour to be, till we knew by the distance run that we must be getting near and it behoved us to be wary how we went. Not a sign of a ship could be seen to ask our exact bearings, and when the lead showed only three fathoms, we had the choice of going on and trusting to luck or of drifting or stemming the tide as best we could; to anchor was not feasible. We decided on the latter course, and so we waited for dawn, with one engine going dead slow to keep us head to sea. Never, I think, has dawn seemed longer coming, or been more welcome when it did arrive, than on that morning.

As soon as the black began to give way to grey to seaward, we looked round for our whereabouts, and, to our intense amazement, found that we were but a mile or so south of the harbour; had we been twenty I should not have been surprised, after such a buffeting in our crippled state. About a hundred yards astern a large tramp steamer was at anchor, but no sign of it had we seen, though we must have been almost cruising round it for the past two hours. Ahead was the beach, not half a mile away, with the wreck of the *White Swan*, a collier that had been driven ashore a few months before in another gale. Had we not stopped where we did, we should have in all probability shared her fate. But the most surprising thing we discovered was the fact that as we made shorewards in the darkness we must have passed right over the Corton Sands, an inshore shoal where the lightship had been blown up by a mine about a year before. Luckily for us, we crossed this shoal on a rising tide, otherwise, with such a sea running, we should never have seen the end of our "perfect night."

When we reached harbour, we made inquiries as to what had happened to our two consorts. One, we found, had soon returned—it must have gone back almost at once after we lost sight of each other; but the other M.L. had experienced, if possible, even a worse time than we had. They had got too far to the northward and, in trying to make harbour in the dark, had run foul of the Scroby Sand. They found by the lead that they had got into a "pocket," and to save themselves from foundering, for it would now have been as dangerous to go back as to go on, they had actually dropped their anchor and ridden out the gale there! To me it is a wonder that either of our two boats ever got back to port at all. And then there are some fools who still cling to the idea that M.L.s are fair-weather craft.

The anti-climax came when we went up to the Staff Office to report and to ask a few questions concerning the ships that were alleged to have been supporting us. "Oh," said the duty officer when he had listened to our stories, "they never went out. About five minutes after you had left another message came through from Lowestoft saying there had been a mistake; the submarine was sighted a hundred and twenty-eight miles off, not eight, and the trip was to be a wash-out!"

"Well, it jolly nearly was," I said, "for us!"

Often the work that the M.L.s had to do was tragic enough, in rescuing men from torpedoed ships or, in some cases, salving the dead from the sea. I remember one such task well, when we had the gruesome job of searching for and picking up bodies from a liner that had been torpedoed some miles away the day before. As a matter of fact, we only found three, but they were enough, and in my mind's eye I can still see them lying on the deck of the M.L.

When we had taken them out of the water, we laid them as reverently as we could by the gun and covered them up with tarpaulin, but the sea was rough, and every now and then, as the boat rolled and pitched, an arm or leg, in ghastly uncontrol, would swing out from beneath the covering with a horrible sense of life in its grim rigidity.

One of these bodies was that of a woman, young, certainly not more than thirty; she was clad in a nightgown only, over which she wore a cork lifebelt, and her dark hair hung about her shoulders like wet seaweed. Her eyes—thank God!—were closed. She wore a wedding ring.

The second body was that of an engineer, clad in a blue oil-stained overall, and the third that of a *lascar*, the most terrible sight of all. His eyes were staring upwards with the whites showing, and his lips were drawn back exposing his set yellow teeth.

The sight of these ghastly pathetic passengers we had on board then haunted me for many a day after. People say "Lest we forget": no one who was on board that day ever will.

2: The Lighter Side

Patrol life, though strenuous often and occasionally a bit monotonous, is by no means without its humour.

Submarine reporting is a common game along the coast; I have even known buoys reported, by people on shore, as the conning tower of a U-boat.

A good many reports come from soldiers, usually men from an inland town, and whose knowledge of matters nautical is distinctly hazy. Of course, the military officer is bound to pass on anything that is reported to him to the Naval Base, however ridiculous it may seem, and then M.L.s are usually sent out to investigate and report. We were sent out on such an errand one night. The message was that a submarine had been reported at a certain point at dusk, about two hundred yards from the shore, and that it had dived three times in a quarter of a mile. Of course, there was nothing there, no one beyond the soldier ever expected that there would be, though he had appeared surprised when it was pointed out to him that at this particular spot there was less than six feet of water at the time, and that sixty feet would be about the least in which a submarine could submerge, and more astonished still when he was told that no submarine yet built could possibly submerge under way three times in so short a distance. Subsequent questioning elicited the fact that he had been at The Red Lion during the early part of the evening, a clue that went far to elucidate the mystery. What he had probably seen was a porpoise.

On another occasion we had a similar trip. A soldier reported that about an hour before sunset—broad daylight—he had seen a suspicious looking small boat leave a large ship which had two funnels and *one* mast. The small boat contained two men and was flying a large red flag. Of course, we had another wild-goose chase and discovered nothing. No ship anchored off the port had sent a boat ashore that evening at all. If we had spent our time looking for such a ship as had been reported, we should be still looking, I'm afraid. The "suspicious small boat" proved to be the pilot motor-boat which was there every day, and the flag was the red ensign. I suppose the vigilant watcher had argued that as it was probably a German boat with a couple of men landing to blow up the port, they had, with true Teutonic thoroughness, flown a red flag to denote that they were about to unload explosives!

Motor launches are always an interest and a puzzle to the landsman; he never knows quite where to place them. Most people seem to think that the letters M.L. painted on the side mean "Mine Layer," and that the depth-charges are the mines, and I have heard them referred to by the curious on the quay-side as almost every class of ship, including submarines, hydroplanes, and torpedo-boats. The greatest compliment, though, ever paid to us was one morning when we were anchored off Brighton.

I had been ashore in the dinghy to see the coast-watching officer, and when I came down to the beach again, I found a large and interested crowd gazing intently at the M.L. as she lay about half a mile out to sea. Many people, not content with the view that could be obtained from the shore, were chartering small boats and rowing round the

M.L., and one old boatman was doing literally a roaring trade as he took party after party out to our ship; and while his boat was filling up with passengers for a new trip, he stood by yelling in stentorian tones, "'Ere yer are, ladies and gents, ninepence round the battleship! ninepence round the battleship!" Some battleship!

The trippers were fond of asking questions, usually silly ones, and they were all answered with the gallantry inseparable from the British Navy! They seemed much impressed; and little wonder, for I'm afraid they heard more things about M.L.s than one dreamed of in the Admiralty's philosophy. One worthy old gentleman went away filled with awe and admiration, and fondly believing that the nozzle of our deck-hose was the top of a captured periscope, while an inquiry in a stage *sotto voce* down the engine-room hatch as to whether the German prisoners had been fed that morning caused one boat-load of ladies to look quite alarmed.

Another name I heard an M.L. called was not quite so grand. We had been out to a large ship to bring two men ashore, neither of whom had ever been on an M.L. before. There was quite a sea running at the time, and the boat was very lively. The two men were standing just outside the bridge dodger, and I could hear all they said. One (the less sea-sick of the two) remarked to his companion, who was leaning over the rails gazing at the waves in a pensive kind of way, "Strike me pink, mate, this 'ere ain't a boat; it's a blankey rockin'-'orse!"

I shall never forget the entry of three M.L.'s into a small south-coast port, which was really a watering-place with a river harbour. It was August, and the place was crowded with London visitors (to whom any sort of Navy ship was a novelty), driven from the east coast by war conditions, and as soon as we made our number to the war signal station, people began to flock from all parts of the beach to the wooden piers that formed the harbour entrance. As we came in with our numbers still flying, they cheered us to the echo; hats and handkerchiefs were waved, and we could not have had a greater ovation had we just returned from a famous naval victory.

It was a great moment, and I wish that veracity would allow me to enlarge on the situation. I should like to be able to tell you how we landed on the pier to the strains from the town band, and listened to an address of welcome from the mayor, and how fair maidens flung their arms around our necks in sheer joy. Our real landing was very different, alas; there was no band, the place did not boast of (or apologise for) a mayor, and no lovely maidens greeted us (at least not then).

No, none of these glories were ours; it was a most prosaic ending to a triumphal entry. We proceeded far up the river and berthed at a coal wharf, and the only greeting we got was from a barge which was being unloaded. Two grimy faces appeared over the side as we approached, and one carbon knight exclaimed to his pal, "Lor, Bill, if this ain't the blinkin' Naivy a-comin'!"

A whole chapter could be, perhaps, written on the remarks overheard by the officers in the wardroom of the men in the galley, from which it is separated by a thin wooden partition. Talkers sometimes forgot how plainly their voices could be heard, and the involuntary eavesdropper in the ward-room often heard some unofficial opinions upon his methods of running an M.L. One instance will have to suffice now. Though I heard nothing interesting about myself in this case, I was certainly entertained.

We were tied up to the quay on a "stand off" day, and in the afternoon, I was curled up on the ward-room seat with a book, more dozing than reading, for it was a baking day in summer. I could hear the cook in the galley busy on some job or other, when I was roused by a fresh voice "whispering" down the galley hatch, "Where's the C.O.?" "Oh, he's asleep. It's all right; come down and I'll show you the steps," the cook "whispered" back. These "whispers" alone would have awakened anyone far faster asleep than I was, without the subsequent proceedings.

The newcomer then descended. I knew from his voice that he was another deck-hand, and I vaguely wondered why he should want to see the galley steps, and what difference it would make to his ambition in this direction if I were awake or asleep. However, I was soon to find a solution to this mystery.

"Now," said the cook, "you keep time with me as I sing the tune. Come on." Then began a noise suggestive of young elephants at play, accompanied by the clapping of the cook's hands and his voice in a combined song-instruction. "The bells are ringing, for me and me gal! Let 'em ring, let 'em ring, let 'em ring—no, you ruddy fool, the *left* foot first—The birds are singing, for me and me gal. Let 'em sing, let 'em sing, let 'em sing—keep your ruddy arms down, you ain't at a semaphore class—Everybody looks knowing, to a wedding they're going, and for weeks they've been sewing—hurry up, you're three steps be'ind—Ev'ry Susie and Sal. They're congregating—faster, you blanker—for me and me gal. 'Ere we are, 'ere we are, 'ere we are—go on, now the left foot again—The parson's waiting for me and me gal—'ere, mind me ruddy shins, you ain't a blankey ballet girl—Let 'em wait, let 'em wait, let 'm wait. Sometime I'm going to build a little 'ome for two, for three or four or more—come on, three steps and two 'ops—in loveland—why the 'ell can't you keep time—for me and me gal!"

All this was to the accompaniment of falling pots and pans, kicked kettles, and sundry other violent noises that naturally accrue when two men in leather sea-boots are dancing in a galley about ten feet by four, half of which space is filled up by the stove and cupboards, with various utensils scattered around. Through all this I was fondly supposed to be sleeping peacefully a few inches away.

"Now," said the cook after a short pause for breath and rearrangement of fallen buckets, kettles, and other movable objects, "we'll do it over again."

They appeared somewhat surprised when I banged on the wall and informed them that though I was sorry to interrupt the worship of Terpsichore, I really thought that they might find a more suitable place to hold their revels.

"Sorry, sir," said the cook, fathoming my meaning, if not the allusion, "we thought you was asleep."

Subsequent questionings elicited the information that there was a men's dance coming on soon ashore, and that the cook, a leading light in this social function, had offered to teach the other deck-hand the mysteries appertaining to such things. Violently expressed opinions had deterred them from practising in the fo'castle, so the galley had been selected as the next best place. I am still in the dark as to what sort of dance they were supposed to be trying to do. It may have been some new form of "jazzing," but my "jazz" education has been too shockingly neglected, I'm thankful to say, to enable me to be certain on this point.

The cook added the most unconsciously subtle touch of humour to the affair when he solemnly informed me, upon my calling him from the galley that evening, that his Christian name was Thomas and not Turveydrop!

There is the Nelson Touch and the Nelson Day Touch. These must not be confused. The former, we are proud to say, is still alive in our Navy, but the latter is quite a different thing. It is the last word in Dug-outitis. An instance? A dozen, if you like. But one will suffice.

At a certain base where there was a large number of M.L.s there was an engineer captain. Having retired many years before the war, at the outbreak of hostilities he came forward at once, leaving his well-earned rest to get into harness again; an action for which we all admired him, as he was an old man. We all liked him; he was one of the most courteous and charming old gentlemen one could wish to meet; but he was apt to forget that during the years of his retirement certain changes had taken place in his sphere of influence, and he did not take at all kindly to these innovations.

A splendid man on steam, he certainly did not understand marine petrol engines or their requirements, and this, combined with a sincere desire on his part to economise at a time of national emergency, often led to some curious conversations. Whenever he was worried his speech assumed a most dismal tone—a voice with a weep in it— which tendency became more marked the more worried he got. The following is a type of conversation we used to have with him, true in spirit if not in actual detail:—

> Engineer Captain (*holding a demand list for M.L. engine-room stores in his hand*): "But surely, Mr So-and-So, all these aren't necessary?"
> M.L. Officer: "I'm afraid they are, sir."
> E.C. (*dismally*): "Oh, they *can't* be. Let us go through the list."
> M.L.O.: "Very good, sir."
> E.C. (*with a "weepy catch" in his voice*): "Twelve ignitor tips! Very extravagant. You know, Mr So-and-So, Nelson never had any ignitor tips!"
> M.L.O. (*thoughtfully*): "I suppose not, sir."
> E.C. (*almost breaking into sobs*): "A new air-compressor valve! Oh, Mr So-and-So, you *do* want a lot; you know Nelson won the battles of the Nile and the Baltic without all these things!"
> M.L.O. (*visibly affected*): "Y-yes, sir, I sup-suppose he did, sir."
> E.C. (*now sobbing like a child*): "Fifteen hundred gallons of petrol!! You can't want all this; why Nelson won Trafalgar without a *single* drop of petrol!!"

And so on. But the dear old boy always signed the lists in the end, though I'm sure it nearly broke his heart.

On one occasion he visited an M.L. to examine the broken bed-plate of an auxiliary engine. He came silently, and stood with saddened countenance gazing at the engine. On the C.O. coming up from aft, he saw the captain emerging from the engine-room hatch with a most woebegone expression on his face (one could almost see the tears coursing down his cheeks), and upon seeing the C.O. he exclaimed in his most weepy tones: "Oh, Mr So-and-So, what *have* you been doing to your engine?" From his tone of voice an onlooker might have imagined that the C.O. had been down with a hammer smashing it up intentionally, with a view to getting leave or some equally fell design! Although he didn't actually mention the fact that Nelson never committed so grave a crime, I'm certain it was at the back of the captain's mind.

To go on relating humorous incidents of M.L. life, however, would be an almost endless task; still the following one will appeal to those who have been on patrol and know the sporting proclivities of an M.L. when it is trying to keep station on larger ships in a rough sea. On this occasion a number of M.L.s were returning from a patrol with a destroyer flotilla, and the high seas running at the time, though not enough to affect the destroyers to any great extent, were sufficient to make the M.L.s try to turn all points of the compass at the same time in their own peculiar way.

As they neared the base the S.O. of the M.L.s wanted instructions from the leading destroyer, and told his signalman to make a signal "What are we to do?" This the man misunderstood and made instead: "From C.O. M.L. 000 to C.O. H.M.S. *Blank*—'What are we doing?'" Now the C.O. of the destroyer happened to have a sense of humour, and back came the very apt answer: "From C.O. H.M.S. *Blank* to C.O. M.L. 000—'Damned if I know!'"

Speaking of rough days at sea, I remember once returning dead-beat from a forty-eight-hour patrol in an M.L., during which time we had been unmercifully and continuously buffeted about by wind and sea, and made our way back to port bruised and battered and full of strange sea oaths. It was somewhere near Christmas-time, and amongst my mail was a card depicting a raging storm at sea above that quotation of J. R. Lowell's—"As the broad ocean ceaselessly upheaveth with the majestic beating of his heart."

Yes! all very well for artists to draw and poets to write about on Christmas-cards, but when you are on an M.L. under these conditions the "majestic" part of it doesn't seem to appeal to you somehow, and you wish that the broad ocean would suffer a bit more from heart failure!

The term "Xmas at sea" has always rather a romantic sound. One conjures up visions of mess-decks elaborately decorated with holly and mistletoe (wasted on warships!) and the captain going round tasting the puddings and wishing all the compliments of the season.

This may be the case on battleships which are in harbour during the festive season, but on an M.L. upon the Belgian coast patrol on this day it is—well, a *little* exaggerated! It was my fate to spend Xmas in this way once when based at Dunkirk.

It was very rough, and owing to several day patrols in succession we happened to be short of victualling stores at the time; and unfortunately, we had no holly or mistletoe, and wet seaweed has certain slight disadvantages which render it a little unsuitable as a substitute for these from a decorative point of view. Again, it is hard to be festive alone, for one officer had to be on deck the whole time; and this, combined with the fact that nothing would stay on the table for more than ten consecutive seconds without bringing up with a round turn against the fiddles (not the sort you play) and toppling over into your lap, rendered any degree of hilarious festivity somewhat difficult of attainment.

However, something had to be done to celebrate the occasion, so we got up an elaborate menu-card, which was fastened to the table with tacks. It was a most chaste and refined effort, and read:—

Hôtel de la Côte Belgique Patrouille.
Restaurant and Grill Room, December 25, 1917.
Menu.
Consommé d'os du mouton.
Boeuf squashée.
Pain du magasin a la marine.
Riz à la M.L.
L'eau ordinaire
(Château Dunkerque).
Pomme de terre.
La margarine.
Fromage de la crême.
Biscuit au chien.
Café.

Well, if you come down hungry after four hours on deck on a winter's day (to say nothing of the stimulation to appetite given by the menu), you can have worse fare.

In writing of the life we led in those days, a "last" example always seems to crop up of some happening that seems worth recording, but I will try and make this one the genuine last in an already extended

55

chapter.

At a certain base in which I happened to be some French ships were also based for a time, and one night when I was about to go aboard my M.L. I came upon a party on the quayside that seemed rather unusual. An excited French naval officer stood in the midst of half a dozen or so British sailors, and from the way he was waving his hands he was obviously trying to make them understand something or other. I went up to the group to see if I could help. "Beg pardon, sir," cried one of the men when he saw me; "'ere's a French orficer as wants a ship called the *Angry Cat*."

"The what?" I said.

"The *Angry Cat*, sir. We've never 'eard o' such a ship, but he says she's in 'arbour. I've 'eard of the *Tiger* and the *Lion*, and I believe there's a destroyer called the *Tigress*, but there ain't no such ship as the *Angry Cat* as *I've* ever 'eard of."

The French officer turned to me, and, speaking in very broken English, explained that he had missed his boat and was willing to pay these men to take him back to his ship, but he could not make them understand. His ship was the *Henri Quatre*, it appeared.

I explained to the men, but stuck to English, for if the native pronunciation sounded to them like an infuriated feline, I shudder to think what zoological interpretation they would have put upon my attempt.

"This officer wants to go out to the French ship *Henry the Fourth*," I said.

"Oh, *'Enerey the Fourth!*" replied the spokesman, with relief in his voice, "I knows where she lays. She's got 'Enerey one vee' on 'er stern."

The Frenchman was profuse in his thanks to me for what I had done, but I did not hear all he said. I was more interested in the remarks of the sailor to the others. I could not catch them all, but overheard him mutter to another as they went towards the boats: "These ''ere Frenchies are rum blokes. Wot the 'ell was 'e carrying on so about 'is *Angry Cat* when he wanted the *'Enerey the Fourth* the 'ole time. *I* can't see no connection between 'em!"

CHAPTER 5

Eternity

It had been a fairly dirty night, with quite enough sea running to make a man glad when his watch was over; and at eight bells I went below from the bridge at the end of the middle watch dead tired, and after a cup of hot cocoa turned in immediately.

I needed no rocking, though on a North Sea patrol plenty is provided, and fell asleep quickly. How long I slept I am not sure, but all at once I returned to consciousness again with the vague feeling that I was not alone in my cabin. It was pitch dark and I could see nothing, but every second the feeling became stronger. "Who is there?" I called out, sitting up in my bunk. For answer the light was switched on, and a man was standing by the hatchway. He was a complete stranger to me, and though he wore a naval officer's uniform it had an unfamiliar appearance. Then my eye fell on his cap badge, and I understood. It was that of the German Navy.

The next instant I found myself looking down the muzzle of a revolver. "Don't move," he said, "resistance will be useless; you must do as I tell you. You are my prisoner." He spoke quite good English, but with a guttural accent. I did not answer, and he went on. "Get up and dress; I will wait for you. If you are sensible, you will do as you are told quietly, then you will not be hurt; but any tricks———" and he tapped his revolver significantly. There was nothing for it; I must obey now and wait for a more opportune moment to give the alarm, though of what might have happened on deck I was in complete ignorance. I got out of my bunk and put on my clothes, the German silently watching me. When I had finished, he said: "Now go up on deck just in front of me and don't make a sound; I shall be close behind you, and I have an armed man waiting by the hatchway."

"Where are you going to take me?" I asked. "You will know all in good time," he answered, and it seemed to me that he chuckled softly

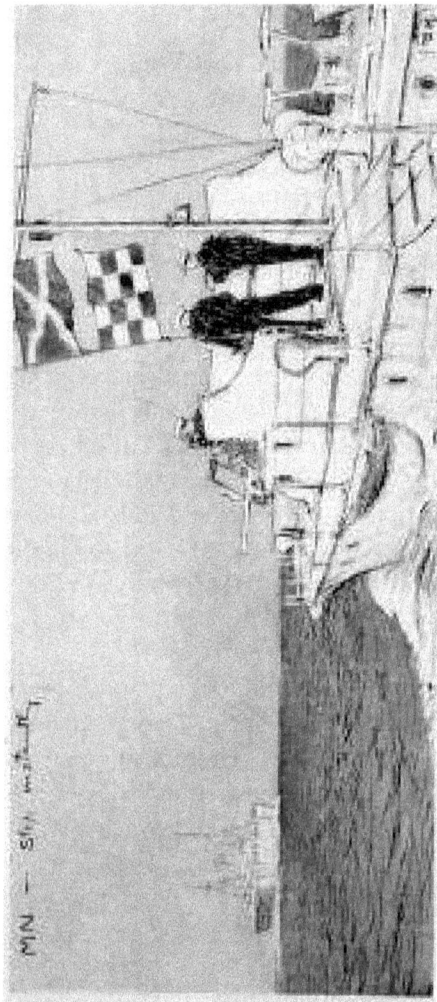

On Patrol—A Suspect; M.L.s engaging a U-boat attacking a merchantman

to himself I went up the ladder with the unpleasant sense of a loaded revolver at my heels. A dark figure was waiting on deck, to whom my captor said a few words in German. I could just discern the outlines of a long dark vessel alongside the M.L., but I was given no time to look about me, for the German stepped quickly on to the strange craft. "Give me your hand," he said to me, "and step straight across." I did so and alighted on the mysterious vessel, but the hand that guided me was so cold and clammy that it sent a shudder through me. The second German came on board directly after me, and the officer flashed a torch for a moment on to some iron steps down a hatchway and said, "Follow me down."

Once below, my guide switched on the light, and the nature of the boat I was in was no longer a mystery; the machinery all round left no doubt as to its identity. It was the control room of a German submarine. For a moment a wild thought of escape filled my mind, but a glance around me showed me the futility of the idea. Close to me stood the two armed men, and to put escape still further away the iron trap door above my head closed with a clang and we began to move forward. Very slowly we moved at first, but soon I felt the vessel sinking beneath the surface, and, throbbing and vibrating from the engines, we began to go ahead at a faster rate.

The German officer—a lieutenant—now took me into another part of the ship, where there was a small table on which there was spread a chart. Here were several other men, nearly twenty I should say—two officers and the rest ratings. They were all sitting, in rather strange attitudes some of them, and two had their eyes closed as if they were asleep. I was struck with the extreme pallor of their faces, and none of them took the least notice of me, but continued to sit with uncanny stillness just as before.

My captor motioned me to a seat by the table and, taking another himself, bent over the chart, looked at his watch on his wrist, and then sat back without speaking. It was a weird journey this, speeding under the sea into the unknown with all these silent companions. For a time I too sat in silence, but at last I ventured to ask again where our destination might be, but to my surprise no answer was vouchsafed to me, though I still saw that the lieutenant had his hand resting on the revolver which lay on the table.

On and on then we sped in silence, and after what seemed an interminable time, we slowed down till we came to a dead stop, and began to descend till, with a slight bump, we rested on the bed of the ocean. Simultaneously with this the light in the cabin went out, and we were plunged into darkness. I felt an ice-cold hand gripping my wrist and the voice of my captor whispered in my ear "Keep still," and then the hand was removed and the voice added, "We are there now." "Where?" I asked, not unnaturally. The answer was a startling one—"Where we must rest for Eternity"; and a low grim laugh, that contained nothing of mirth, came from the other occupants of the vessel, the first sign they had given yet of being anything but dummies.

My blood ran cold at this horrible sound, but before I could speak the voice continued: "Have you not guessed yet whom you are with—here in the middle of the North Sea—this silent company who will never speak or move again and whose laughter is but the echo of mockery of former days, and with whom you are destined to be till the sea gives forth its dead?"

Then I understood who this grim and awful company were. "But you," I cried, "you surely are living?" I heard the voice laugh bitterly again before it replied: "No, I am also as the others; but the Fates that rule over us have decreed that I alone shall speak as a mouthpiece, ere I too am silent for ever. My mission was to fetch you here and tell you what your own fate is to be."

"But why me?" I asked.

"Why not?" it replied; "you are an officer of the accursed Navy that doomed us to lie here. If you went forward, you would see a hole in our bow made by a shot from one of your destroyers, which sank us like a stone and drowned us all. And so, I determined to get at least one of your race to share our torture with us; for by some evil enchantment a spell has been cast upon us that we, though dead, can still understand, hear, see, and suffer, and here we must lie till the end of all things."

As the German, or his wraith, ceased speaking, there was a succession of heavy bumps against the side of the vessel, accompanied by loud and hollow groans.

"What's that?" I exclaimed involuntarily.

"That," replied my captor, "is part of our eternal punishment. What you hear is the bodies of men from passenger or merchant ships sunk by our submarines bumping against our side, which they will do for ever now, while we are forced to listen all the while to their groans."

Wailing sounds now fell on my ears, plaintive and heart-rending cries as a child might utter.

"Those cries," exclaimed my ghostly guardian, "are those of the children we have murdered—they too will never cease."

A strange luminous effect at the far end of the ship now attracted my attention; confused masses at first then slowly took shape, till a hundred pair of eyes were gazing down at us. Never have I seen such eyes; at once reproachful and terrible, they seemed to burn like living fire into the soul of the beholder.

"The eyes you see now," went on the voice at my side, "will be our only light as we wait here through the years of an everlasting tomorrow. They are the eyes of the women our submarines have drowned. Nor can we by stopping our ears or closing our eyes shut out either sight or sound for an instant; for ever now we must lie at the bottom of the sea and take our awful punishment."

"A living death in an eternal hell is only your due——" I began.

"But you forget," broke in the voice, "that you too will share our fate and torture."

"But I am living, while you—you—are dead," I cried in horror; "surely——"

"Oh, that is soon remedied," the voice again interposed, but with a complete change of tone—it now snarled like a wild beast, "you damned pigdog Englishman."

I heard a movement in the darkness, and raised my hand sharply to strike up the revolver that I felt instinctively was being levelled at my head. I seized his wrist, determined to fight this grim battle to the end before I gave in, and as I did so I heard again the mocking laughter of the dead all around me. Slowly, inch by inch, I felt the hand was bearing me backwards, ever backwards, and I felt my strength gradually failing, but with a last despairing effort I——

★★★★★★★★★★★★★★★★★★

The signalman was touching me on the shoulder as I opened my eyes, "The officer of the watch wants you to turn out at once, sir," he said, and I could trace the excitement in his voice; "a periscope has just been reported on the starboard bow."

CHAPTER 6

'Ell

He was a veritable "Old Bill of the Sea." The fact that this was the third time he had been torpedoed did not seem to him anything remarkable. He had a sort of unconscious fatalism about him that set his mind above worrying over such everyday things in war-time.

He had been picked up in an open boat with half a dozen others, and was now being taken back to port in an M.L., with the boat in tow. He was sitting in the ward-room drinking hot rum and water with the greatest contentment.

"You must have had a hell of a time," remarked the C.O., "all night in that open boat, this weather too."

"Oh, I don't know," replied Old Bill; "might 'ave bin worse, you know, sir. Might even 'ave bin drownded," he added, as a rather unlikely afterthought.

"Well, all I hopes is," broke in another of the rescued men, "as how one of you navy boats has now caught the ——s and sent 'em to hell themselves."

"Ay, the right place for 'em, damn their ruddy eyes," put in another.

"Well, you knows," went on Old Bill, sipping his rum and becoming reminiscent, "'ell ain't allus a place o' everlasting brimstone and treacle, as they tells us in the Bible or the Prayer Book—I ain't quite certain which, but I knows it's one o' them 'oly books wot tells yer about 'eaven and 'ell and 'ades, and all them such-like places."

"And what is *your* conception of hell?" asked the C.O.

"My contraption o' 'ell?" he answered; "well, I reckon, sir, as 'ow I once came pretty near to knowin' wot sort of contraption it were."

"I see, you mean a hell on earth?"

"Well, no, sir, it weren't on earth at all; it were on water," warming to his subject. "It 'appened many years ago when I was quite a young man. I was a deck-'and aboard an emigrant ship on 'er way to

Canada at the time. She were a largish sailin' ship called the *Sleepin'
Beauty*. On this voyage most o' our passengers seemed to be wimmin
and children. They was goin' out, so one woman told me, to join their
'usbands wot 'ad gone out about a year afore. The number o' babies
on board was terrible, and you couldn't 'ear yourself snore in the
fo'castle for their cryin'. The langwidge them babies caused among
the men was something awful. We *did* bless 'm, I can tell you. One of
'em complained to the skipper about it (one o' the men, I mean, not
the babies), but 'e only larfed and said it would make us domesticated.

"Whatever part o' the ship a man would go to for a quiet pipe, sure
enough 'e 'adn't been there more nor five minutes when a wailin' and
a cryin' would begin within a yard of 'is 'ead. Them babies seemed
everywhere; it was like spillin' a gallon o' parryfeen in a cupboard—it
finds its way into everything. Try that when you get 'ome, and you'll
'ave some idea what a shipload o' babies is like. Those that could just
manage to crawl did crawl, and them as couldn't, rolled or wriggled.
The skipper 'appened to be very fond o' babies and was in 'is element,
which was rather curious, as 'e was very stern and strict, and most o'
the men feared 'im.

"The first Sunday arternoon as we was out from Liverpool two
or three of us were leanin' over the side smokin' and tryin' not to 'ear
the kids.

"'This 'ere ship's name ought ter be changed,' I ses to Ern Watson,
who was next to me; 'it's ridikilus to call it the *Sleepin' Beauty*, with a
row like this goin' on.'

"Ern nodded. 'Wot 'ud you call it?' he asks.

"'I should call it the *Creech*,' I answers.

"'The wot?'

"'The *Creech*.'

"'The *Screech*'?

"'No, the *Creech*.'

"'Wot's wrong with the *Screech*?' 'e ses; 'ain't there enough of it
goin' on to please you?'

"'Granted; but if you will only 'ear wot I 'ave to say you will see
that the name I suggests 'as scientific reasoning be'ind it,' I answers,
superior like.

"'Well?' 'e ses.

"'Why I say that this 'ere ship ought to be called the *Creech*, is becos' no other name is 'alf so sootible.'

"'I don't call that very scientific,' put in Ern.

"'That's becos' you 'aven't 'ad the advantage of early edication when young,' I replies; 'if you 'ad, you would know that "*creech*" is the French for "babies."'

"'Oh,' 'e ses, crushed like.

"'When I was livin' at Lime'ouse,' I went on, 'there was a district lady wot used to visit in our street sellin' magazines, and givin' a lot o' free advice nobody wanted; well, she 'ad got *one* rather good idea, and that was when she started a sort of nursery place where the wimmin could leave their babies when they went to work of a mornin' and fetch 'm as they came 'ome o' nights. Over the door she 'ad "*Creech*" stuck up, and wimmin knew when they saw this that they could leave their babies there. I know "*creech*" is French, becos' a man told me what was courtin' the widow of a I-talian baker. The noise you could 'ear as you passed that 'ouse was exactly the same as you 'ear on this ship. That's why I say she ought to be called the *Creech*.'

"Meantime the skipper 'ad been standin' near the mainmast talkin' to several of the wimmin, and admirin' the babies they was carryin'. We wor too far away to 'ear what 'e was sayin', but the mothers looked mighty pleased, so I suppose 'e was crackin' up the kids; though 'ow anyone can tell one baby from another at all is a mystery to me.

"Suddenly the skipper calls out 'Brown!'

"'Sir,' ses 'Arry Brown, who was alongside o' me.

"'Come 'ere, I wants yer,' ses the skipper.

"'Arry swore under 'is breath, but 'e 'ad to go, and we all edged up nearer so as to 'ear what were goin' on.

"'You're a married man. Brown, ain't you?' asks the skipper, when the other gets near.

"'Yes, sir,' ses Brown; which was true enough, only the skipper didn't know that 'is wife 'ad run away with another man three months arter they was married, and 'e 'adn't seen her for five years.

"'Then you're fond of babies?' went on the skipper in a louder tone.

"It was a 'abit of 'is to repeat all 'is sentences in an angry and loud voice if 'e didn't get an answer at once; and if this failed in its desired effect, 'e would yell each remark in a conversation louder than the one afore, so that by the time 'e 'ad finished wot 'e 'ad to say 'e was usually nearly black in the face and yellin' at the top of 'is vyice. 'E 'ad a very 'asty temper and was mighty short with the men.

"'You're fond of babies,' he roared for the third time at poor Brown.

"'Yes, sir.'

"'You like nursin' 'em?'

"Brown stared at him.

"'You like nursin' 'em?' repeated the skipper.

"'Y-y-es, sir.'

"Poor 'Arry was a rather nervous man, and got sort o' flustered when the old man spoke to 'im like this afore the wimmin, who was all grinnin' at 'im like Cheshire cats; and as the skipper raised 'is voice, Brown raised 'is too in 'armony, unconscious like.

"'You're quite used to nursin' 'em?' yelled the skipper.

"'Quite,' roared Brown, who as a matter of fact 'ated 'em, and 'ad never been near enough one to nurse it; but he wanted to please the old man, for this was the first time 'e 'ad sailed with 'im.

"'Brings back pleasant memories?' bellowed the skipper in a voice like the Bull of Bashan.

"'Very pleasant,' shrieked Brown in a 'igh falsetter.

"'You'd like to nurse one of these now?' shouted the skipper.

"'Yes, sir,' bawled poor Brown, who by this time was far beyond knowin' what he was sayin'.

"'There, mum,' ses the skipper, lowerin' 'is voice and turnin' to a woman 'oldin' a baby, who stood by 'im, 'I told you my crew was not the 'ard-'earted baby-'atin' lot you believed, and I was right. Why, 'ere's one as ses 'e would like to nurse your baby, 'e's that fond of 'em. You 'eard 'im say so, mum, with your own ears.'

"The woman looked much impressed.

"'Let 'im 'old the little dear, and give the poor man a treat. Can't you see 'is 'eart is yearnin' to nurse it.'

"Afore the flabbergasted Brown could escape, I'm blest if the woman 'adn't actually thrust the baby in 'is arms and then stepped back to the captain's side, and they both stood lookin' at 'im and smilin'.

"Poor old 'Arry looked as if 'is last hour 'ad come, and stood there, the picture of misery, 'oldin' the kid as though 'e expected it to come to pieces at any moment.

"'Charmin' picture of domestic 'appiness, ain't it, mum?' ses the skipper. 'I'm sure this 'ere voyage will 'ave an 'umanising influence on the crew, and make a great difference in their opinions of babies.'

"'E was quite right in the last part. Afore we used to just take no notice of 'em, but arter this we all shunned 'em as we would the plague.

"Just then the baby Brown was 'oldin' began to cry.

"'Comfort it,' ses the skipper.

"Brown shook it about a bit, but it only cried more.

"'Kiss it,' cried the skipper.

"Brown stared at him as though the old man had told 'im to chuck it overboard, which I'll warrant 'e'd rather 'ave done.

"'Kiss it!' yelled the skipper.

"In desperation Brown bent 'is 'ead and touched the baby's face with 'is cheek, but as 'e 'adn't shaved for three days, it only made the ungrateful little thing scream at the top o' its voice as though it was bein' murdered.

"'In'uman brute!' yelled the mother, rushing forward, ''e's 'urtin' the precious pet,' and she wildly clutched her orfspring and looked at Brown as though she would like to skin 'im.

"'Never mind, mum,' ses the skipper, affable like. 'I'm sure 'e didn't mean no 'arm. The men'll soon get used to 'em, bless you, and I always 'olds as there's nothin' like a baby to bring the 'uman qualities out of a man.'

"We took poor old 'Arry Brown below, and 'e wasn't 'isself again till 'e 'ad gulped down three glasses o' stiff grog.

"Well, this 'ere 'umanisin' went on more or less the whole v'yage, and we was pretty near worn to skeletons with all the skipper's silly 'umbuggin' ways, tryin' to make us fond o' babies. I think it showed wot a really Christian lot o' men we was on board the *Sleepin' Beauty*, when you thinks that there was no murder done, seein' 'ow easy it would 'ave been to 'ave dropped one or two o' the little brats overboard as it was gettin' dark. The temptation was terrible; we very nearly all turned pirates and made the 'ole bally shoot, captain, wimmin and kids, walk the plank.

"We were just gettin' near the end of our v'yage, in fact we were in sight of the American coast, when we ran into a most almighty fog, so thick that you couldn't see two yards fore or aft. We took our soundin's, but it was too deep to anchor, so there was nothin' for it but to run on under shortened sail and trust to luck. There was not much wind, o' course, and for about twelve hours we drifted about without the fog liftin' at all; it seemed to be gettin' thicker and thicker. We 'ad shut all the babies down below, which was just as well, as temptation is an awful thing and opportunity a worse one.

"We must 'ave made some progress, 'owever, for towards evenin' we was sittin' on deck cursin' the weather, when all at once, *bang! crash!* and we had grounded; on rocks too!

"In a minute all was confusion: up rushed the passengers, men, wimmin, and children, mostly in their nightgowns. Everyone was shoutin', and the babies was yellin' fit to bust. Then the carpenter comes up and tells the skipper that there is a rent on the starboard side and that she is making water fast. This news, o' course, makes things worse. The fog didn't exactly improve matters, and no one knew 'oo was 'oo. We soon 'ad the pumps a-goin', and then the skipper orders the boats to be lowered. This was easy—when you could find 'em—but we got one down at last.

"'Wimmin and children first!' yells the skipper and comes up to see 'is order is obeyed.

"'You and Watson get down into the boat,' 'e ses to me.

"This we did, though it was tricky work in the fog, and then they passes down a lot o' blankets for the kids to lie on.

"The wimmin was for clamberin' down any'ow with the babies in their arms, but the skipper stops that.

"'No,' ses 'e. 'It's too dangerous in this fog. We'll lower the babies first and then the wimmin.' "They was forced to agree to this, and someone fetched a basket with a rope on it, and then they begins to lower the babies; me and Ern took 'em out and made 'em as comfort- able as we could on the blankets. I must say that though they 'ad been a deal of worry to us all the v'yage, I was a bit sorry for the poor litde brats, bein' 'oisted about as though they was frozen mutton. We must 'ave packed over a dozen away in the blankets, when we 'eard a shout from the deck. We both looked up, and blest if somehow the painter 'adn't slipped and we was driftin' loose.

"I made a dash forward, but missed the ship's side by an inch, and 'ad 'ard work to keep myself from followin' the rope into the water. There was a fairish tide runnin', and we was already close to the stern, and afore you could count three we 'ad drifted clear of the ship and out o' sight in the fog. We could 'ear the shouts of those on deck, and Ern got out the oars, but the stream must have been stronger than we thought, or else Ern quite misjudged the position of the *Sleepin Beauty*, for we 'eard the voices gettin' fainter and fainter till they was lost in the sound o' the water on the rocks.

"'My eye,' ses Ern, stoppin' rowin' and lookin' woefully at me, ''ere's a pretty go, Bill.'

"'You're right, mate,' ses I; 'wot in the name o' fortinge can we do?'

"Ern shook 'is 'ead; the problem was too much for 'im. 'This 'ere boat's a bloomin' "*creech*," and no mistake.'

"It were only in the natur' o' things that the babies should all be yellin' at the top o' their lungs; you couldn't expect nothin' else from 'uman kids. 'We must pacify the poor little things,' I ses, 'and then decide on a course o' action.'

"We started by countin' 'em, and there was thirteen. I never 'ad much faith in unlucky numbers afore, but this was evidence enough to convince the most pig-'eaded spectre, as the sayin' is. The babies ranged from a few months or so up to about a year and a 'arf, so none could talk much, and I picked up one who looked as if it would 'ave two or three fits the next minute, and tried to soothe it.

"Ern went one better than me and picked up two, but it was 'ardly a success, for 'e knocked their 'eads together in 'is enthoosiasm. We gave up tryin' to nurse 'em after a bit as it only seemed to make 'em cry more.

"'I've 'eard as babies always cry when they is 'ungry,' I ses, 'but wot on earth can we give 'em to eat?'

"For answer, Ern began turnin' out 'is pockets; 'e had a plug o' baccy, a bit o' tarred string, an old pipe, a match-box, and a candle-end. I followed 'is example, and found I also 'ad a pipe and baccy, as well as a knife, a cork-screw, and a small flat bottle 'arf full of grog. Just as I 'ad given up all 'ope of findin' anything really nourishin', I came across a piece of oiled-rag I used to clean the winch with. We laid out all these articles on the seat and began to wonder which we ought to start on.

"'You've got a married sister, ain't you?' ses Ern, brightenin'.

"'Yes, I 'ave, but——'

"'Well, then, you ought to know all about babies,' replies 'e, with a tone o' relief in 'is voice.

"'No more than you,' I ses, 'in fact not 'arf so much; you was brought up in a orfan asylum, wasn't you?'

"'Yes, but I don't see that 'as much to do with it.'

"'Don't yer? why, if you was brought up in an orfan asylum you lived among kids and ought to know all about 'em.'

"Ern grunted 'It don't signify,' and lapsed into silence. He may not 'ave been to blame for not 'aving much early edication, but 'e didn't even seem to 'ave taken advantage of what was literally chucked at 'im, so to speak.

"By this time, we was both nearly deaf with the noise the kids was makin', and we started to comfort 'em in earnest. I began with the candle-end, and it was more of a success than I 'ad 'oped in my most sanguinary moments. The kid I give it to seized on it and began suckin' it like winkin'. The next kid we give a bit of tarred string to, and it treated it just the same. We worked all through the lot, givin' some one thing and some another, such as pipes and the paper the baccy was wrapped in, and our success in quietin' the kids was astonishin'. The oiled-rag seemed a great favourite, and I tore it into four pieces to make it go further. But there was a baby 'as wouldn't be comforted no-'ow, and wouldn't suck none of the temptin' delicacies we offered it.

"'I know,' ses Ern all of a sudden. 'I've seen my aunt do it. I'll sing it a lullie-by.' With that 'e picks up the baby and shakes it about in 'is arms and starts singin' in a voice that a respectable raven would 'a put in the dust-bin.

"This o' course sets several o' the other kids off yellin' again, and as for the one 'e was tryin' to soothe, it nearly busted itself with cryin'.

"'Stow it,' I says, 'I'd rather 'ear the kids.'

"With that 'e gets a bit offended, but 'e could see that 'is singin' did no good. 'I'll pat it on the back,' 'e ses, ' p'raps it's in pain.'

"I don't know whether it was in pain afore, but I should think it was arterwards; 'e seemed to think 'e was a grocer and the kid a pat o' butter, by the way 'e went about it.

"Ern looked at the baby in 'is arms and then at the water, and looks at me and 'eaves a big sigh. I sighs too, and ses in a 'usky voice:

"'Temptation is a terrible thing, Ern, but we must fight agin' it; it's sent to try our moral characters.'

"'First time I knew you *'ad* one,' ses Ern, grinnin', but I forgave 'im, as 'e 'adn't 'ad no early edication.

"Well, we couldn't pacify that baby at all, and we simply 'ad to let it yell, as we took turns at the oars while the other one acted as nurse. But it was no use, we couldn't come upon the ship, and we decided the only thing to do was to wait till the fog lifted, or else we might be only gettin' further and further away, and p'raps run on to rocks ourselves.

"For five solid hours we 'ung about and worked like 'eroes to keep them babies warm and nourished. As fast as we cover 'em up with the blankets they kicked 'em off again, and Ern used langwidge as weren't fit for them tender ears when one of 'em chucked 'is best pipe into the sea. We tried givin' the kids a sip of grog apiece, but it only made 'em cough and splutter, so we finished it up ourselves; and we was glad of it, I can tell you.

"Well, at last the fog lifted when a fresh breeze sprung up, and lor' bless me life if we weren't within 'arf a mile o' the *Sleepin' Beauty* all the blessed time.

"They gave a yell when they sighted us, and we pulled as 'ard as we could over to 'em, and you bet your boots we was that thankful to get aboard that we could 'ave kissed the deck.

"It appeared as 'ow the 'ole in her side was nothin' much arter all, and the carpenter 'ad patched it up easy. They was not above 'arf a mile from the shore, and at 'igh water they 'ad floated and was only waitin' to find traces of us.

"And now comes wot is p'raps the saddest part of my story, and that is the base ingratitood o' them wimmin arter all the tender care and self-sacrificin' devotion me and Ern 'ad showed them bloomin' kids all the while.

"They rushed at the babies and seized 'em as though they was a-goin' to eat 'em, and then stood glarin' at us.

"'You're wicked, wicked men,' ses one big lanky female, 'to play such a crool joke on us poor wimmin 'oo as done you no 'arm.'

"Ern and me looked blank at each other.

"'It weren't no joke, mum,' I ses, 'at least not for us.'

"'You 'ear that,' cried another, "e ses it were no joke; then it must 'ave been done a-purpose. I know what they was a-goin' to do if we 'adn't spotted 'em; they was going to take the poor little mites ashore and sell 'em to organ-grinders and beggars. I've 'eard o' that sort o' thing bein' done. We'll have the law agin you, we will.' Then they glared at us all the more.

"'We couldn't 'elp it, mum,' ses Ern weakly; 'we was sort o' taken aback like.'

"'Then it's accessory without the deed!' ses another woman, with a superior sniff. 'I knows all about the law; my old man's done time, and you can't git over me.'

"'They've been tryin' to pysin 'em,' cries the big woman, whose baby was still suckin' a bit o' oiled-rag.

"'Oh, you're wicked, sinful men!' ses one of 'em, reproachful, 'and you'll both go to 'ell, that's w'ere you'll go.'

"Ern and I looks at each other again.

"'P'raps you don't know wot 'ell is,' she ses, 'you sailors is such bad men.'

"'Oh, yes we do, mum,' answers Ern; 'it's thirteen babies and two seamen in a ship's boat.'"

CHAPTER 7

The Hundred Minutes

THE M.L.S AT ZEEBRUGGE

If St George's Day 1918 is a great one in the annals of the Royal Navy, it is even a greater in those of the Royal Naval Volunteer Reserve, for whereas in the former case but another brilliant page was added to its already glorious traditions, in the latter tradition itself was born, for in the early hours of this now famous day the R.N.V. R., represented by the flotilla of motor launches, played an important part in a naval engagement which thrilled the world, and one which will make history, for I venture to think that in years to come *Vindictive* will rank among the historic ships, alongside vessels like the Elizabethan *Revenge* and Nelson's *Victory*.

Of the action in general I do not propose to deal here, save as far as regards the motor launches. The former has been described many times, but of the experience of the particular part played by the M.L.s, this, I think, is the first detailed account to appear.

Almost the worst part of the whole affair was the waiting and the anticipation of the unknown. Before the action we had two abortive starts, both of which failed to materialise on account of weather conditions. The ten days that elapsed were certainly trying to the nerves, and we were glad when we had orders to leave harbour. Word went round that it was to be the real thing this time.

The M.L.s made a fine showing as they left Dover harbour and formed up in three divisions line ahead, but the best sight was at "A" position, where the other forces joined us and we started in earnest. Vice-Admiral Keyes led the flotilla, flying his flag in the destroyer *Warwick*. *Vindictive* came next, with *Iris* and *Daffodil* in tow. Then came the blockships *Thetis, Intrepid, Iphigenia, Brilliant*, and *Sirius*. On each beam of the line were the M.L.s, and outside them the destroyers. It was a most imposing sight in the twilight. *Vindictive* seemed to loom up above everything else, and she was a weird-looking craft, with no mast, tall funnels, and boarding gangways swung up high upon her port side.

At "D" position *Brilliant* and *Sirius* left us for Ostend, while we continued our way to Zeebrugge, each ship going to its appointed station for the attack. As we neared our objective the Huns must have learned of our approach by aeroplane, and star shells began to go up. They were wonderful star shells, and lit up the sea like day. The last I saw of *Vindictive* that night was when the first star shell soared up above her; there she was, like some grim phantom ship, ploughing her way towards the dim outline of the Mole (for our smoke-screen had already begun); close behind pounded the squat-looking *Iris* and *Daffodil*, and all were surrounded by M.L.s and C.M.B.s.

The smoke began to thicken and blotted out everything in its fumes. Still, the relief when one of those brilliant star shells lit the water and went out was great, for it seemed while their light was shining that, in spite of the smoke-screen, every ship approaching the enemy harbour must be an easy mark for the shore batteries, and it gave one a very "naked" feeling. Thicker and thicker grew the smoke as more floats were dropped, till all sight of the Mole and the happenings on and inside it were blotted out from our sight if not from our ears, for we could still hear the guns' incessant roar and the greater single roar, that seemed to rend the very night, as the old submarine blew herself up to destroy the viaduct connecting the Mole with the shore.

The action, from the attack on the Mole by *Vindictive* to the retirement, lasted exactly one hundred minutes, and during those fatal minutes history was made. It is indeed good to hear R.N. men say, as we all have since, that had it not been for the smoke-screen put up by the M.L.s and C. M.B.s, and the rescue work done by the former, the action could never have succeeded, in fact could not have taken place at all.

I am saying very little in this book about the part played by the "hush boats" (coastal motorboats), not because their work was not as good as ours (in many ways it was far more wonderful, for although they have double our speed they are only half our length and are practically open boats), but because I think it far better that someone who was on one of the marvellous little boats should describe the "stunt" from their point of view, which I hope will be done. Their personnel is, of course, a mixture of R.N., R.N.R., and R.N.V.R.

Of all those M.L.s which took part in the attack on Zeebrugge the doings of some naturally stand out, though I think that it can be safely said that all officers and men did their duty faithfully and well on that now famous night.

The first two M.L.s to get inside the Mole were those of Lieut. H. A. Littleton (M.L. 526) and Lieut. P. T. Dean (M.L. 282), and these two boats constitute the keystone of what credit is due to the M.L.s for their share in the action. The first of the block-ships to enter was *Thetis*, and close on her quarter was an M.L. Next came *Intrepid* and another M.L., with *Iphigenia* close behind. Of the two other M.L.s that were also to attempt the enemy harbour, one was that of Lieut.-Commander Young, which was sunk before she got there, and one which had engine trouble and could not reach the entrance in time.

A very brisk fire was opened on the ships as they came round the end of the Mole through the gap between the barges and the boom to the shore, and the old cruisers plunged on to their objective— the blocking of the entrance to the Bruges Canal—at the same time briskly answering the fire of the shore batteries with their guns. Then *Thetis* had the bad luck to fall foul of the net boom to the beach with her propeller, which left her at the mercy of the guns on shore, so her Commander was forced to sink her where she was, where she would be an obstruction, though not in the spot intended.

Heedless of the heavy fire from the shore, Lieut. Littleton closed her in his M.L. and picked up the crew, who were already in the boats waiting for the explosion. When all were aboard, he turned to leave the harbour, but just as he did so a shout was heard from behind, to the effect that another boat-load was coming, and right back into that inferno of fire Lieut. Littleton took his M.L. and got the crew aboard and turned once more to clear harbour, but stopped again to pick up a man who had fallen in the water from one of the ships' boats. Then with a surplus crew of sixty odd, the M.L. found her way outside the Mole amidst the smoke and hail of shells, to arrive finally at Dover without mishap beyond a machine-gun bullet through her after-hatch and a piece of shrapnel through the roof of her bridge-house. A wonderful achievement, and a wonderful escape.

To the Number One, Lieut. Lefroy Geddes, genuine praise is due for his untiring efforts and nerve throughout the whole affair, ably seconding his skipper in the rescues and in the running of the ship under heavy fire, bringing it safely out of the danger zone while Lieut. Littleton was doing his best to make the wounded comfortable with the limited accommodation a motor launch affords.

Meanwhile *Intrepid* and *Iphigenia* were making their way into the mouth of the Bruges Canal, followed by Lieut. Dean in his M.L. His achievement was possibly the most remarkable of any M.L. throughout the whole action, for he was instrumental in saving over a hundred men from *Intrepid* and *Iphigenia*. Curiously enough, they managed to get inside the Mole with hardly a shot fired at them, by using one of the blockships as a screen from the enemy guns. Still following close behind *Intrepid* and *Iphigenia*, Lieut. Dean managed to get his boat straight into the mouth of the Bruges Canal and waited alongside the western arm while the block-ships swung into position, putting up an effective smokescreen which certainly hampered the shore batteries, which had by this time transferred their attention from *Thetis* and were submitting the two ships in the mouth of the canal to a devastating fire.

After the explosion which sank the block-ships Lieut. Dean closed them and took off the crews, who were already in the boats casting off. These he got aboard and was just going to leave the harbour when his boat grounded on the sloping side of the canal, damaging the propellers. At that moment he perceived at the stern of the *Intrepid* a Carley float with one man on it, so he went ahead again and took off the occupant, who happened to be the captain of *Intrepid*.

So intense was the fire all around that the M.L. was forced to back out to save time, and as this had to be done with damaged propellers it was certainly a wonderful piece of work, laden as the launch was at the time; and it must be remembered that all the while the brilliant star shells made the whole scene as light as day. During the manoeuvre three men on the launch were killed, including the coxswain at the wheel. Still coming astern, the C.O. brought his boat round the stern of *Thetis*, when he managed to turn her and commence the perilous passage out of the harbour, passing the gap in the Mole which was clearly visible by the light of the star shells.

It says much for the coolness and resource of Lieut. Dean that he thought of the daring plan of running his boat close along the wall of the Mole, thus rendering ineffective many of the larger German guns which could not be depressed sufficiently to bear upon the M.L., although of course the manoeuvre could not prevent the heavy fire from the machine-guns being directed upon her. Just as the boat was clearing the harbour, in fact as she was passing the last of the anchored barges which marked the entrance, a shell from the shore batteries

ZEEBRUGGE, ST. GEORGE'S DAY, 1918. H.M.S. *VINDICTIVE* APPROACHING THE MOLE THROUGH THE M.L.'S SMOKE-SCREEN.

burst right over the dinghy and killed several men, and carried the deck pump away, while another hit the forecastle, killing three men and wounding several others.

It is certainly a little less than a miracle that the boat managed to get to the open sea at all, for at this point the steering gear jammed, owing to a body getting entangled in the wire, and several valuable minutes elapsed at this vitally critical juncture before the cause could be discovered and the wires cleared, during which time the boat had to be steered by the engines alone.

The behaviour of the Number One, Lieut. Keith Wright, throughout the action deserves the very highest praise for the way he helped his C.O., especially in leaving the harbour, acting as a look-out forward in this perilous passage, where his help was invaluable; this he continued to do in a very exposed position until he fell very dangerously wounded.

Subsequently Lieut. Dean managed to pick up *Warwick* and put the rescued crews aboard her, except one or two dead men and a few of the more seriously wounded, whom he took direct to Deal Pier, where an ambulance had been summoned by wireless.

That an M.L., whose full complement is ten men all told, should have been able to get out of harbour with over a hundred men on board at night, would have been wonderful under peacetime conditions, but when we consider that the feat was performed amidst a tornado of gunfire, some idea of the achievement can perhaps be imagined, for by the time *Vindictive* was clear of the Mole all the attention of the enemy was directed on the M.L.

The first R. N.V.R. officer to be killed was the senior M.L. officer in the action, Lieut.-Commander Dawbarn Young, who was in command of the first boat (M.L. no) to approach the Mole with the purpose of laying flares to guide the blockships in. This he was never destined to do, as when he was about four hundred yards away his bridge was struck with three shells from a shore battery, killing the coxswain instantly and severely wounding Lieut.-Commander Young, Lieut. Lee, and members of the crew. Although mortally wounded, Lieut.-Commander Young stuck to his post and gave orders for the dinghy to be lowered. Lieut. G. F. Bowen, the first lieutenant of the ship, had perhaps what was one of the most marvellous escapes of the whole action, for although he was standing on the bridge close to his C.O. and Lieut. Lee, he himself escaped without a scratch.

Great credit is due to Lieut. Bowen for his coolness at this time, for with the M.L. still under heavy fire, with the unwounded members of the crew he launched the dinghy and managed to get the C.O., who had now collapsed on the deck, into it. Then when all the rest were aboard, he wrenched off the ship's compass, passed it down to them, and got the Lewis gun and emptied two trays into the already holed hull of the M.L., also smashing her in several places under the water-line with an axe, refusing to leave the ship till she was already settling down by the head. The plight of nine men, many of whom were wounded, in a little tin dinghy in such an inferno could hardly be worse, but they stuck gamely to it. It was found that Lieut. Bowen and the chief motor mechanic were the only two who were in a fit state to row; all the rest were either badly wounded or prostrated with shock.

I think the circumstances in which Lieut. Lee happened to be on board this M.L. are interesting. He had just arrived at Dover for the "stunt," and found to his disappointment that his boat was not ready to run owing to some important repairs being done, so rather than miss the action Lieut. Lee obtained special permission to go on Lieut.-Commander Young's M.L. as a spare officer. Even now, while they were in the dinghy, Lieut. Lee, though unable to row, refused to be a passenger, in spite of his wounds, but held the compass between his knees and with his uninjured hand managed to work an electric torch and set the course.

For about half an hour they toiled on, heading away from the Mole with a strong easterly tide. Three C.M.B.s dashed by them, but were lost again in the darkness and the smoke before they could hear the hails of those in the dinghy. Then M.L. 308, under Lieut. H. W. Adams, loomed up in the thick gloom and luckily heard the shouts of the others and took them aboard. Lieut.-Commander Young died on the way across. He was conscious till the last and wonderfully plucky over his wounds. His left arm and right leg were very badly hurt, but it was a gash in his left lung which proved fatal. The death of Lieut.-Commander Young will be a very great loss to the R.N.V.R. in general, and to the Dover Base in particular, where he had been for over two years.

Young was a "white man" in the best sense of the word; a mean or lying action was impossible to his nature, and no man ever set or kept a straighter course than he. He was a most efficient officer and a very hard worker, and expected others to be the same, but he would never ask a junior officer to do what he would not willingly do himself, in fact he often did far more work than he need have done in his position rather than impose on anyone, a fact which all who served under him appreciated. I have often heard men say "You'll always get a straight deal from Young," and it was quite true. And what finer epitaph could he have than the above words? He was the essence of fairness in all his dealings, and we sincerely mourn the loss of a true friend and a very gallant comrade, who died, as he would have wished, at his post of duty.

Lieut. Oswald Robinson was the second M.L. officer to be killed. The circumstances were not dissimilar to those connected with the death of Lieut.-Commander Young. Lieut. Robinson's boat, M.L. 424, was hit while off the Mole, and again it was the bridge that was struck, the shell killing the C.O. and the coxswain instantly. Lieut. Robinson's body was never recovered; he must have been blown away. The only mercy is that death was certainly instantaneous and he could not have suffered. Another incident that was almost the same as the first boat to go was that the Number One, in this case Lieut. J. W. Robinson, was also on the bridge the time the M.L. was hit and came off unscathed.

The dinghy was launched, but before it could be manned, M.L. 128, under Lieut. R. Saunders, came up from out of the smoke and took them off. Lieut. Oswald Robinson will be missed by all, and his cheery personality is a great loss to our little fleet. Only a few days before the action he was one of the principal performers in a concert we got up in the ward-room of *Arrogant*. He was a wonderfully clever mimic and actor, and his impersonations were the making of that concert. To his young wife the sympathy of us all goes out very fully and very sincerely.

Some of the M.L.'s had remarkable escapes during the action, and one of the narrowest was that of M.L. 558, under Lieut.-Commander L. S. Chappell, on which the Flag-Captain, Captain R. Collins, R.N., who was in command of the motor launch flotilla, hoisted his flag. Throughout the hottest part of the action Lieut.-Commander Chappell kept his boat right off the Mole, on the beam of *Vindictive*, to screen, as much as possible, the latter vessel with his smoke. Every now and then when they came to the end of their short patrol the smoke blew away from them, exposing the M. L. to the full glare of the searchlights from the Mole, and the only thing to do was to turn sixteen points into their own smoke and make their way back again and renew the manoeuvre.

This the M.L. kept up during the time that the storming party from *Vindictive* landed on the Mole, and undoubtedly saved them from much of the fire from the western shore batteries. It was Captain

Collins himself who hailed the blockships during the earlier part of the action and directed them to the entrance of the enemy harbour, after Lieut.-Commander Young's boat had been sunk, whose duty this was originally. It was during one of the exposed moments that I have mentioned that Lieut.-Commander Chappell's M.L. had its miraculous escape.

A 6-inch shell landed on their magazine hatch, ricocheted on to a box of six-pounder ammunition, and blew up the latter without, however, exploding every shell. The iron top of the hatch was blown clean away, but fortunately the explosion expended itself upwards instead of downwards, otherwise nothing could have saved the ship. Some of the cordite from the six-pounder shells exploded in mid-air after the shells had been blown to pieces in a very curious way, for the force of the explosion really burst the shells instead of detonating them. The only real damage it did was to set the foredeck on fire, but once again the magazine was saved by the quick action of the Number One, Lieut. C. C. Calvin, who extinguished the flames very promptly with pyrene.

Another of the boats which was screening the searchlights on the Mole was M.L. 252, under Lieut. T. Hedberg, which came in for a good deal of attention from the enemy; but though hit several times the boat seemed to bear a charmed life, for she escaped without casualties if not without signs of her rough handling. To Lieut. Hedberg the credit is due for rescuing another M.L. from what might have been a fatal position, at the retirement. After smoking *Iris* away from the Mole till she was taken in tow by the destroyers, he was on his way to the rendezvous when he saw distress signals from a boat well inshore, and picked up a Morse message to the effect that it was an M.L. in trouble. He went back at once and found the signal had come from M.L. 420, which had been in collision in the "fog" and had her bows very badly smashed in.

At first it was thought that it might be necessary to abandon her, but Lieut. H. Tracey, the C.O., decided that now he had another boat to stand by him he would make an effort to save his ship, and stuck gamely to his task. The engines were still in good order, but owing to the condition of the vessel's bows it was impossible to steam at anything more than dead slow even if she were taken in tow.

Crawling away at this pace from an enemy harbour with the dawn not so very far off was no pleasant journey, but it was either this or transferring the men and sinking the damaged M.L., a proceeding possibly likely to attract the enemy's attention and one which would be accompanied by considerable risk in such a position after the main forces had retired. They steamed on, therefore, and by the time day broke they had luckily managed to get enough miles between themselves and the enemy coast as to be safe from gunfire from shore batteries, if not from pursuing craft.

With daylight a stop was made and the damage to the M.L. examined more closely than had been possible in the darkness, and it was decided to try and rig up a collision mat of sorts. The only difficulty was what to use for this purpose, till someone thought of the canvas recognition signal from the top of the bridge-house. After a good deal of difficulty this was secured over the bows, and the two boats proceeded on their way.

A good deal of anxiety had been caused in Dover by the non-appearance all the morning of M.L.s 252 and 420, and many thought that they were lost, but at about 2.30 in the afternoon we were all glad to see them enter harbour, the last of all to return from the action. The red-white-and-blue bow of M.L. 420 was certainly something new in camouflage.

There were many narrow escapes in M.L.s that night, for instance, a shell fell into an engine-room without exploding. But it is impossible to narrate every story, or to pretend that this account is that of an eye-witness; the dense artificial fog or smoke in which the whole action took place would render such a thing impossible. All that I have told, however, is from the accounts of the actual participants. As regards the eye-witness point of view, I can speak only of what happened on my own boat, M.L. 314, and, as I trust this will be interesting, perhaps I am justified in telling the story.

We were the most westerly boat of unit "G," whose duty it was to find No. 4 Buoy, previously laid down by a coastal motor boat. This, in the darkness, we failed to pick up, so when we considered that we were in the approximate position (fairly accurately, we subsequently discovered) we dropped our first smoke buoy and stood by as the smoke patrol boats passed us, turned, and disappeared to the eastward. It was a signal for a fresh shower of shrapnel and pom-pom shells around us, a good deal closer than was pleasant. This gave us an idea. If the Germans liked to fire at those buoys, why shouldn't they, as long as the position of the buoys in question was where *we* wanted them?

Accordingly, under cover of the thick pungent smoke, we steamed northwards for a minute and then westward at full speed for about two miles, and then more cautiously we made our way inshore. We must have been about five hundred yards or so away, for by the light of the star shells over Zeebrugge we could see the beach and the sandhills beyond quite plainly. All at once the beams of a powerful searchlight blazed out from the shore and swept about us. At first, we were not located, but after a moment they picked us up and then the batteries opened fire. A smoke buoy was dropped at once, and we managed to dodge the beams of the searchlight behind the thick smoke that poured off. We drew off for about a quarter of a mile, but the batteries still continued blazing away and the searchlight was trying to pierce the smoke to discover what was behind the flare.

We then dropped a second buoy, and about a quarter of a mile further on let go a third. All these sent up the same bright flare—we made certain of this by removing a small plate before we dropped them—and a perfect fusillade from the western shore batteries was poured forth at them. We put out to sea again, and as no shots came near us, we waited to note the effect of our little ruse. It certainly seemed to be answering, for we undoubtedly had the Hun guessing. Those lights so close inshore, away from the main operation, evidently puzzled him; possibly he imagined that something in the nature of a landing was being attempted, which was just what we wanted him to think. But whatever he thought he certainly wasted a lot of ammunition on nothing, which meant less for *Vindictive* alongside the Mole.

It appealed to our sense of humour to think that one solitary little M.L. a couple of miles away from its friends and relations could put the "wind up" the Hun to that extent. Had we not been getting short of buoys and in need of what we had left for our correct position, we should have been tempted to repeat the experiment, but we steamed back to our original place in the line and carried on smoking till the time for the retirement. We had nothing much near us for the rest of the night beyond stray shots. I think the western batteries were still waiting for the fictitious landing party somewhere Blankenberge way.

Some of the credit for the success of our ruse is certainly due to my Number One, Lieut. Gordon Ross, who carried on during the whole action with a broken finger, superintending and assisting in the dropping of the buoys, no light articles, and awkward to handle on the narrow gangways of an M.L.

On our way to the rendezvous, we waited for about half an hour off Zeebrugge in case we could be of assistance to any men or vessels in distress. *Vindictive*, *Iris*, and *Daffodil* we knew had gone, for they were working to a schedule of time, but we saw nothing, though we kept a good look-out for any pursuing German craft. Apparently, none came out; I think they were too rattled and too thankful that the British had gone to worry about pursuit.

Then full speed for the rendezvous, but there were no ships left there by the time we reached it. And so on, still full speed, for Dover. I shall never forget that run, tearing through the blackness of night "all out." About half-way across we had a bit of excitement; a dark shape was sighted on our port bow; it was a ship of sorts, and looked very like a submarine. We challenged it at once, and by the reply knew it to be a friend, so we closed it and discovered that it was an M.L., curiously enough the next boat to us of our own unit. They also had seen no one since leaving Zeebrugge, so we sped on in the darkness together. When dawn broke, we were still out of sight of land, and a slight haze on the water made visibility bad. The first thing we picked up was a wreck on the Goodwin Sands, which loomed up suddenly out of the mist rather nearer than we thought ourselves to be. Soon a white line of breakers warned us that we must alter course to the northward.

We reached Dover Harbour just as *Vindictive* had entered. That entry will live in my mind for ever. About six M.L.s were converging out of the fast gathering mist, and I am afraid we all raced for the eastern entrance. M.L. 314 won, and we had the honour of being the first M.L. to enter harbour from the Zeebrugge action.

Then came what was to me perhaps the most stirring part of the whole affair. As the six M.L.s passed *Vindictive*, battle-scarred and covered with the signs of her wonderful fight, all eyes were turned upon her and the men who thronged her deck, many of whom also bore signs of their fight in the way of slings and bandages. Then these men, remnants of the landing party and the ship's company, each of whom deserved the V.C., waved their caps and cheered again and again as the M.L.s steamed slowly past. We could scarcely believe our ears, that these men, whom we felt we ought to be cheering, actually got in first with a cheer for the M.L.s who had helped them in their wonderful achievement

That cheer went straight home to the heart, and its echoes will sound there to my dying day. Our little ship's company replied lustily, and our whistles added their voices. But to be cheered first—well, I am not ashamed to own that a lump came into my throat. To lead the first M.L.s into harbour from Zeebrugge and to be cheered by *Vindic-*

tive's crew—it seems like a dream now that I look back upon it.

During the next few hours, the M.L.s returned to port in driblets, some bearing the marks of their narrow escapes from enemy gunfire or collision in the fog. These hours were anxious ones for us, waiting to learn who was safe and who had fallen. At length all had returned but two, and of these we had received reports of their loss. Then we knew the fate of all who had gone into action with us. The feelings in our hearts were mixed: genuine sorrow for the good comrades who had made the Great Sacrifice and thankfulness at our own escapes, and, being human, a certain amount of pride that we had helped in an action that will live in the naval annals of the world.

ZEEBRUGGE, APRIL 23, 1918. M.L.s RESCUING THE CREW OF THE BLOCKSHIPS IN THE MOUTH OF THE BRUGES CANAL.

CHAPTER 8

The Double Offensive

THE M.L.s AT OSTEND

At the same time as the operations at Zeebrugge were in progress another naval force was attacking Ostend with the intention of blocking the harbour entrance there with the old cement-laden cruisers *Brilliant* and *Sirius*, and although these blockships were not destined to be so successful as those at Zeebrugge, the M.L.s at this action carried out their part of the programme as efficiently as did those farther up the coast.

To describe the smoke screen made by the M.L.s here would be repetition, for it was similar in working to that put up at Zeebrugge. The operations at Ostend were under the command of Commodore Hubert Lynes, R.N., though the organisation of the M.L. flotillas at both actions was the work of Captain Hamilton Benn, D.S.O., R.N.V.R., who personally led the M.L.'s into action.

The M.L.s were again responsible for rescuing the blockship crews, under conditions which, if not quite so difficult as those at Zeebrugge on account of there being no Mole to negotiate, were at least dangerous enough, for here the attention of the shore batteries, undistracted by any landing party, was directed fully on the blockships and the accompanying M.L.s, As a matter of fact, opinions differ as to whether Zeebrugge or Ostend was the more difficult to attack, for although the Mole at the former presents an obstacle, and one difficult to overcome, it at least stands high out of the water for over a mile, and is therefore a good mark at night; while the piers at the latter place are comparatively short and low, with a background of houses close behind; the water is very shallow, with the Stroom Sandbank a mile from the shore and the entrance to the channel at an acute angle with the shore line.

With a pluck which everyone admires, Captain Benn selected the most dangerous work for himself, that of following the blockships into harbour and rescuing their crews. The other M.L. which accompanied him on this work was that under Lieut.-Commander K. R. Hoare. Lieut. M. S. Kirkwood was the Number One on Captain Benn's boat, while Lieut. A. G. Bagot occupied a similar position on the second rescue M.L.

The scene at the first rendezvous of the Ostend attacking forces on April 22 was a memorable one. Monitors and destroyers were all busily getting up steam and anchors to form up in their appointed positions in the line for the advance. All was ready, and they were but awaiting the signal to start from the S.O. on the flagship.

The captain of the monitor was watching the mouth of the harbour at Dunkirk, a mile or so away, and giving his attention to a long line of little grey ships that were emerging and fast approaching the rendezvous. These were the M.L.s, which formed in two divisions line ahead on the beam of the monitors, looking very like toy boats alongside the floating fortresses with their great guns and tripod masts. The whole force then started on its way, and the captain continued to watch the M.L.s on each side of him with a thoughtful eye, so much of the success or failure of the operation depended on these "pocket warships," which were responsible for the smokescreen and the rescue work from the blockships; then, turning to a signalman, he told him to make a signal to the leading M.L. The semaphore flags waved the message "From C.O. H.M.S. *Marshal Soult* to C.O. M.L. 532, Good luck to the movies." Thanks were flagged back from the M.L., and then down the two lines of "movies" the message was passed. It was a sportsmanlike and a spontaneous act to send such a message, and was appreciated to the full on all the motor launches, which were rolling and pitching on their way alongside the almost rocklike steadiness of the monitors.

At "R" position the monitors and M.L.s separated, the former going to their bombarding positions and the latter carrying on towards Ostend with the destroyers. On reaching "K" position, all ships stopped for a while until the direction of the wind had been signalled by Commodore Lynes from the destroyer *Faulknor*, and so on again to position "W," where the destroyers made off eastwards, leaving the M.L.s to continue inshore alone and start their smokescreen ere the arrival of the blockships.

The rescue M.L.s waited at the Stroom Bank buoy, where they

were to pick up *Brilliant* and *Sirius*. A slight drizzle commenced, which was viewed by those on board with mixed feelings; it would certainly help to keep the smoke-screen low down and prevent it from drifting away too rapidly in parts and getting "patchy," but on the other hand it meant that weather conditions "upstairs" were probably not such as were suitable for our airmen to operate. This unfortunately proved to be the case both at Zeebrugge and Ostend. On this night the attacking forces were deprived of the help of the airmen, who were to have played a big part in the operations at both places; a great loss to the inshore craft, as it left the batteries and searchlights practically unmolested and able to give their full attention seaward instead of skywards as well.

The failure of the blockships to find the narrow entrance between the piers on this night was due to the Germans having shifted the Stroom Bank buoy some two thousand yards to the eastward, and shortly before they arrived the wind, which until then had been N., shifted to S.W., carrying the smoke-screen across the mouth of the harbour and blotting it from view, at the same time exposing the blockships and some of the M.L.s to the shore batteries.

When *Brilliant* and *Sirius* arrived at the Stroom Bank buoy they were followed in shorewards by Lieut.-Commander Hoare in M.L. 283 and Captain Benn in M.L. 532, the former close astern of *Sirius* and the latter on his port quarter. It was originally intended that the rescue work should be done by these two M.L.s alone, but Lieut. R. Bourke asked and obtained permission to back them up in M.L. 276, a fortunate arrangement as it turned out.

When about a mile from the shore searchlights picked up the approaching ships, and the batteries concentrated on them; one in particular, to the eastward, was very vigorous. M.L. 532, therefore, put on speed and went ahead of the two large ships, making smoke, which screened them for a time, returning to take station on *Sirius* when this vessel was close in to the shore. It was now observed that a dense volume of smoke was issuing from the after-part of *Sirius*, and she stopped almost immediately, so M.L. 283 went alongside under heavy fire to take off the crew.

Nothing could be seen of *Brilliant* owing to the smoke from the other blockship, which shrouded everything like a black pall. Captain Benn, therefore, determined to go through the smoke after *Brilliant*, but while still enveloped in its density his M.L. came bow-on to the port side of *Brilliant*, which had run aground and swung broadside-on, an action which was expedited by the nose of *Sirius*, which hit her on the port quarter.

The bows of M.L. 532 were completely smashed by the impact as far as the forward bulkhead, while both engines were shifted on their beds and the exhaust pipes broken, filling the engine-room with fumes. The boat was therefore useless for rescue work, in fact it was more than doubtful whether she would founder or drift on to the beach. However, she kept afloat, and thanks to the efforts of the engineers and, later, of Lieut. Kirkwood, who all in turn were gassed and became insensible, one engine was started with great difficulty and kept running. The vessel made her way, at a crawling pace almost, out to the Stroom Bank buoy, where, in response to distress signals, another M.L. came to her assistance and towed her to within a mile or so of Dunkirk, when, the engines having been patched up a little, she was able to get into port under her own power.

It was certainly very hard luck for Captain Benn that he was robbed of the fruits of his risky work just at the very moment that it seemed as if he had achieved his object, that of rescuing men off the blockships, and that, having taken his boat into that living hell of gunfire which the enemy were concentrating at this spot, he should meet with so unlucky an accident at the critical moment that not only rendered his boat unable to carry out her original plan in the operation, but came within an ace of ending her career then and there. He is to be congratulated not only on his plucky and skilful work in reaching his objective, but also on bringing his boat out again in her damaged condition, and, with all others on board M.L. 532. on remarkable escapes from death both from the enemy guns and by drowning if they had foundered after she had struck *Brilliant* in the dense smoke, which at the moment alike blotted out those who had come to rescue and those who were waiting to be rescued.

The other two rescue M.L.s had, in the meantime, been busy at their strenuous and dangerous work in the dense smoke, for not only was our own smoke over everything, but the Germans had apparently put up a counter smokescreen over the harbour mouth, which fact, combined with the shifted buoy, made the finding of the pier heads almost impossible before the blockships grounded in the shallow water by the beach. A raking fire was kept up on both vessels the whole time, and *Sirius* was badly holed quite early and began to settle down. Before long, both blockships had been hit repeatedly, but though badly damaged they returned the enemy's fire fiercely, the gunners continuing to serve their guns till the last.

Star shells lit up the scene, as far as smoke would permit, at frequent intervals, and "tracers" and "flaming onions" (strings of small star shells) went whizzing past. As soon as the blockships grounded Lieut. Commander Hoare closed *Sirius*, no easy task in the dense "fog" and hail of shells which were falling round her. He found a whaler in the falls full of men; this could not be launched, as it was badly holed, but the occupants were soon transferred to the M.L., which stood off while the captain and his assistants fired the charges which blew the bottom out of the ship. Lieut. Commander Hoare closed *Sirius* once more and took off the remainder of those aboard, and on the way came across the whaler of *Brilliant*, full of men, but badly holed and in a sinking condition. He stopped to rescue these before proceeding to complete his work alongside *Sirius*. This M.L. had now some seventy-five men aboard, and seeing that the other boat was closing *Brilliant* they put out to sea, subsequently landing all their "passengers" at Dunkirk.

Lieut. R. Bourke in M.L. 276, with whom was Sub.-Lieut. Young, was doing equally good work alongside *Brilliant* all this time. In the dense smoke they missed the whaler which had already been launched, but closed the blockship and took off the captain and thirty-five men who were still on board. In addition to this, Lieut. Bourke went to the assistance of Captain Benn's M.L. when it was in danger of foundering, and towed it into safety.

At the second, and more successful, attempt to block Ostend harbour on the night of May 9, the M.L.s were again literally to the fore, when they were once more under the command of Captain Hamilton Benn, who led us to the attack.

On this night the wind was westerly all day, an unsatisfactory quarter for the operation; but towards evening it began to veer round towards north, and, all other conditions being favourable, *Vindictive*, which had been got ready for blocking Ostend, left Dover for the rendezvous with Commodore Lyne's forces from Dunkirk.

On reaching the appointed position off Ostend, the M.L.s and C.M.B.s parted from the destroyer flotilla and went on into the inner roads, where they put up their smoke-screen in accordance with the programme. None of the harbour buoys were seen that night, but as it was anticipated that they might have been removed by the Germans, no time was wasted looking for them. Captain Benn, who was on M.L. 105 (Commander W. W. Watson), put a Holmes light in the charted position of the Stroom Bank buoy and a C.M.B, put two in the charted position of the Bell buoy, as marks for *Vindictive*. The wind kept fairly steadily from the northward during the operation, and a clear lane in the smoke-screen was maintained throughout.

The enemy appeared to be taken by surprise on this occasion, for although the inshore flotilla began making smoke at 11.30 p.m. the batteries did not open lire until 11.45, when our monitors began to bombard; and then the firing from the shore, though violent enough, was mostly at random, with a heavy barrage at one and a half miles and half a mile at intervals.

Vindictive arrived exactly on time and proceeded in for the shore, followed by Lieut. G. H. Drummond in M.L. 254 and Lieut. R. Bourke in M.L. 276. A few minutes later two C.M.B.s found the piers and discharged two torpedoes at them, but when *Vindictive* got close inshore she could not see anything but smoke; it is possible that the tall houses on the sea-front deflected the wind somewhat and caused the smoke to bank up at this point. *Vindictive*, therefore, cruised up and down for some fifteen minutes, but could not find the harbour mouth until a Dover flare (one million candle-power) was lighted by CM. B, No. 23 (Lieut. the Hon. C. E. R. Spencer), which showed up the entrance directly in front of her, so she carried on right in.

Meantime she had been seen by some of the shore batteries, and a heavy fire was opened up on her and the attendant M.L.s. M.L. 254 was hit by several projectiles, and Lieut. Drummond was wounded by a piece of shell in the right leg. Lieut. Ross, who was working the Lewis gun, was unfortunately killed outright, together with one of the crew. A moment later the coxswain was hit and Lieut. Drummond was again wounded in the shoulder and right arm by machine-gun bullets, but, undeterred by this, he followed in between the piers and brought his ship alongside *Vindictive* as soon as she came to rest in the spot where she now lies.

Two officers and thirty-eight men were got on board despite the continual heavy fire, and, as no one else could be seen, Lieut. Drummond backed his vessel out of the inferno and turned seawards. It was then found that she was badly holed forward, but the pump was got to work, and with the aid of the rescued men bailing with buckets she was kept afloat until she was picked up by *Warwick* half an hour later. It was found necessary to abandon the M.L., and the Admiral gave orders for the gallant little boat to be sunk to avoid any possibility of her falling into the hands of the enemy before she took her final plunge.

Lieut. Ross died in a gallant way and one, I'm sure, he would have chosen, for he was by nature one of the most glad-hearted men I have ever met and always ready to take his share in any adventure. He was the first Canadian to join the R.N.A.S, which he did early in 1915, subsequently transferring to the R. N.V.R.

In the meantime, Lieut. Bourke in M.L. 276 had sustained considerable damage while waiting off the harbour, and two of the crew had been killed. When he saw M.L. 254 backing out, Lieut. Bourke decided to go in to *Vindictive* and look for any survivors that might have been left behind. After considerable search, Lieut. Sir John Alleyne and two seamen were found in the water alongside the blockship and rescued. All three were badly wounded and would undoubtedly have perished but for the opportune arrival of the M.L. Sub-Lieut. J. Petrie managed to get the three men out of the water at great risk to himself.

The M.L. was under very heavy fire all the time, and her dinghy was hit by a six-inch shell, which fortunately went right through without exploding; the steering-wheel was badly damaged and the hull hit in more than fifty places by machine-gun bullets. The engines were hit several times, but the boat was successfully got out of the more immediate danger-zone under her own power before she had to be taken in tow by another M.L. and the wounded men transferred to a monitor. M.L. 276 presented a singular appearance in Dunkirk harbour the next day, with part of her mast shot away and her many scars. Of machine-gun bullet marks alone, she had fifty-five.

All the time that these rescues were taking place Captain Benn was in ignorance of what was happening inside the harbour, and, being in doubt whether M.L.s 254 and 276 had succeeded in taking off *Vindictive's* crew and fearing that they might have come to grief, sent in M.L. 283 under Lieut.-Commander Hoare and M.L. 128 under Lieut.-Commander Saunders to see if further assistance was required, and followed them with Commander Watson in M.L. 105. The rescue work was done, however, but all three boats came under heavy fire; but, with the exception of M.L. 128, they were lucky enough to escape casualties.

The escape of M.L. 128 under Lieut.-Commander R. Saunders deserves more than a passing reference, for it was certainly one of the most thrilling during two actions filled with thrills. As this launch was approaching Ostend piers she suddenly emerged from the smoke-screen to find herself almost on the beach, not more than two or three hundred yards away. By the houses on the front Lieut.-Commander

Saunders knew he was to the westward of the piers, and turned to make for them at full speed, but it was too late to escape attention from the shore, for up went a succession of star shells and a hail of bullets from machine-guns clattered on to the deck. One man standing just behind the C.O. was killed instantly, but the rest of those on board seemed to bear charmed lives.

The glass of the telegraphs on which Lieut.-Commander Saunders' hands were resting was shattered by a bullet, but he was untouched; the coxswain also escaped without a scratch. Lieut. F. F. Brayfield was slightly wounded in the leg, but he had a truly marvellous escape, a bullet actually passing in and out of the crown of his shrapnel helmet without touching his head. The detonator box in the chart-house also had a bullet clean through it, but without hitting a detonator. Escapes from death, literally by fractions of inches, these. No one else was hit before the boat managed to get into the smoke again, but the bullet-riddled hull tells the story of escape very vividly.! believe this boat holds the record of "scars" from machine-gun bullets during the three actions, sixty-six being counted upon her return to harbour.

Owing to a slight eleventh-hour alteration in the plans of the M.L.s, it became necessary to find someone almost at the last moment to take on the none too enviable task of marking the Bell buoy, which is well inshore from the Stroom Bank and not far from the harbour mouth. Lieut. R. Proctor undertook to do this in M.L. 556, in spite of the fact that his boat was so newly commissioned as to be incomplete in many important details, and possessed a crew who were as new to M.L. life as the boat itself. However, by very strenuous hustling, Lieut. Proctor managed to get some semblance of order out of chaos, and to instruct his crew (first having to learn it himself) in the art of dropping smoke-floats.

From Stroom Bank to the Bell buoy was an exciting run under fire, but covered to some extent by a smoke-screen put up by a C.M.B. which had gone on ahead to lay a calcium light float to mark the position. In this important and dangerous spot Lieut. Proctor remained until the blockships and attendant M.L.s and C. M.B.s had passed, laying his smoke buoys to screen their advance, and at the same time keeping the channel clear of smoke, no easy task with the variable wind, and one that required constant care and forethought; to lay buoys at haphazard in such a position would have been worse than useless, as it would have impeded instead of helping the passage of the blockships.

After this the M.L. still stayed by the buoy until the retirement to lay floats to cover the retreat of the eastern forces. In spite of her prolonged stay in this exposed inshore spot, the brisk fire that was. kept up at the position, and the numerous searchlights that were playing around her, the boat was only hit by a single bullet, which did no damage, a result doubtless partly achieved by the excellent use the M.L. made of its own smoke-screen.

The alteration of the direction of the wind in the middle of the operations this night was a distracting factor for the attacking forces, as it necessitated alterations in the original scheme for smoking and that each boat should act on its own initiative in altering its position. This naturally affected the boats near the clear channel rather more than the rest, who had to exercise great care lest their smoke should blow across. In this matter Lieut. S. D. Gowing in M.L. 551 showed fine judgment.

Finding that the wind had shifted and that his present position was quite unsuitable, he made his way to the southward of the eastern edge of the channel, and then running inshore laid several floats with the purpose of masking the eastern batteries during the inshore progress of the blockships. The boat was subjected to considerable fire and certainly had a very narrow escape at one time, for a shell struck the foredeck, tearing out a stanchion, narrowly missing the gun, and passed on without exploding.

Lieut. A. A. Webb in M.L. 23 also showed excellent judgment in laying his smoke-floats on the opposite side of the channel; coming at one time on to a large uncovered area by a smoke-screen, he decided to leave his original position for a time to smoke this unprotected part. By a skilful use of his floats he managed to keep this portion screened as well as his own. It appeared subsequently that, owing to an accident, the boat that should have done this work was not in her position, so, had it not been for the strenuous work of Lieut. Webb, this area would have been devoid of smoke at a critical time.

Much of the success of the smoke-screen at both the actions against Ostend is due to Commander W. W. Watson on M.L. 105, who, as senior divisional leader, led the boats to their positions, a task which called for skilful and accurate navigation under trying conditions. An error or a miscalculation of tidal conditions at the commencement of the proceedings, as can easily be seen, might have led to very serious results to the attacking force.

Again, it is not possible here to record the doings of every M.L., and there would be too much repetition if it were done when nearly every boat was engaged on work of a similar nature. But there are several facts which would be of interest were there unlimited space at my disposal in which to record them, even though the incidents had no direct bearing on the operation taken as a whole; such as the action of Lieut. Mackie in M.L. 279, who broke a shaft early in the proceedings, but who carried on with one engine during the whole time until the retirement rather than leave his position or even distract the attention of another boat by making distress signals. To elect to remain in a crippled condition off an enemy harbour until the end of the action, and take his chance of getting away with the rest rather than retire as soon as the accident occurred, as he would have been quite justified in doing, shows grit of the right sort.

The second action against Ostend differed in some details from the first; the main part of which was a very heavy bombardment to which the inshore monitors were subjected on the latter occasion. For over two hundred missiles, nearly all of a high calibre, were reported as having been fired at them during the operations. Of this part of the "stunt" I can speak from personal experience, for, my own boat being disabled, I asked and obtained permission to go as spare officer on M.L. 17 under Lieut. T. Jenkins. During the latter part of the action, owing to an accident to our smoke gear, we were left absolutely exposed in the full glare of the star shells, which appeared suddenly, soaring above the smoke-screen in a surprising manner, while some were seemingly dropped by a spotting aeroplane which must have been hovering above us.

Each brilliant flash that lit up the sea, sky, and shore was a signal for a fresh salvo from the enemy batteries, and I cannot but pay a compliment to his range-finding on this occasion. The fact that neither monitors nor the attendant M.L.s were hit was marvellous, for there seemed a constant whirr of shells over our heads and the sea was torn up into giant splashes on all sides. One salvo I especially noticed that fell around M.L. 30 under Lieut. A. Chumley. So large were the splashes that they hid the boat completely, and every moment I expected to see a burst of flame as she went up in a roar of exploding petrol tanks; but when the splashes subsided the M.L. was merely rocking with the concussion, but quite unharmed.

It is not to the officers alone on the M.L.s that all the credit should be given: the engineers stuck to their "guns" nobly, unseeing and unseen at their work so vital to the ship. And to the deckhands too a meed of praise is due for their coolness and efficiency under what was for most of them their baptism of fire at close quarters.

Summing up the rescue work done by the M. L.s at Zeebrugge and Ostend on the two nights, eight M.L.s were engaged in this special work apart from those employed making smoke, and two of the former went in twice on the same night, and between them they brought over three hundred and fifty officers and men from the blockships. Two of these M.L.s were sunk, but all alive on board were taken off, and four of them, though badly damaged, were brought home safely.

It requires courage of no mean order to stand on the unprotected deck of a frail wooden craft and go steadily on into an enemy port under a murderous fire, and go alongside a ship that is being hammered by half a dozen shore batteries, as the blockships were hammered by the German guns; yet M.L. 283 was alongside *Brilliant* once, and twice alongside *Sirius*, on the night of 22nd April, and M.L. 532 was with her until her accident. M.L. 276 was alongside *Brilliant* that night, and twice alongside *Vindictive* with M.L. 254 on the night of 9th May. While at Zeebrugge, M.L.s 283 and 526 were both inside the Mole taking off men from the blockships there.

In conclusion I might, perhaps, quote a remark made by an R.N. captain to an M.L. officer on our return to Dover after the second Ostend action. Meeting him on the flying-bridge of *Arrogant*, the captain said: "Congratulations! I hear the M.L.s were up to sample again." A little remark, but one with much meaning.

CHAPTER 9

Dunkirk

My first sight of Dunkirk was characteristic. I had crossed from Dover in the duty destroyer on a winter's afternoon to join my M.L., which was already there. I had been on forty-eight hours' leave, and it had been taken over by my Number One. Darkness had already set in by the time we passed the Dyck Light Vessel, and I stood on deck watching the dim black outline of the coast, unrelieved by a single glimmer of light.

When we were almost abreast of the harbour mouth, or so I was told though it seemed all one black line to me, there suddenly broke upon the night a loud and weird moaning. The remark of one of the after-gun's crew, who were closed up, gave me the clue as to what it was: "There goes old Mournful; now for the ruddy fireworks."

The show was not long starting; it was opened by a flash and roar, followed by a fusillade of bursting shrapnel high in the air. The destroyer now dropped anchor, and we all stood on deck and watched. Flash followed flash and roar followed roar in quick succession, and the bursting shrapnel seemed continuous. At first it was hard to distinguish from a bursting bomb or the flash of a gun, but a little scrutiny soon enabled one to tell the difference, while above all the voice of the siren—the famous Mournful Mary—kept up a moaning obligato.

It was an awful but a fascinating sight. I had been in plenty of air-raids before in England, but nothing to equal this. To know what an air-raid is really like one must go to Dunkirk. We could hear distinctly the whirr-whirr of the Gotha engines overhead, and before long splashes in the water told us that we were in danger of being hit by stray shrapnel from our own barrage. Then all at once, with a roar and a burst of flame shooting high into the night, some building in the docks caught fire to add intensity to the weird night effects. For the best part of an hour this "firework display" kept up, with little intermission, and then a strange silence, doubly intense by the contrast, hung over all, and save for the burning building all was peace again.

We entered harbour, and I made my way to the corner occupied by the M.L.s, and was just going to have some supper when Mournful Mary kindly said grace for me. "Come along," said my sub, and when a man says that under these circumstances there is only one objective—the dug-out. The "fun" had already started by the time we had got on deck as a flash and a roar from the quayside told us. The decks of the moored M.L.s were full of dark scurrying figures, and strange nautical oaths filled the air as men fell over things in the pitch darkness. The sound of a great splash behind us told its own tale—a bomb had fallen near the tier and luckily had not exploded. It happened to be low tide, and this meant getting up a slimy wooden ladder with the two bottom rungs broken. Quite strenuous going enough, without an air-raid.

There was no panic, but there was "some" haste. About twenty men tried to get on the ladder at once in the darkness; one man missed his hold altogether and went into the water, and we had to stay to haul him out. We all got on to the quay at last, though, and in those days the nearest dug-out was across a lock-gate and an open space surrounded by barbed wire with a narrow opening. We all tore along (and our breeches at times) to the accompaniment of bursting bombs and shrapnel, with Mournful Mary cheering us encouragement. I often regret that no official times exist for that course. It was the most exciting obstacle sprint race I have ever been in. It was a chance of the devil getting the hindermost with a vengeance!

For another hour we sat in the dug-out illumined by an odd candle here and there; it was half-full of French soldiers when we arrived, most of whom seemed to take the matter quite philosophically, and curled themselves up on the rough benches or on the sandy floor and went to sleep, mingling their snores with the other discordant noises of the night.

It was very boring down there; it was far more interesting to stand close to the entrance and watch the show, taking your chance of a strafing. It was a good deal pleasanter too. The art of ventilation in dug-outs had not yet reached perfection.

This dug-out life was for those who did not happen to be on patrol on those nights when an air-raid was sometimes doubtful, owing to weather; but on fine nights when a "hate" was almost a certainty, a different programme was arranged for our amusement. This was the interesting event known as "Clear harbour," which meant that at the first sound of Mournful Mary all ships in harbour, except the duty monitor and a few others, had to get out and anchor in Dunkirk roads. This had an excitement of its own, as may be imagined, when about twenty M.L.s are trying to get out of one corner of the docks in the darkness, without lights as a rule; though even with, in such a melee, it is little better. Everyone is going all ways at once, whistles blowing one, two, or three blasts all round you, and just ahead a number of drifters and minesweepers doing the same manoeuvres. It is a wonder that there were not more accidents than there were. But, as a Scotchman sagely remarked, "I expect there really were, only in the darkness you couldn't see them!"

When you were once out in the roads at anchor you were fairly safe, and we used to stand on deck and watch the raid going on over the land. Of course, here again you had to take your chance with the shrapnel and a stray bomb, unless a direct attack was made on the shipping, when naturally it was another story! Then the whole roads seemed alive with bursts of flame and whistle of shell and machine-gun bullet. But I think I am right in saying that during all the time no ship was hit in the roads from an air-raid; at least while I was there, I never heard of it.

However, to go on talking about air-raids at Dunkirk gives one an almost inexhaustible subject, but for those who like statistics about this sort of thing the figures are:—

Air-raids	175
Bombs dropped	5092
Long-range bombardments from land	32
Shells fell in town and docks	165
Bombardments from the sea	4
Shells fell in town and docks	119
People killed	548
People injured	1114

Mere figures, however, are but cold and unromantic things, and can never hope to express for an instant what Dunkirk was like in these days, especially when there was an air-raid, a bombardment from the sea, and one from the land too, all going on at once, as happened one night, I remember. These figures are compiled from a chart recently issued, but personally I can't understand the low number of air-raids here given; I know to us they seemed almost nightly. I suppose they have not counted here those times when the Gothas visited us, either on their way to or from Calais and dropped half a dozen bombs or so as a gentle hint that we must not feel slighted at their neglect of us that night.

How one is to arrive at the definite number of bombs dropped in an air-raid seems a little hard to understand; how can the number of those that fell in the water be counted accurately? On one night in September 1917 there were supposed to have been 360 bombs dropped on the town and docks alone; how far this is accurate I don't know, but I do know that it was a great night!

The figures quoted will show that air-raids were not the only excitements to be found in Dunkirk. There were a few quite exciting bombardments from the sea, and the long-range bombardments from the land were at one time fairly frequent. One of the latter lasted for four days, and during the course of this we had, on my boat, the narrowest escape from being blown to eternity that we ever had had, even in so warm a corner as Dunkirk. We had just come in from night patrol and had turned in to get a little much-needed sleep, when *bang! splash! crash!* our boat was lifted up by some unseen agency and banged down again upon the water with a bump, and the after cabin was filled with black pungent smoke, which poured down the after-hatch, and was so thick that I could not see my Number One in the other bunk, some six feet away, though it was broad daylight.

Thoughts of poison gas filled my mind as the smoke filled my lungs, but it was not so, luckily for us, for our gas masks were up in the chart-house at the time. We went on deck while the boat was still rocking, and it seemed as if some freakish giant had got a huge brush and splashed us all over, from mast to keel, with soft mud. No part of the deck or upper works had escaped; you could not see the original paint work at all, so thickly were we coated. The water was still circling in great ripples about us from a centre some thirty feet or so astern, where a long-distance shell had dropped. It was low tide and it had exploded in the soft mud, which had saved us; a few more feet in its flight, and it would have struck the quayside, when instead of soft mud we should have been spattered with broken masonry if not fragments of the shell itself.

My Number One suggested a move, but I decided to remain where we were, on the theory of the argument that in the days of the old "wooden walls" the safest place to put your head was the hole made in the ship's side by a cannon ball. This theory was justified, and we had nothing more to disturb our slumbers. It was a consolation to us to learn that the next long-distance shell, some half-hour later, passed right over Dunkirk and killed thirty German prisoners in a camp at St Pol; and I cordially agreed with the cook's remark when the coxswain gave him the glad news down the galley hatch, "*That's* the stuff to give the ——s!"

A footnote came out in M.L. orders next day, which I have kept as a memento of this escape:

Dunkirk, March 26, 1918.

M.L. 314 is to be much congratulated on her escape from being struck by a shell during last night's bombardment. The extent to which she was splashed with mud is some evidence of the narrowness of her escape.

Dunkirk was the place for night patrols, especially in the winter. The West Roads patrol was fairly simple; this was practically up and down about a mile out in front of the harbour mouth. The Hills Bank patrol was a bit worse; outside the shelter of the sandbanks you had a rougher time. But both these were play compared with the Zuidcoote Pass patrol. This was one of the most nerve-racking patrols I have ever been on, and meant all hands on deck and a devilish sharp look-out, for it was the usual track of Hun raiders from Ostend or Zeebrugge. The patrol lay some ten miles to the eastward of the roads, through the Zuidcoote Pass into West Deep, and here on all nights, winter or summer, two solitary M.L.s kept watch and ward during the hours of darkness.

It is an eerie feeling to be out in the pitch darkness close up to the German waters and lines ashore, and to know that there is nothing but two small 80foot boats between the enemy bases and the fleet in the roads, and that it is up to you to give warning any moment if some indefinable shapes loom up suddenly out of the blackness ahead. Of course, we were not expected to engage destroyers; our duty then was to "beat it" over the top of a sandbank (this was a high-water patrol) inshore, firing rocket signals and Very lights as we went; though it was comforting to know that a strong fleet was ready behind you to engage the enemy. The passage over the sandbanks would probably have been accelerated by a few rounds from a Hun destroyer, when one had but to pray that the little cherub that sits up aloft and looks after poor Jack would deflect the course of the shells.

In the case of German motor-boats attacking, then it was our job to engage them and "do our damnedest," but it was never my luck to be in a scrap like that; for an action at equal odds would have been a sporting event in motor-launchery.

On one occasion in the Zuidcoote Pass patrol two M.L.s encountered six Hun destroyers, when the latter turned tail and fled as our rocket signals went up. The Huns did not fire a shot even at the M.L.s. I am not trying to say that they fled from two motor launches, but they knew that warning had been given to the fleet and that the element of surprise was foiled, and the Huns had a very wholesome respect for the monitors' guns and the destroyers that were straining like hounds on the leash ready for them. Our destroyers gave chase that night, but the Hun won the race; he is a wonderful sprinter on the "home run."

The next night the Huns came again, but a different way from out to sea (a compliment to the M.L.s, anyway). This was the night of the fight off Dunkirk in the spring of 1918, when six British destroyers turned back twelve German and sank three of them. We were anchored in the roads that night, and we had "front seats" for a very merry little scrap, though all one could see were flashes to seaward, and hear the guns.

Yes, night patrols in those days were never dull, especially in the winter when the seas came off the tails of the sandbanks like a mill-race. The "Dirty Mile" off Dover was bad enough, but I think the Franco-Belgian coast was worse. It was a perfect canal system between all the sandbanks, though it was wonderful how one could get used to it. Then latterly a new move in this water maze was added to our troubles in the shape of a huge explosive floating barrage all round the anchorage, in which the gaps were unlit, and through these we had to pass to our patrols at night.

There was one thought that often used to come vividly into my mind on these nights, and that was the fact that some 330 years before one of the most famous British naval victories had been won on the very waters that we were now patrolling; for it was off Gravelines (between Calais and Dunkirk) that Drake had finally defeated the Spanish Armada, driving them along the coast, past Ostend and where Zeebrugge is now, to be scattered and wrecked in the North Sea. It was to Dunkirk itself that the ships of the Armada were making, where the army that was to invade England was waiting to embark.

Surely these were memory-haunted waters. Here the naval might of Spain was broken, and here the maritime power of Germany was dealt a blow—at the Zeebrugge raid—from which it never recovered; but the King's ships still hold the narrow seas. And may they continue to hold them 330 years hence.

I think that the signal staff at Dunkirk must all have been members of the Navy Branch of the Practical Joke Department mentioned by Ian Hay in his fine book, *The First Hundred Thousand*. Their favourite joke, and one they seemed to love above all others, was to watch for the return of the M.L.s after night patrol, and then, being careful to allow the tired occupants "to get their heads down," to come and wake up the C.O. by yelling down the after-hatch, "A signal for you, sir!" The tired C.O. would sit up in his bunk and take the signal held out to him, imagining at least that something awful had happened or was to happen. He would then read:

The so-and-so buoy off the N.E. coast of Iceland has been moved 3 cables to the S.W.

This he would sign with a curse (*not* muttered, but very outspoken), and promptly forget all about Icelandic buoys in dreamland again. Then about a quarter of an hour after, "A signal for you, sir!" would again be yelled down the hatch, when he would wake up and read:

Admiral Brasshat will hoist his flag on H.M.S. *Blank* with the Grand Fleet today at 1400.

This he would sign with remarks concerning Admiral Brasshat of a lurid and pointed nature, and go to sleep again.

The next interruption was similar to the last, and the C.O. then gained the invaluable information that:

All X★ type depth-charges on ships attached to the Dover patrol would be superseded by Z★ type on the 10th of next month.

The C.O.'s remarks were by this time not only unprintable, but unthinkable also to any respectable person.

The next piece of somewhat startling information that he would be awakened to learn was to the effect that:

Dame Pince-Nez will inspect the members of the W.R.N.S. at Dover on Sunday next, and C.O.'s are to see that all women under their command are properly dressed.

And so, it would go on. The poor wretched C.O. would be awakened at intervals of never more than half an hour during the morning to be informed of changes at the Admiralty; to be told that all ships having twelve-inch guns were to send in ammunition reports forthwith (we had no larger guns than three pounders at that time); to be informed of a sunken wreck in the Persian Gulf; and to learn that a perfect game of general post seemed to be being played with the buoyage system round the British Isles.

The C.O. would soon give up all hope of sleep, and, long since reduced to a state of incoherent but intense expletives, would throw a boot at his Number One (who all this time had been sleeping peacefully, a privilege enjoyed by Number Ones on signal occasions), and ask him how he *could* stay and snore like a pig this beautiful morning, and then proceed to get up and smoke a pipe on deck to calm his shattered nerves.

Day patrol was better, in fact even pleasant given fine weather. At some unearthly hour, any time between two and six a.m., the "Circus" used to assemble at "Y" buoy. The performers usually consisted of two big monitors, two small ones, a couple of sweepers, a drifter or two, and half a dozen M. L.s; and this flotilla used to proceed upon B.C. patrol (B.C. = Belgian coast). About daylight half a dozen destroyers used to rush up (incidentally nearly upsetting the M.L.s with their wash) and take up their stations on our beam slightly ahead of all ships, save the sweepers.

Our course lay right up the war channel to the northward of Zeebrugge, and every day this procession would set out as a gentle reminder to the Hun that he had to behave himself, at least during daylight hours. About three times a week we used to bombard the coast, and therein lay our use for making smoke-screens a little inshore from the monitors who fired over our heads. One cannot help giving the Hun all credit for his range-finding, for in *three shots* I have seen the monitors straddled at twelve miles. It was the shorts that we had to fear; but it was pure "joss" if they hit an M.L., for eighty feet by twelve is a small mark at twelve miles. We had some pretty narrow shaves, though, and I have seen M.L.s rocking often with the wash of a tower of water some hundred feet high from a shell that just failed to find the range of the monitors. These bombardments were some of the grandest sights I have ever seen at sea and full of excitement.

It was very seldom that the Hun ever showed his nose outside harbour on these little strafes, and then only at a safe distance, on the chance of cutting off stragglers. During all the time I took part in these affairs I can only remember one hit on one of the British ships,

B.C. Patrol. Monitors bombarding the Belgian coast behind M.L.'s smoke-screen.

though once an M.L. was almost telescoped by the concussion of a fifteen-inch that fell just astern of her.

But even this B.C. patrol was not without its humour; though when you have to turn out and put to sea on a bleak winter's morning at 5.30 it is a bit hard, perhaps, always to see the funny side of things, I can recall one morning in particular, though, when an incident, small in itself, occurred that seemed to take the edge off the unpleasantness. It was a particularly blustering morning when we turned out on deck in the pitch darkness; the wind was biting, and the general conditions spoke of a nasty sea running outside. Six M.L.s were to go out, and on five of them preparations for departure were going forward busily.

On the sixth, however, there was not a sign of life; they had, as our French master at school used to say, "slept over themselves," seemingly. The S.O. M.L.s sent his coxswain to give them a gentle reminder to this effect. The man went forward to the forecastle of the belated M.L. and roared down the hatch with a voice like the bull of Bashan, "Now then, you ruddy swabs, wake up and come and do something for your —— king and country!"

Such patriotism at 5.30 on a cold winter's morning was surely a noble thing.

On another morning we were leaving harbour just before dawn at the same time that the night patrol M.L.s were coming in. Now a monitor is rather an unwieldy thing to manoeuvre in a harbour mouth, and the tug that was towing one of these floating fortresses to the open sea managed to get her almost broadside on in the mouth, to the discomfiture of an incoming M.L., which in the pitch darkness fouled the monitor's blister, and, unable to stop in time, found herself with her bow high and dry upon the flat surface, being carried out to sea again very much against her will. It must have been a humorous sight for those who could see anything (I was too far ahead, and only heard the shouting), though I don't suppose those on the M.L. appreciated it to its full extent at the time. The captain of the monitor came down from the bridge and stood for a moment looking down at the dark shape by his port bow, and then said in a most aggrieved tone to the M.L., as if addressing a stowaway, "But you *can't* stay here, you know."

The subsequent signal the captain sent to the commodore reporting the incident, after the M.L. had managed to get clear by the combined efforts of both crews, was a delightful touch, a climax to an affair that luckily ended without much damage. It read:

I beg to report that the monitor, H.M.S. *Blank*, has just been rammed by an M.L.

Dunkirk was a great place for rumours, and one of the most extraordinary of these was in full force when I first got there. How much truth there was in it I never discovered, but it was to the effect that frequent murders took place in the docks, and horrible stories were related of men being found in the water with their throats cut or knocked on the head! Where this originated is a mystery—probably from some sailor having fallen in after "looking upon the *vin blanc* when it was red,"—but I know these stories were always told with lurid details to newcomers. We thought it might take their minds off the air-raids a bit! Various reasons were assigned for these happenings, ranging from French hooligans, *via* German spies, to "Chinks" or members of the Chinese labour gangs that used to work in the docks.

Although Dunkirk may have been a "city of dreadful night," it was an intensely interesting place in the daytime to the eyes of imagination; though even the dullest intellect could not have failed to note the living tragedy that lay in its heart, when none of the inhabitants knew what terrors the night would hold, or who would be alive to see the dawn.

Historically, much could be written of Dunkirk, though there is no space here for such an account; but it is interesting to note that for a few years in the seventeenth century it belonged to England, and, although history did not exactly repeat itself recently, it was certainly the English that kept it going during these dark days, both by reason of the protection given to it by our Fleet and the money spent in the town by the "Navy of occupation."

Commercially, too, its own story could be told, for in pre-war days it was a busy place—the third largest port in France; but here again the story must be told elsewhere. The size of the docks, partially deserted as they were, gave indication of the commerce that must have flourished here to keep such a huge place going. To a rambler the docks seemed never ending, and in the remote parts a scene of desolation; ruined buildings abounded on the quayside, broken bridges stopped the wanderer's way, and here and there the wreck of some deserted merchantship or fishing vessel told its own tale.

In the town the ruins were even more frequent; there was hardly a street without some shattered house in it; sometimes half a dozen were practically razed to the ground, while others bore many scars from bombs that burst near; windows were boarded up everywhere; in fact, glass once broken was never replaced, for obvious reasons, and in some quarters of the town there was hardly a whole pane to be seen. In the poorer quarters sacks and rags were used in the place of wood for, protection against the weather. It was indeed a city of desolation in those days. I shall never forget a walk through Dunkirk during one of the long-range bombardments. Every now and then a bang from somewhere around would announce a new arrival, and one could see the black smoke shoot above the housetops.

It was like walking through a city of the dead; scarcely a soul was to be seen in the streets, for on these occasions, and on every night, Dunkirk was a town of Troglodytes, when all folk returned to their cellars or the dugouts. Cellars were apparently open to all, and most had a red flag hung outside and the notice "*En cas d'alerte*" pasted on the wall outside. But a stuffy cellar full of excited French people was, to my mind, a far worse pandemonium than a half-hourly explosion which was just as likely to be a mile away as a yard. Air-raids, of course, were different, in comparison with which a long-range bombardment is a leisurely and gentlemanly strafe.

The French clearly thought the English mad on these occasions, especially at one time when such a bombardment had been going on for four days, with a shell at more or less regular intervals (for the Hun is methodical in this as everything). Fearing that our nerves might become "jumpy" under this strain, we got up a football match—"Dover M.L.s v. Sheerness M.L.s,"—while later in the afternoon the M.L, officers played the Commodore's staff at hockey. This was a most exciting and strenuous game, and played in a paved courtyard to the accompaniment of bursting shells, sometimes near and sometimes in the distance. No damage was done to us by these. I wish I could say the same of the hockey, played under strict Dunkirk rules. We bore the honourable scars of this fierce fight for weeks. I forget who won, but I think we had more bruises than our opponents. French paving-stones are no respecters of persons.

Of social life there was practically none in Dunkirk; all the better-class people had left it long since, and only those remained whose business kept them here. But at the same time, I was surprised at the number of shops open, which apparently seemed to be doing well. The scene in Jean Bart Square on a Saturday morning and afternoon was a very busy one. The whole square was full of booths and a general market was in progress, people coming in from the surrounding villages to do their weekly shopping. This was the only day the place was ever crowded, though on most afternoons there was a fair quantity of people about; but after sunset very few seemed to venture abroad. It was not a healthy place at night.

All the public buildings were closed, with the exception of the Hôtel de Ville, which seemed to bear a charmed life; only once was it hit, and then only by flying shrapnel. The cathedral church of St Eloi was badly smashed up; the nave was but a debris of broken masonry, and the Lady Chapel almost completely wrecked. The tall tower at the opposite side of the road seemed to have escaped. This tower was far older than the cathedral itself, of which it had once been part. On the top of this was "Mournful Mary's little sister," a smaller and shriller syren that went off directly after, and seemed like an echo of its famous relative. Mournful Mary herself was in these days quite a public institution. It was really an old light-ship that lay in one corner of the docks. I think they ought to preserve it in the local museum.

I was glad to see that old Jean Bart, the seventeenth-century buccaneer-admiral, escaped all injury, and to the last still waved his sword in the centre of the main square. The Dunkirquois are very proud of him, and they have reason to be, for he is one of the few Frenchmen who have ever been too good for the English at sea.

The country round Dunkirk is flat and uninteresting, but for those who cared to indulge in the sport of "lorry-hopping" there were some interesting places to see. The best of these, I think, was Bergues, about eight miles away, one of the most delightful old-world French walled towns I have ever seen. To go to Bergues was almost like going back into the Middle Ages save for the costume of the people, and even that had very little of the modern about it.

Malo-les-Bains was interesting, but quite modern. It is really the seaside quarter of Dunkirk and far more typically French than Dunkirk itself, which is very Flemish in parts. Malo-les-Bains lies a mile or so outside the walls, and was a favourite walk of ours. It was badly knocked about; half the Casino was in ruins, but in the other half they still had a weekly cinema show on Sunday afternoons, about the only excitement the district still retained—beyond air-raids, that is.

Dunkirk is surrounded by walled fortifications and dykes, the former now quite obsolete as regards modern warfare; but they made a picturesque ramble. The gates of the town were always closed at night in quite the old-fashioned way.

Just outside one of the gates is the cemetery, a place with a rath-

A GERMAN MINE ASHORE

M.L. EXPLODING A MINE.

er pathetic interest of its own. The French, always elaborate in their mourning, are very fond of erecting glass-houses, not unlike small green-houses, over the graves, in which they put a great quantity of artificial flowers and usually a photograph of the departed. It can be imagined what havoc the air-raids had played with these. But better here, I thought when I saw it, in this garden, whose inhabitants had passed to a world that cared not for the largest bomb, than in the quarters of the town among the living.

This cemetery supplied evidence of the origin of Dunkirk, for quite half the names on the stones were Flemish, and not French. It had quite a cosmopolitan air, this only spot in Dunkirk whose dwellers slept in peace at nights. In one corner were the French war-graves, each headed with a small wooden cross that bore a tri-colour rosette; in another lay the English, sailors and airmen chiefly, whose graves all bore crosses, some very simple, with bits of tin slips from an automatic machine to show the identity of the occupant, while others were painted, with one or two very well carved in oak.

One airman had the propeller of his machine at the head of his grave as a cross. In one far corner, apart from all the rest, were half a dozen or so graves with large crosses painted with white signs of which I could make nothing, but I presumed them to be the resting-places of French colonial soldiers, from Algiers or Morocco, who had fallen in this sector of the war-zone, this cold northern clime so far away from their native desert. There was even a German—an airman—buried in this cemetery. Here they slept undisturbed, friend and foe alike, in the Great Peace that must come to us all in this life of strife, caring nought for the red tide of war that ebbed and flowed but a few miles away, deaf to the thunder of the big guns from the sea hard by and the fierce nightly combat that was waged high in the sky above them.

At one time during the war "The Man who dined with the *Kaiser*" wrote an account of it, and earned thereby a certain amount of notoriety; but "The Man who smoked out the King," though well-known at one time at Dunkirk, is at present unknown to fame. I was unlucky enough to be the latter individual.

It happened when the king came to inspect the naval forces at Dunkirk, and my boat was told off, with another M.L., to give a demonstration of smoke-screening. The king was on a monitor which was moored to the quay at a narrow part of the harbour, near where we had to pass as we made our way from the entrance smoking furiously.

Now the signal for us to stop smoking was the negative flag hoisted on the monitor, instead of a blast on the syren, as it ought to have been. This was all right for the leading M.L., and she cut off accordingly, but, as it takes some little time to clear the smoke from the pipes, the monitor ahead was completely hidden from us. So, on we came, belching forth a lovely cloud of smoke, which, by the time we saw the signal, was far too thick to be cut off in an instant.

The result was that the wind carried it, rolling full and strong over the monitor's quarter-deck in thick pungent fumes. I could see nothing of monarch or monitor as we passed; but looking back after the smoke had cleared a little, I saw the king holding a handkerchief to his face and apparently coughing violently.

I half expected to be "strafed" for this little episode (for to get into trouble over another's blunder or error in judgment is not unknown in the annals of war), but nothing happened. In fact, I was told subsequently by an officer from the monitor that the king took it in a very sporting spirit, and was more amused than annoyed at being smoked out by an M.L.

When I said there was no social life in Dunkirk, I was forgetting an incident that befell me in those days in that stricken city, which, since it contains certain humorous elements and a lucky escape from what might have been an embarrassing situation, is perhaps worth recording here.

It came about through my habit of wandering and exploring back streets; always more interesting to my mind than main thoroughfares. I don't think there was a street or lane in the whole of Dunkirk that I did not explore, usually to the no small astonishment of the inhabitants. It was in the course of one of these rambles that I came upon the adventure. I was going down a street, not a back street this time, though not one of the main roads, when I saw a small shop that sold postcards, tobacco, and things like that. Not that there is anything remarkable in this fact, and it was purely chance that made me enter it to make some small purchase. Those humble doors were the portals of romance; rather too much of it, as it turned out.

A pleasant-faced middle-aged woman served me; she was very gracious, and I stayed to chat with her for a while, if very halting remarks in bad French on my part in reply to her voluble flow could be so-called. I was just about to make my departure when Marie entered.

Now the dark eyes of Marie were all the trouble, for had they not smiled on me then I probably should never have entered the shop again. I mean this literally, it was her eyes that smiled; her little mouth was very demure. Marie, it may be explained, was an exceedingly pretty girl of some eighteen summers, and *Madame* introduced me to her as her daughter, Marie knew a little English, and the conversation took a new lease of life, and by the time that Palmyra made her entry things had brightened up considerably. It is perhaps unnecessary to say that I had long since given up all thoughts of a speedy departure.

Palmyra was some four years older than Marie, and equally good-looking in a rather more typically French, but equally delightful, way. She knew no English, but that was no bar to her joining in the conversation.

So that was the beginning of it all. I often called at that little shop and bought enough postcards and other useless trifles to stock a shop of my own. *Madame* was always very gracious, and explained that she was most anxious for her daughters to learn English, and it was so good of "*Monsieur le Capitaine*" (they promoted me at once up to four stripes) to come and talk to them, and she hoped that I would learn French at the same time. Artful mamma! I hoped so too. Anyhow, it was better to stay and talk to two pretty dark-eyed French damsels than look at ruined houses.

By degrees I learned their history. They were refugees from Lille, who had fled with sundry of their relatives before the advancing Huns; but though they had saved themselves they had lost everything. The father was a lawyer's clerk, but was now with the French Army near Verdun, and he had managed to settle his wife and daughters in this little business by the help of a relative.

Time went on, and I certainly soon found that it was easier to talk French than it had been, and before long I was able to converse comparatively fluently, if a little colloquially, with *Madame* and the two girls. Then I did a rash thing: I asked *Madame* if she would let me take Marie to the cinema at Malo-les-Bains on the following Sunday.

"*Mais oui, m'sieu,*" she replied, beaming on me, "*certainement; c'est très amiable de m'sieu le Capitaine!*"

(This French is quoted entirely "without prejudice": at least it was *something* like this.)

Well, Sunday afternoon, and I accordingly arrived at the little shop. There was Marie, looking prettier than ever in her Sunday best, and I was introduced in state to one or two relatives, who had, I thought, come round to see us start, as they appeared to be very interested. So, we soon set off, and I was looking forward to an afternoon of Marie's company alone. But I had counted my eggs a bit too early, as I discovered when, to my horror, a middle-aged and very stern-looking aunt detached herself from the little group round the door and ranged herself alongside us with great determination.

There was no escape. I did my best to lose Auntie, but she would not be shaken off. As a chaperon she did her work well—too well. We ran for a tram, hoping (at least I did) that Auntie would lag behind and lose it. But not a bit of it. At the first sprint I saw Auntie "up petticoats" and start off like a two-year-old. In the crowd round the cinema entrance, I tried to lose her again. No use. Coming out, I repeated the manoeuvre. Futile. We turned quickly down a side road, when Auntie was a bit in front, to get to a certain tea-shop, but Auntie went astern at once and soon caught us up.

After that I gave up the struggle, and reconciled myself as best I could to her presence. Marie made no comment about my efforts to lose Auntie, but I think she understood. What girl wouldn't? It seems that in France one cannot go out with a girl alone as one might in England, in a friendly way. A sort of "*aut Caesar aut nullus*" state of affairs. You apparently either have to be engaged or married to a girl or shun her like the plague. A respectable girl, that is. (I know "respectable" is a hateful early Victorian sort of word, but in this instance, it seems to meet the case without a lot of explanation.)

Who, if they have been based at Dunkirk, does not know that little tea-shop at Malo, where "*les Anglais*" were, by a special act of grace on the part of *Madame*, invited to a back room, and where *Madame* would produce her special cream-cake, even on "cakeless days" (which were bi-weekly in France at that time), explaining in dumb show, aided by sundry nods and winks, the extreme secrecy of the transactions on these days, and how we must be on our guard in case Monsieur le Food-Controller (or his French equivalent) should pay a surprise visit? Ah, *Madame*, your cake was all that French *patisserie* could be. We eat your health!

Well, to return to Marie and the romance that was fast hurrying to its tragic climax. At one of my afternoon calls next week, I could see that *Madame* had something special to say to me, and as soon as we were alone she came up to me in a confidential way: "Would *m'sieu* do them the honour of taking the tea with them next Sunday?"

Monsieur, who had been thinking over the advisability of offering to take Palmyra to the pictures that afternoon on the hope that she, being older than Marie, would be allowed to go auntless, accepted this invitation with profuse thanks. Palmyra and the pictures would have to wait.

That tea was one of the historic events of the war, as far as I was concerned. An afternoon of thrills. I arrived about three and got my first shock early. As soon as I was ushered into the room behind the shop it was to find it crowded with people, to whom I was solemnly introduced, to discover them all to be aunts, uncles, and other assorted relatives. They were very profuse in greeting me. Several aunts even kissed me (on both cheeks). I finally discovered Marie among the throng, looking prettier than ever by reason of a slight flush on her usually rather pale face. She greeted me somewhat shyly, I thought, but this I put down to the publicity given to things by the gathering of the clans.

Then began the tea, an event which in itself was sufficiently entertaining without the additional excitement. We all sat round a huge circular table at which Marie and I were given the place of honour; at least I think it was the place of honour, though at a round table it is a little hard to tell—anyway it was opposite *Madame* and the fattest aunt.

I was not used to French afternoon tea-parties, and the courses surprised me a little. The first was chocolate blancmange. We all ate this in silence. The plates were cleared away by some mysterious female I had not seen before; she was hardly a servant, and apparently not an aunt. The next course was red wine. This we all drank standing, and to my horror all the others raised their glasses towards Marie and myself as they drank. Very embarrassing. We sat down for the next course, which was white blancmange, and so course after course succeeded each other in amazing rapidity. We had (all in separate courses) coffee, tea (of a sort), white wine, beer, biscuits, pink blancmange, buns, gateaux, and finished up as we had begun, with chocolate blancmange.

The lively running conversation that began to spread round the table after the red wine episode was only partially understandable to me, but the frequent references to Marie and *M'sieu* and the glances in our direction gave me the first clue of the horrible truth! In a sensational novel I suppose a cold sweat would have broken out all over me, but as a matter of fact I felt uncomfortably hot. The rest of the tea-party seemed like a nightmare, and I must draw a veil over it.

As soon as I could with decency I urged important duty, bade farewell, and broke through the barrage of slightly astonished but still affectionate aunts to the road. I think there must be some subtle connection in France between betrothals and blancmange, eaten at tea. I feel sure that had I partaken of a few more of these delicacies, in the presence of the girl's relatives I should have found that, by some almost forgotten French mediaeval law, we were married! It was a providential escape.

At that moment I would rather have gone through the Zeebrugge raid again than told the aunts that I had only taken Marie out in friendship and already had a wife in England. And what would have happened had I taken Palmyra to the pictures also, as I hoped to do, I dare not think. I should have been looked upon as a potential bigamist, I'm certain.

I never went near that shop again, but a few days after I met the two girls and told them the reason of my sudden exit. Marie's very real enjoyment of the joke told me that, on her part at least, I need have no qualms of conscience about my "base deception." The aunts—— Ah, that is a different matter!

But still, "sarner fay re-ang," as the British sailor so eloquently puts it about almost anything that happens at Dunkirk!

★★★★★★★★★★★★★★★★★

A chapter on Dunkirk would hardly be complete without some mention of Commodore Hubert Lynes, R.N., who was S.N.O. there during nearly all the time when the real "Dunkirk days" were in being. His very sporting and generous treatment of the M.L.s and his appreciation of our efforts to "carry on" at all costs rendered us doubly keen to do our best.

In conclusion, I should like to quote from a letter I received from him after we had both left Dunkirk, when he wrote:

"Of all our naval war units the M.L.s were, I think, the most delightfully Bohemian element, comprising as they did the very widest scope of varied talent. I am sure it was an excellent sauce, both morally and physically, to our stodgy *haute école* of the R.N. I am always proud to remember that we did get the greatest *use* of our gallant M.L. flotilla for its solid labour and unpleasantness."

Which quotation calls to mind the apt remark made by Captain Hamilton Benn when I showed him this letter. "Well," he said, "whatever the Commodore thought of the M.L.s, there was never any shadow of doubt of what the M.L.s thought of the Commodore."

And there never was.

CHAPTER 10

The Gimlet

A STUDY IN WAR-TIME ECONOMY

We learn many things in the R. N.V.R., some according to the schedule laid down by the authorities and others according to our observation, and the chief among the latter is never to be surprised at the humorous ways of the government. If things happen which in ordinary life would seem Gilbertian, we must try and realise that this is merely the normal way of government departments. I wonder what would happen to any private firm that tried to run on these lines, or any engineering workshop that founded its methods on, say, Portsmouth dockyard? But no, I don't wonder, I know, and so does everyone else who thinks a moment—bankruptcy.

The little episode I am about to relate occurred at a time when we were all warned to economise in paper, as there was likely to be a serious shortage. We did our best, but the Government had a method of doing this in a way peculiar to themselves—a very peculiar way.

When our M.L. left Portsmouth, she was short of one or two things, among which was a gimlet. The cost of this gimlet would, I suppose, be a few pence at any ironmongers. We left in November and managed, with an effort, to carry on quite well without this gimlet—some rash rich man bought another one, I think. We had forgotten the existence of the one we had never had (I had an Irish sub at the time, which will explain this sentence), but not so the Admiralty, or the Naval Store Office at Portsmouth.

At the end of March some eagle-eyed inspector discovered our loss, and, thoroughly shocked at the lack of full fighting efficiency in one of His Majesty's ships, at once sent us two large printed forms in a long envelope. One form was for us to keep and the other to sign and return as a receipt for the gimlet we had never had. I wrote to the N.S.O. pointing out that as I had never had the gimlet, I could not sign a receipt for it with a clear conscience, or words to that effect in official parlance. I then received a note saying that if I signed the receipt saying that I had already got it the gimlet would be sent to me. This seemed rather a tail-about-face way of doing things, but I did it.

Then there was a long pause, and at the end of about a fortnight an important looking package arrived, for which I signed some paper or other. I opened the box, and there, carefully wrapped in tissue paper and packed in shavings, reposed the gimlet, *and* two large printed forms. I signed one again and sent it back to Portsmouth, and put the other with the ship's papers. Any reasonable man might now be excused for considering the matter closed; but it wasn't. About a week later I heard again from the N.S.O., with two more forms enclosed. One, a receipt for my receipt, was marked "8876/4 S.A. N.S.B. 11 255. To complete. To be returned at expiration of service," and the other was a receipt for me to sign saying that I had received this receipt.

This I duly signed and returned, and, rather to my surprise, heard no more of the matter. It had begun to be quite interesting, and I was thinking what splendid writing exercise it would afford my grandchildren to fill in these forms when I was too old to write. It left quite a blank in my life for a time.

Note: The following day the gimlet fell overboard, but I did not report the matter. With paper so scarce and expensive it would have seemed unpatriotic, for I dread to think of the forms I should have had to fill up explaining the full details of the loss. Also, I am rather nervous as to my fate when the loss is discovered by the authorities. I expect it will mean dismissal from the service with disgrace, for it was evidently a very valuable tool, possibly an Admiral's gimlet, supplied to an M. L. owing to a shortage of the common or workshop kind.

Chapter 11

"Dover Guyed"

So much has been written of the Dover patrol that the general public must be, by this time, almost as familiar with it as we were in those unforgettable days.

No need to describe again those never-ending night patrols, the famous Dover flares, or the wonderful minefield so cunningly laid from the English to the French shore. So instead of vain repetition I want to present a side of Dover life that I am certain is new, and that is the only effort in journalism for which the M.L. flotilla were responsible. It may not have been a very brilliant effort, and it was only a one-man show, I'm afraid.

It came out at that time, just before the Zeebrugge-Ostend actions, when everyone was very fed up with endless manoeuvres and orders and counter orders that were buzzing about like flies at that strenuous time. It was meant for a tonic for overtired and strained nerves, and though it never got beyond manuscript form, and was only passed from hand to hand among the M.L.s, I hope it achieved its object. I was told it did, and I like to think it did not fall flat. It was topical if nothing else.

One or two of the items I have omitted, especially from the glossary, as they dealt with personalities or things known only to those concerned with events at the time and would be quite pointless to others.

Nothing is more painful than the laboured explanation usually given before telling a "family" joke to a stranger. Even now I'm afraid it will appeal to those who were at Dover on the M.L.s rather more than to others, but as I have been asked many times to publish, it I do so now. Those who saw the original will know why certain personal and pointed items are omitted!

𝔇over 𝔊uyed
𝔄nd 𝔇unkirk 𝔅omb=𝔅urst

Vol. I., No. 1.   April 1918   Priceless

It has long been felt that the Base should have a paper of its own apart from the daily issues of the *Motor Launch Routine*. Although we cannot hope to equal the brilliant wit of our sparkling contemporary, we still feel we shall be supplying this long-felt want in bringing out this paper. So, with this conventional lie we make our bow to the public, who will find in our pages surprising news of all that has happened and a good deal of what has not.

Dover Daily Orders

(M.L. Comic Cuts, formerly *M.L. Routine)*

Night Patrols.—Owing to a separate peace having been signed between the Dover M.L.s and the enemy, there will be no patrols to-night.

Leave.—All officers must apply for leave under the Bribery and Corruptions Act of 1872. Length of leave will depend entirely on amount of bribe.

Navigation.—Any officer wishing to ram the eastern wall of the harbour should set his course due E. from the western wall.

Refit.—Any M.L. wishing for a refit can proceed to Sittingbourne at once without permission for any period up to six months.

Dunkirk.—The following will sail for Dunkirk (weather permitting or not) at 0200: H.M.S. *Arrogant*; M.L. Office (on pontoon); Floating Dock; South Goodwin Light Ship.

Weekly Reports,—The senior officer requests that C.O.'s will not forward these *less* than twenty-eight days late, as the shock might kill him.

Decorations.—The C.O. of M.L. 1001 has been awarded the Order of the Milk Tin by the Swiss Navy.

Lieut. Blank has got the M.L. Office Cross (frequently).

Complete History of Dover

(Compiled from latest and most reliable sources for use of M.L. officers and men)

Dover is a seaport town on the S.E. coast of England, except during a smoke stunt, when it is moved to the S.W. by skilful camouflage. It is one of the Cinque Ports, but it is known to the M.L.s as the Sink Port, from the clean and pure nature of the water surrounding the M.L.s in the submarine basin. The term Stink Port is also applied during smoke stunts.

Many pleasant moonlight walks can be enjoyed around Dover, especially along the harbour front during air-raids. The close proximity of the M.L. berths to the town is much appreciated on wet nights by M.L. officers. The town itself (when you *do* reach it) abounds in innocent amusements, from whelk-stalls to shove ha'penny, thus partly accounting for the tremendous popularity of Dover as a base among R.N.V.R. men, in whose ranks can be found some of the finest living exponents of the latter sport.

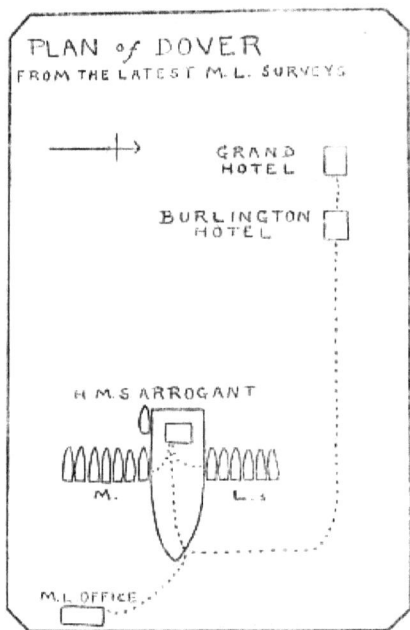

Jellicoe's remark "The Battle of Goodwin Sands was won on the shove ha'penny boards of Dover" is world-famous.

Officers get so attached to Dover that they never want any leave, which is perhaps just as well, for they don't get it if they do.

Dover Glossary

M.L.R.—Motor Launch Routine (see D.C.C.).

D.C.C.—Dover Comic Cuts. A daily humorous paper having a large circulation among the M.L.s. Published as a kindly thought to brighten the lives of the officers.

Bathing Parade.—Morning swim across harbour at 5 a.m. from October to March. The Number One is to see that this is carried out. The C.O. can attend or stay in his bunk as he likes—he usually does!

Submit, Request, and Report.—Interchangeable naval terms meaning anything or nothing.

M.L.—A sort of boat.

Manifold sins and wickednesses.—A series of crimes committed in M.L. engine-rooms.

Brake.—An anchorage for M.L.s off Ramsgate.

Broke.—An anchorage at the end of the month.

Naval Peer.—?

M.L. Office.—The haunt of a little band of humourists.

Linguista Fruita.—A plant readily grown on Dover soil.

Pleasant afternoons with Uncle.—A happy gathering of boys on the naval pier, which meets for a chatty hour. Parlour games are indulged in, such as "Follow my leader," and games with toy boats. The only thing that never flags is the interest.

H.M.S. Burlington.—Flag-ship of the Dover Squadron (see Crossing the Bar).

Refit.—The Promised Land.

Blue Sixteen.—An expression indicating the turning point in the career of every M.L.

Drifter.—See Engines—Dud.

Mixture.—A combination of soot and water supplied to M.L.s instead of petrol.

Leave.—A pleasant fiction.

Smoke Stunt.—1lb. a month can be drawn from victualling stores.

Grand.—A Pilgrim's Rest.

Strafe.—A heart-to-heart talk with Uncle.

Line ahead.—An imaginary straight line drawn from the leading boat to the last one.

Line abreast.—A more imaginary line still.

Masks, gas, one in number.—Should be worn by all officers who go up to be strafed for not attending signal classes or church parade.

Camouflage.—From the Latin "*camou*—I love," and "*flage*—Dover"; a term indicating deception, or a damned lie!

Depth-charge.—A contrivance for killing fish on eatless days. Has also been used for submarines by wasteful people.

Wash-out.—See Leave.

Naval Store Demand Books.—Too serious a matter on which to jest.

To Lieut. (G),
H.M.M.L. Flotilla.

April, 1918,

Sir,

2½ pounder gun on M.L. 000.

I have your request for the History Sheet of our gun, but regret same is lost, but as I think it a pity that so wonderful a history should be lost to the nation, I am putting down as much as I can from memory.

This grand and war-scarred veteran first saw the light in the Trojan war. The fact that this was centuries before the invention of common (or garden) guns, only makes this history the more remarkable! At the siege of Troy, it was cunningly concealed in the mouth of the famous wooden horse; and at its first firing its thunderous bellows completely deceived the innocent Trojans, who mistook the noise for an imitation of a hoarse cough. This was the first instance of camouflage in history.

This gun also made its mark at the Norman Conquest, Bannockburn, the defeat of the Spanish Armada, Marston Moor, Ramillies, Waterloo Station, and the Crimea. I regret that the details have been lost, but rumour has it that Cardinal Wolsey remarked:

> Had I but served this gun as I have served my king it
> would not now have left me naked to mine enemies.

(I don't quite know what this means, but it sounds *fine* for a history sheet!)

Coming down to more modern times, in 1891 this gun was re-modelled by Hotchkiss and Cie of Paris (Monsieur Cie himself, I understand, attending to the matter personally). The range and deflection of the gun are in centipedes—hence the *Entente Cordiale.*

A few years later this fine weapon went out to the Land of the Cherry Blossom (I forget whether this was Japan or the boot-polish factory, but judging by the hieroglyphics engraved on various parts I incline to the former view).

I am sorry that these few facts are all I can remember of the gun's history, but I shall be pleased to take a month's leave (at double pay) and search for more details at the British Museum Library, which, I have no doubt, contains much information regarding this gun that would be of vital importance. At the same time, I should be pleased to search for two missing articles belonging to you, *i.e.*:

1. Your sense of humour, which seems to have been mislaid for some time.

2. The temper you *may* lose on reading this "official" report.

I would suggest—request—report—submit (please take your choice) that this 2½-pounder gun be placed in a prominent position on Dover front after the war, when, with very slight adaption, it could be used as:—

(*a*) A telescope to see the wrecks on the Goodwin Sands.

(*b*) A chestnut roaster.

(*c*) A combination of the above two things.

And at all times to be a lasting memorial of Britain's naval power!

I have the honour to be. Sir,

Your obedient servant,

I. Bangit,
Lieut., R.N.V.R.

ANSWERS TO CORRESPONDENCE

(Fed-Up.)—The verses to which you refer are thought to be a collaboration of William Shakespeare and Charles Garvice, set to the tune of "A Little Bit of Heaven."

The chorus runs:—

Just a little bit of Heaven fell from out the sky one day,
Though I don't know where it landed, but it wasn't Dover way!
But when a bit from realms below roamed from the other place,
It landed just by Dover Cliffs and formed an M.L. base!
So, they sprinkled it with Movies just to make the Navy grow;
It's the hardest place they work them, no matter where they go;
And they dotted it with half-stripes just to make it look so well,
Oh, and when they had it finished, sure, it was a second . . . .

The original MS, was unfortunately torn just at the last word, and up to the present the closest search has failed to find any existing copy of this rare document. A special Naval Court of Enquiry is shortly to be held at the M.L. office on the eastern arm of Dover Harbour to try and throw some light on this baffling mystery.

(M.Ell.)—Dunkirk is a pleasant French watering place where M.L. officers go to recuperate after the strain of Dover. Their life there is in the nature of a yachting holiday and they take little trips to sea at intervals. Social life is very gay in this miniature Paris.

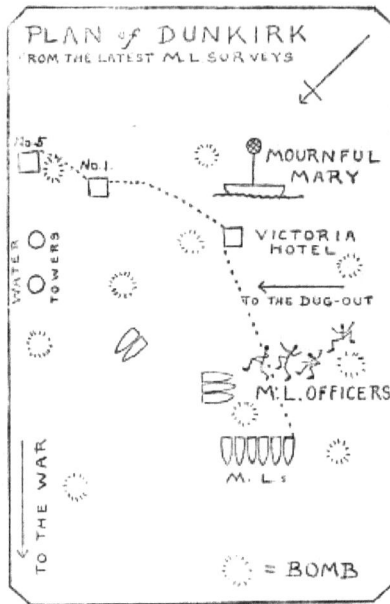

PLAN of DUNKIRK
FROM THE LATEST M L SURVEYS

No.5
No.1
WATER TOWERS
MOURNFUL MARY
VICTORIA HOTEL
TO THE DUG-OUT
M.L.OFFICERS
M. Ls
TO THE WAR
= BOMB

DUNKIRK GLOSSARY

Mournful Mary.—A famous French *prima-donna* whose soul-inspiring voice has moved many people and attracts huge crowds nightly to the Troglodyte Theatre.

Bomb.—A nasty noise.

Dug-out.—Where we dig in.

Hills Bank.—Cheques cannot be cashed here—it's a wet idea, anyway. You may possibly get a check out there some night, however.

Zuidcoote.—A large fish found on the Belgian coast in France. Immortalised in Tennyson's well-known lines

As I wandered out on night patrol
I saw a Zuidcoote Pass."

Monitor.—An unfortunate leviathan frequently rammed by M.L.s.

Baby Monitor.—By M.L. out of Erebus.

Wind up.—That 'orrid feeling.

Cold Feet.—Thick woollen socks and railway carriage footwarmers can be demanded (at the point of the depth-charge) from the naval stores before any stunt.

Ostend.—A seaside resort on the Belgian coast with a fine beach. Interesting to shell-collectors.

Zeebrugge Regatta.—Noted for the famous race between a monitor going broadside on and an M.L. going astern. The result was a draw, as neither reached the winning-post (the harbour mouth) owing to the unsportsmanlike action of the Hun in opening fire at the most exciting part of the race. At the subsequent Court of Enquiry, however, the cup (the only unbroken one left in the M.L. flotilla) was awarded to the monitor, the M.L. being disqualified for having dropped a depth-charge from the bow with a view to increasing her speed by the recoil.

Period d'alerte.—Waiting for the "negative patrol" signal on extra duty nights.

Negative—A positive blessing at times.

Firework Shows.—Nightly entertainments kindly provided by the Hun to brighten our lives.

The Circus.—A merry performance at Y Buoy at 5 a.m. on a winter's morning. Much patronised by M.L.s.

DUNKIRK DAILY ORDERS

No M.L. is to capture either Zeebrugge or Ostend single-handed without filling in triple-quadruplicate copies of Form XYD-5678931BF before starting.

Any officer asking for leave will be given it. If he recovers from the shock, it will be washed out!

If the weather is favourable a diver will be employed astern of M.L.000 to salve the empty whisky bottles. Six barges will be in attendance to take these away.

All M.L.s in future will be moored in Jean Bart Square, stern to Hôtel des Arcades (for convenience of officers). Motor lorries will be waiting after each patrol to take boats to their places.

Top hats are not to be worn with No. 1 uniform except at sea.

Any officer smoking a *hookah* in the streets will be interned in a Turkish *harem*. (*Hookahs* can be obtained at *Le Magasin de Turco* in Jean Bart Square. Come early to avoid the crush.)

NOTICE—TO MUSIC LOVERS AND OTHERS
(Chiefly the others)

A fairly musical, but very dramatic, entertainment will be given in the wardroom of H.M.S. *Arrogant* on April 21, 1918, (the night before

125

the Zeebrugge raid), by certain R.N.V.R, officers whose modesty (together with the uncertainty of getting them up to the scratch) forbids the mention of all their names, though the poster in the ward-room will tell you of the more hardened and unblushing ones who will positively appear.

This concert has been arranged with a view to getting the R.N.V.R. used to the horrors of war, for if they can stand this the capture of Kiel Canal by M.L.s will be child's play, as it would be nothing like as terrible as what they will go through listening to this concert.

Lance-bombs must on no account be thrown at the performers unless the detonators have been removed.

Special emergency exits will be provided through the port-holes to avoid crushing.

The usual joke about the egg-proof curtain being lowered after each item for the protection of the performers to be taken as made for the purposes of this announcement.

A stretcher-party will attend for the benefit of the *"artistes"* after the show.

Admission to Front Seats   Nil.

Seats near the Door   10s. each.

Doors open all day. Commence (about) 9 p.m. Finish Heaven knows when!

It is *hoped* that H.M. the King will attend this concert.

God save the King!!!

ADVERTISEMENTS

Attractions for Visitors

Food Shortage

All those who feel this should come to Dover, where they will be very soon fed up.

Shakespeare's Cliff

So called because the poet tried to commit suicide from here after being in Dover a day—and little wonder.

Lovely Sea Trips

Fast, well-equipped motor launches will run daily (war permitting) to the Goodwin Sands at low tide. Fares: Single 1s. Return 30s. Passengers can have the option of remaining on these famous sands till the lifeboat calls or paying the return fare.

Channel Tunnel

Dover has always been noted as a boring place, and was consequently chosen for the start of this.

CLASSIFIED ADVERTISEMENTS

For Sale.—Motor launch in good condition (once). Has been to sea. Fine large engine-room containing a quantity of very useful metal. Wonderful 2½-pounder gun. Never fails to hit the sea first shot when fired. The boat has no stem to worry about. Owners disposing of same to save cost of refit. Might exchange for a bowl of goldfish or anything equally useful. Apply M.L. Office, Dover.

Two Lonely Sailors (R. N.V.R. officers) at Dunkirk wish to meet two young and beautiful ladies with a view to sharing a home to save expense. Real sailor's jumper and trousers provided for camouflage purposes owing to old-fashioned and narrow-minded regulations on part of Admiralty. Comfortable quarters on real M.L. at Dunkirk. Frequent air-raids. Shower-baths over bunks (where decks leak). Charthouse for chaperons. Apply M.L. 1001, Dover.

To Let Furnished.—A *bijou* detached marine cottage (now used as M. L. Office). Fine sea views. Beautifully furnished. Good letter-rack; several chairs. Would suit M.L. officer on leave (if obtained). Apply Movie Villa, Eastern Arm, Dover.

Printed at the M.L. Press, Crowded Tier, Dover.

We kept going in those strenuous days by leg-pulling; it seemed to ease the strain at the other end. If it were not at each other's expense, it was at that of the Base. Yet if any outsider made a disparaging remark about Dover M.L.s, he was answered, unanimously, in a few "well-chosen words."

Which is as it should be, after all.

CHAPTER 12

The M.L.s in the Mediterranean

A man who was based somewhere in the Mediterranean once said to me: "You know, you Dover M.L.s, though you get your share of the hard work, certainly get most of the limelight as well. Now, out East the M.L.s have a pretty gruelling—and sometimes grilling—time, but we don't get much limelight."

There was truth in this remark, and perhaps it was inevitable that more should be heard of the M.L.s at Dover and Dunkirk for the simple reason that they were attached to so famous a flotilla as the Dover Patrol.

So, it is out of fairness to the splendid work done by the M.L.s in the Mediterranean that I am writing this, though my information is of necessity second-hand, and I have had to rely on what has been told me by men who served on these Eastern patrols for my facts.

I wish it were possible to write a full account of the work of the M.L.s at every base, and to tell of their activities in such divergent waters as their patrols called them: round the cold Scottish coasts, in the sweep of the Atlantic off Ireland, in almost every port in England and Wales, under Oriental skies, and even in far-off Trinidad. But one man could not write such a book from his own observations. Perhaps one day someone will take the trouble to compile a book of this nature, from the stories of others; let us hope so, at least, for such a record would be invaluable in the history of the R.N.V.R.

Nevertheless, it would be hardly fair to ignore entirely the work of the Mediterranean M.L.s here, and so "from information supplied," and with a due realisation of many sins of omission, this chapter is written.

The principal bases for M.L.s in these waters were Gibraltar, Malta, Taranto, Gallipoli (Italy), Otranto, Mudros, Lemnos, Mitylene, Alexandria, and Port Said, with various sub-bases and ports of call. Of one

"Parlez-vous Anglaise". Semaphoring a French battleship in the Mediterranean.

of these I had an amusing account from the illustrator of this book in a letter written shortly after the Armistice, when the spectre of the censor had faded a little. He wrote:—

★★★★★★★★★★★★★★★★★

"The little harbour at Tricase will always live in the memory of motor launch adventures in the Adriatic, for it was used exclusively by M.L.s, no others of His Majesty's ships being able to adapt themselves to its Lilliputian proportions. Those boats at work on the Otranto anti-submarine barrage were wont to run in there for shelter, and as many as six have been known to berth there at once. Airmen reported that on these occasions a more splendid imitation of a newly opened sardine tin could not be imagined when viewed from a height, and the first glimpse vouchsafed to a traveller coming along the coast road was that of a cunningly staged musical comedy at Daly's.

"There is a legend out here, firmly believed in by all M.L. men, concerning the shoal in the fairway at the entrance to the harbour. The story goes that the commanding officer of an M.L. was showing a brick to his sub. How he came to have a brick on board in a country where only stone abounds, I do not know, unless it was for this reason regarded as a curio, or why he was leaning over the side of his boat when handling it is not apparent.

"However, for some reason or other he *had* a brick and he was holding it out in the manner stated when, owing to some momentary carelessness, he let it fall overboard, and the fairway was blocked! Efforts on the part of the whole fleet to recover this were unavailing, and boats after that were constantly going 'aground.' The general locality of this obstacle was known, however, so it was marked on the chart as a shoal, and by cautious navigation M.L.s were still able to make their way in and out of harbour.

"I was told another good story recently. A certain M.L. out here has a C.O. who prides himself upon his knowledge of French. One day on patrol he met a French battleship, on passage in Italian waters, and the temptation was too much for him. He made some excuse to speak to her, and, as the larger ship eased up in response to an international code flag signal, the C.O. took the semaphore flags himself and made a signal in his best French.

"When he had finished there was an awkward silence for a while, then the Frenchman semaphored back in English, 'We are a French ship, and do not know Italian. Please use French; or we can understand English.'"

The Suez Canal also lay in the M.L. patrol, and with reference to this a letter I received from one engaged on this work contained some information which is certainly novel. He wrote:

"Have you ever heard of camels being used in connection with minesweeping? I know it sounds like a yarn, but when I was on the Suez Canal, I saw them for myself. It was not exactly minesweeping, but next door to it. The M.L.s swept the water of the Suez Canal, but a camel 'sweep' of two flat boards was run over the sandy approaches to the canal every evening, so that any footprints made in the night would be clearly visible, for the Turks had a trick of bringing mines overland and dropping them into the water during the dark hours."

The same letter, which I have quoted at more length in another book, (*The Naval Front*) had, among much interesting information, brief accounts of two amusing incidents at which the writer was present. He went on to say:

"The capture of Alexandretta, a small harbour along the Palestine coast, had a quaint touch of humour about it. Intimation was sent to the Turks that the place was to be surrendered or blown to hell. The Turks would not surrender, but at the same time offered no active resistance. So a 'landing' was arranged. A scratch crew was got together to man a ship's boat to go ashore; this party consisted of one lieutenant, four deck hands, two marines, one cook, and a few odd volunteers who were seeking excitement.

"But alas for their hopes, no excitement was forthcoming; no one opposed the 'storming party,' which proceeded to land in a leisurely fashion and went up the small main street to the centre of the little town. Here they hoisted the Union Jack over the Government building, to the intense interest of the local inhabitants, while the Turkish garrison merely looked on with a bored indifference! So, when you read in the paper that 'the port of Alexandretta was captured by our naval forces,' you can picture the scene. It was just like an act from a comic opera, even to the 'chorus of villagers.'

"On another occasion the Turk had his leg very neatly pulled. During the retreat near Gaza two barge loads of 'dummy troops' set out from Ismailah accompanied by a small flotilla of M.L.s and other craft. These 'troops' were in reality members of the Egyptian Labour Corps, and at night they were 'secretly' landed in front of the flying Turks. This landing was a great stunt; boat-load after boat-load was put ashore, and a light 'accidentally' shown at frequent intervals for the benefit of the enemy outposts, who were known to be watching.

Then with *real* secrecy these Labour Corps men were re-embarked and towed away.

"The next day the Turks hurried up several regiments to search for the landing-party that were thought to be ambushed for a secret attack in the rear. Of course, there was not a man there, but it made them very uneasy till they discovered how they had been 'had,' when I expect their uneasiness gave way to some stronger feeling!

"When I was on the Otranto-Albania barrage, I was interested in the towers that are built along the coast on the Italian side. They are something like the Martello towers one sees on the S.E. coast of England. These towers out here were built by the Crusaders against the Turks. Well, we are still fighting the Turk for the possession of the Holy Land, though we use tanks instead of towers these days.

"Many of the M.L.s out here are camouflaged with broad white stripes painted over the dark-blue grey. They look weird, but effective."

★★★★★★★★★★★★★★★★★

There is one story that comes from Gibraltar which was told me during the war by an M.L. officer, who was a participant in the adventure, and who, before he related the story, made me promise not to divulge it during hostilities, as the matter was being kept very secret owing to the fear of international complications. Even now he wishes to remain anonymous, but I do not think I am breaking any confidence when I mention that he was subsequently awarded the D.S.C.

At one period of the war secret service information proved the fact that a good many U-boats were successful in negotiating the Straits, in spite of the very close watch which was kept at night by our patrols. At the same time many Spanish fishing-vessels were disappearing in a somewhat mysterious manner, though no one at the time ever thought of connecting these two things; storms are sudden in these waters, and the Spanish smacks were small and open boats.

It was owing to the astuteness of an M.L. officer that the truth concerning both matters was discovered, and in solving the mystery of the disappearing fishing-boats the reason of the German submarines' success in eluding the vigilance of the British ships was learned.

On one fairly dark night two M.L.s were carrying on their patrol, and as the night wore on it seemed as if it were to be the usual dreary watching for a foe that never appeared. A good many Spanish fishing-boats were seen, but that was not unusual; some of these passed by in silence, some hailed the patrol boats or were hailed in their turn if near enough. Generally, these boats worked two or three together, but soon the two M.L.s saw one proceeding by itself away from all the rest; but there was nothing very much out of the way in this, and had it not been for another thing about it the smack would, in all probability, have been left to its own devices. The other thing that attracted attention was the unusual fact that it carried a stern light close to the water, which none of the other boats did, and that as soon as the M.L.s approached this light was extinguished and did not appear again.

Signalling to the other M.L. to stand by, the senior officer approached the smack and hailed it. He was answered, and the smack at once altered course. He spoke to them again through a megaphone, and the same voice made reply. But there was something in the intonation of the voice that aroused suspicion: the words were Spanish, but the voice did not sound like a Spaniard's.

Closing the smack, the M.L. suddenly switched on her searchlight and played it on the strange boat, and the muttered exclamations from the two occupants showed that this attention was by no means a welcome one, and again the small sailing vessel altered course.

"I'll swear these men are no Spaniards," said the C.O. to his Number One. "I'm going to board the boat. I'll take two armed men with me. You take the M.L. alongside, and then make her fast when I have got aboard."

This the Number One did, and the C.O. and two deck hands, all armed with revolvers, boarded the smack.

"Look after the man in the bows while I speak to the helmsman," said the C.O. to the men, and, making his way aft, he flashed an electric torch full in the face of the man there, who had remained motionless, as had also his companion, while the boarding was in progress.

"Now, my man, let's have a better look at you," said the British officer. The man tried to hide his face and began to speak, and then checked himself. But one look was enough; it was no Spanish face upon which the torch flashed, and before the man had time to turn his head aside the blue eyes, the fair skin, and bullet-shaped head of closely cropped hair had betrayed him. It was unquestionably a German face.

"If you move, I shall shoot you," said the C.O. "You can understand English, can't you?"

There was no answer, but he kept still. A pointed revolver is better even than *Esperanto* to make foreigners understand that they can play no tricks.

"One of you two," called out the officer to the men aft, "keep your

133

man covered, and shoot him if he shows fight; while the other, go back aboard and bring another man, with two lengths of heaving line.

As soon as the two prisoners were safely bound the C.O. examined them more thoroughly, which revealed the interesting fact that although they had on the coats and hats of Spanish fishermen, they wore blue naval trousers and sea-boots of obvious German make.

A further search of the boat brought to light a bundle which lay at the bottom, which set all doubts on the matter at rest. This bundle consisted of two naval coats—one apparently of a petty officer and one jumper—and two hats to correspond. They were German, and the man's cap bore on the ribbon the wording *"Unterseeboot Flotille Mittelmeer."* Nor was this all the search revealed, and the next finds were gruesome ones. A dark stain on the deck and some splashes on the gunwale proved to be blood; while a sailor's clasp-knife, found in the pocket of the warrant officer's coat told its own ominous story.

"If I gave you your deserts," cried the C.O. to the German prisoners, "I should shoot you both now. Can you speak English?" he added to the warrant officer.

"A little," replied the man this time, sullenly.

"Well, it will be best for you to tell me the truth. Though part of it seems pretty obvious, why did you murder these fishermen and then put on their coats and hats?"

"I only obeyed orders," said the man. He seemed reluctant to speak at all.

He did not reply to this. "And why," went on the C.O., "were you showing that light over the stern?"

The man again kept silent.

"Very well," said the officer, who had been doing some rapid thinking, "it's evident you are up to some damned dirty game, whatever it is. We will see."

He returned to the M.L., and spoke rapidly to his Number One for a few moments. "Leave me here with three deck-hands, and go over to the other M.L.," he said when he had explained matters, "and tell them how things stand. Warn them to be ready for instant action, and to see that their depth-charges are properly set. It's obvious these Huns are acting as a guide to something, and what that is I will leave you to guess. Keep within half a mile of me, and drift as much as possible, using your hydrophones. When I flash 'C' on my torch, close me at once."

The M.L. then drew off into the darkness, as soon as the C.O.

had boarded the smack again. His first act on returning was to relight the old oil lamp, and to set one of the deck-hands to hold it over the stern as near as possible where it had been before. He told one man to watch the prisoners, and bade the other stand by in readiness to help with the sail if necessary. The tiller he took himself, and set the boat on a course as near as he could remember to that she had been on when he had overtaken her.

He had taken the precaution to bring a pair of night-glasses with him, and through these he made frequent sweeps of the sea behind him. For over an hour they sailed on in dead silence. The night was not as black as it might have been, though there was no moon, and the sea was moderately calm.

The hour grew into two, and still they sailed slowly on. Was it to be a fruitless experiment, and was his idea all wrong? mused the C.O. as he sat at the tiller. If so, what *was* the explanation? The two Germans could not have dropped from the skies, the only other alternative being that they had risen from the depths. And so, he watched and waited.

All at once, during one of his searchings of the waters through his glasses, he gave a gasp and peered more closely still at the waters astern. Was it the night shadows playing him tricks, as night shadows will, or could he see, about a hundred yards away, a long black shape with a small whitish wave behind it? He was tremendously excited, for it was for such a thing that he had been waiting so patiently. With his glasses glued on this object, he whispered to the man beside him to extinguish the lantern. This was done, and a moment later the black shape disappeared: nor could all his searching reveal any further sight of it.

The C.O. was still thinking hard and for some moments sailed on, and then, taking his torch, flashed a succession of "C's" over the port-quarter, and waited. A few moments later "R D" was flashed back, and soon the sound of an M.L. running slow on one engine was heard, and a minute later she loomed up out of the darkness.

"Come alongside," morsed the C.O., "and make fast."

This the M.L. did, and the Number One stepped aboard. "Any luck?" he asked. The C.O. informed him of what he had seen, and told him to see to moving the prisoners on board, together with their spare clothes, and to lower the sail of the smack. While this was being done, the C.O. lit the lantern once more, and his last acts before joining his own boat were to lash the tiller and set the light, so that it could be seen astern.

Then the M. L. drew off again, leaving the smack tenantless, and joined its consort. A short talk between the two C.O.s followed, and then they separated, and the waiting game began afresh.

They kept about two hundred yards on the quarter of the drifting fishing-boat, and themselves drifted too with their hydrophones out. For an hour or so they waited, but at first there was no sound but the gentle "swish" of the water, though at length a faint whirring throb could be heard. This was enough, and the order "Up hydrophones, and prepare for instant action," was sent from the senior M.L. to the other.

All at once the searchlight of the leading M.L. flashed out and swept the water astern of the abandoned fishing-boat. This time there was no mistake, for a dark-grey stick-like object with a bulb-head was slowly rising out of the water.

The gun's crew was already closed up, and at a sharp order from the C.O. fire was opened, and three shells from the thirteen-pounder splashed the water into long columns close to their target. There was no hit. But that did not matter; the object had been achieved, for the periscope began to sink again beneath the water.

"Now for it," cried the C.O., and with the Number One aft to see to the depth-charges, he rang the telegraphs down to full speed ahead. By a prearranged signal, a sharp single note on the ship's bell rang out a few moments later, and two depth-charges were released, to explode a few seconds later as the M.L. sped out of danger. Great columns of water spurted high in the air, and those on the M.L. felt as if some giant hammer had suddenly hit the bottom of the boat.

Then the second M.L. came into action, and within a few feet of the widening of circles let go her own depth-charges. The boats then stopped their engines and waited, with their searchlights sweeping the white patches, and their guns trained on the same spots. Nothing happened, however, and soon the two patrol boats approached the place where the depth-charges had exploded, for a closer inspection of the surface of the sea.

"Can you see anything?" called out the senior C.O.

"Damned little," replied the other; "there's a patch here that *might* be oil, but I'm not certain."

The M.L. closed her consort and examined the streaky lines on the water.

"Well, I *think* it's oil, but there's not much of it, and in this light, even with a searchlight, it's hard to tell. We'd better hang about for a bit. Just go and take the fishing-boat in tow; we shall want her as evidence."

★★★★★★★★★★★★★★★★

Such was the story told to me, and there is not much to add as a sequel. On their way back to port the M.L.s met two destroyers which had been attracted by the sound of the depth-charges. To these the C.O. of the M.L.s reported what had happened. The destroyer commander told them to carry on back with their captives, and he would wait till daylight in the vicinity in case of emergencies. Nothing was, however, seen of the submarine again, and it was subsequently assumed to have been destroyed.

The full story came out when the naval authorities questioned the two captives, who in hope of saving their own skins made a fairly complete confession. They had been ordered aboard the smack from the U-boat, it appeared, and told to cut the throats of the occupants— knives make less noise than revolvers—and to throw them overboard, weighted, for, despite the adage, dead men *do* tell tales at times, though seldom from the bottom of the sea. The light over the stern was to guide the following U-boat through the straits: as long as this light was showing all was well, but as soon as it disappeared there was danger, and the submarine, which was travelling with nothing but its periscope above water, was to submerge entirely and lie "doggo" till a furtive look-round showed them the friendly light again.

Those on the smack trusted to their disguise to escape attention, and in nine cases out of ten would probably have been taken for ordinary Spanish fishermen upon their lawful occasions. But this was the tenth case, and the M.L.s scored.

★★★★★★★★★★★★★★★★

In another of the letters I received from my brother he told me some M.L. news concerning the ancient harbours of Tyre and Sidon.

"I am writing this, on a drifter off Sidon, where I have come to make sketches. I know you will be interested to hear of anything to do with M.L.s, and two have just passed us bound for Port Said. They had been patrolling on this coast together with trawlers and drifters, and were the only ones of all H.M. ships small enough to go into Tyre and Sidon, once the greatest naval bases in the world.

"The first British vessel to enter Tyre was M.L. 248, in fact she was the only ship that could *enter*. The other craft—trawlers, drifters, food hulks, etc.—were forced to anchor outside the harbour. The army had pushed on from Haifa, and was marching up the coast towards Tyre

137

and Sidon, and was dependent to a large extent for supplies from the sea. The flotilla arrived off Tyre at dawn; two minesweeping trawlers swept a channel, and the M.L. went right into the ancient harbour, feeling her way along by the lead. It is not an easy entrance even for an M.L., and in some places was only a matter of clearing by inches. All sorts of snags and obstructions strewed the channel. When all was arranged with our advance troops on shore, the surf boats began the work of unloading the hulks, plying to and fro to the beach, Sidon was victualled in the same manner.

"I had a yarn with the C.O. of M.L. 206, who went into Tyre shortly after this, and he described a weird and extraordinary sight. Tyre is a miserable place, as seen from the north side, where there is an apology for a harbour. It is really the ancient site, and broken traces of the old mole abound. Jagged fragments of masonry stick out from the water and jumbled masses of columns, which make it a tortuous channel. A few small fishing-boats constitute its shipping. A more desolate scene it would be impossible to imagine, her walls shattered and her towers broken down.

"Night fell, and the minesweeping fleet came to anchor. In the failing light, while still a dull red glow showed in the upper sky, the M.L. put on her searchlight and started creeping in towards the entrance. On her starboard hand a pile of stones that looked like a ruined tower, on her port hand a low line of debris and fallen pillars ending in a tower-like mass of masonry; ahead, on every accessible fragment of building, hundreds of weird and ragged figures, gesticulating and shouting and making strange movements indicative of astonishment, fear, or welcome. The skyline was black with people.

"We felt as though we were dreaming or taking' part in some extraordinary pageant. The Dantesque weirdness of the scene belonged rather to the Inferno or to some vision of the prophet Ezekiel.

"It is surely prophetic that Isaiah should have written of this very place:

"'Is this your joyous city, whose antiquity is of ancient days?

"'How art thou destroyed that was inhabited of seafaring men, the renowned city that was strong in the sea.'"

★★★★★★★★★★★★★★★★

Lieut. A. C. Turner has given me some interesting news of the doings of the M.L.s in the Mediterranean, and his account of the special secret service work upon which he was engaged in these waters reads like a romance. He writes:

M.L.S 200 entering Tyre

M.L.s off Sidon Nov. 1918.

OFF THE PALESTINE COAST

"My M.L. was based at Mitylene at the time, on the Turkish Asiatic coast some miles south of the Dardanelles. We were then acting under special orders from the Intelligence Department, working under the British Vice-Consul, who were responsible for the secret service work out there. What I am going to tell you happened on several occasions, but I will relate one instance which will be typical of the rest.

"When we left harbour on this job we timed our departure so as to arrive at a given part of the Turkish coast under the cover of darkness. After stopping our engines some distance from the shore, the dinghy would be lowered, and with muffled oars the spies, whom we had brought with us, would be rowed ashore and landed.

"Before I speak of the mission that these men had before them, I may as well tell you something about the men themselves. They were, of course, natives, and they lived on a special island by themselves, so that any information they picked up should reach no other ears than those for whom it was intended. These men were a weird crowd, and looked more like a set of brigands from the pages of a novel than participants in a modern war. They were dressed in loose and very baggy trousers, small, close-fitting, highly decorated waistcoats with long sleeves; in addition to this they usually had brightly coloured shirts and invariably wore large cloth sashes wrapped round the middle of their body, in which they carried knives and revolvers. Their head-dress was another slip of cloth worn turban-fashion, while cowhide boots completed their picturesque attire. All the provisions they took with them were a couple of loaves of brown bread, a few olives, and a water-bottle.

"As soon as they were landed on Turkish soil, they began their long and perilous journey either to Smyrna or Constantinople. This was, of course, a journey attended by very great risks, as their way lay over the rocky mountainous country that surrounds the coast in these parts, and as this was well patrolled and carefully watched by the Turks, it was necessary to travel by night and hide by day. After gaining information in the cities, where they passed themselves off as native countrymen, they would return to the coast several days afterwards, where, by previous arrangement, our M.L. was waiting off a certain spot. They would give us a signal by striking matches, which we would answer, and then pick them up again in the dinghy. It was not always, of course, that they returned. We could only guess at their fate then.

"After some experimenting it was found that the safest place to land these spies was not, as might be imagined, at a lonely spot on the coast, but almost under the very noses of the guns of a Turkish cliff-fort, where, curiously enough, a far worse look-out was kept than at the more lonely spots. I can never remember being fired at from one of these forts, though at some apparently deserted part of the coast we frequently met a pretty hot reception from machine-guns and rifles.

"As regards the general work of the M.L.s in these waters, I can speak best of that which took place from those boats based at Mudros, in the Isle of Lemnos. We used to go out in divisions of six with one of the M. class monitors as flotilla leader. We would leave harbour before sunset, and would remain out for twenty-four hours, when another division would relieve us at sea.

"We were all wireless M.L.s, and at night we would take up a special listening formation with our hydrophones down. When a U-boat was detected by any M.L., information would be signalled to the leader, who would plot on the chart the position and probable course of the submarine, after which the division would be ordered to move into a new formation to intercept it. Everyone who knows anything about U-boat hunting will, of course, understand that the chances in a case like this are nearly always in favour of the U-boat if it wishes to escape. In these particular instances it usually happened that the submarines would be forced to return up the Dardanelles again. Sometimes they did not either return or get past our patrols—you can guess what happened!

"This meant that those waters covered by our operations were made comparatively clear and safe for the passage of troop, hospital, and provision ships to and from Salonika. In fact, it is not too much to say that the work of the M.L.s from Mudros in submarine-hunting was, to quite a considerable extent, the reason that the loss of shipping in these waters through U-boat activity was reduced to a minimum."

For the following exciting account of the entry of an M.L. into a Turkish harbour at night, I am indebted to Lieut. G. H. Menhinnick, who accompanied Lieut. S. F. Strang in M.L. 196 on this perilous duty.

"We had been sent by the S.N.O. on H.M.S. *Forward* at Samos with orders to proceed to Sivriji, a Turkish port on the Asiatic coast, where we were to enter the harbour and to put on our searchlight and search the harbour for an enemy submarine which had been in action the day before with a trawler, and was supposed to have been damaged and to have sought refuge in this harbour: so the report of the Intelligence Department stated.

"This promised to be an exciting adventure enough, for our orders were that if we were successful in locating the submarine, we were to do as much damage as possible to her before leaving.

"We took on board Lieut. Lorimer, who was in charge of the Samos section of the Intelligence Department, and set out, having landed all our confidential papers and signal books, for it was likely to be touch and go, and if we *did* happen to fall into enemy hands, it was as well to be prepared. Another M.L. under Lieut. E. S. Sacret, with whom was Lieut. H. G. C. Hutchinson, accompanied us till we were outside the enemy harbour, where we left them to keep watch, and to warn us if any enemy vessels should approach. We went alongside them before proceeding to give them some final instructions, and there was quite a touch of humour in our farewell.

"Someone on the other boat was horrified to discover that M.L. 196 had thirteen on board and was actually entering an enemy harbour under this cloud of ill omen. 'Couldn't you leave one behind?' they asked. 'No, we can't do that, but we will take a volunteer if you like,' we replied. However, none was forthcoming, and so we cautiously made our way inshore. I'm certain the waiting M.L. never expected to see us again.

"Besides the intelligence officer, we had on board a local guide— he was a refugee from the locality, and with his beard, turban-like *fez*, and baggy trousers, he looked the typical brigand to the life; but he was useful, and we stationed him in the bows to act as a pilot. We had taken the precaution to fit outside silencers over our exhausts, and, 'slow on one,' we crept towards the shore. There was a small island in the mouth of the harbour, and, acting on the advice of our brigand, we left this on our starboard hand. The night was dark, and we could see precious little ahead, though we could make out the shore very dimly outlined.

"When we got well in, we stopped the engines and switched on the searchlight, and swept the little harbour from end to end. The signalman's hands were a bit unsteady, I'm afraid, for he was in an exposed position for the fire that was certain to be opened up on us soon, and at times the searchlight looked rather like Morse. But it was enough, and not a sign of a submarine could we see. It was impossible for it to have been submerged; there was not enough water for that.

"A few bullets began to whistle round our heads by this time, and the order 'Off searchlight!' was given, much to the relief of the signalman. I sympathised with him: it could not have been pleasant on the top of the chart-house under such conditions! Lights began to show on shore by this time, and we could distinctly see the houses now, we were so close, less than a hundred yards away. We could also see the numerous small flashes of flint and steel being struck as the shadowy figures on the beach lit lanterns and began to run about. Someone suggested they were looking for the guns! Evidently, they managed to find them, for just as we had put the helm hard over, a deeper roar and a large splash ahead of us told us that we'd better be off.

"I was at the wheel and suddenly felt the boat stop, though the propellers were still turning. We had fouled some obstruction, possibly a wire of sort, with our stem, and were 'brought up with around turn' with a vengeance. How we had managed to get over this wire, or whatever it was, on our way in was a mystery, but we had. All efforts to clear ourselves were unsuccessful, and the rifle fire was getting fierce, and larger guns were firing with increasing vigour. Their marksmanship was happily atrocious.

"The unlucky thirteen occupants of M.L. 196 were indeed in a sorry plight; we could not go forward, and there was no retreat. There was nothing for it but to give the order to 'abandon ship' and to get the dinghy ready to try and row to the other M.L. Thirteen is an unlucky number for an M. L.'s dinghy, whatever it may be elsewhere. Petrol-soaked waste was prepared ready to set the ship on fire as soon as she was abandoned; but luckily it never came to that, for as this was being done all at once she floated clear from the obstruction on her stem and began to go ahead. What it was we had fouled, or why we had suddenly got clear, are still mysteries to this day. We did not stay to satisfy our curiosity.

"Even now we were within an ace of a fresh disaster. I was at the wheel, and our brigand in the bows suddenly gave a warning cry, and one of the deck-hands shouted 'Hard aport, sir.' I swung her over, but only just in time, for a dark mass that suddenly rose on our port hand told me that in the excitement of the moment I had been trying to leave harbour on the wrong side of the island at the mouth, where there was less than eighteen inches of water! However, we eventually managed to get clear of the harbour, aided by good luck and bad shooting, but it was a near thing. The waiting M.L. thought there was something almost immoral in our turning up again in one piece after venturing into an enemy harbour with thirteen aboard; when they heard the firing, they thought it was all up with us.

"We had a good many interesting experiences in those days apart from this adventure, especially on those occasions when an M.L. was ordered to proceed in daylight through the straits that lay between Samos and the mainland for the purpose of drawing the enemy fire. I remember one particularly hot time we had on this job, when we had Captain Lake, R.N. aboard. The Turkish guns on the mainland were extremely well camouflaged, and we had to steam along the straits and act as a target for them, while Captain Lake did his best to locate their positions from the flashes. There were also special observation-posts for the same purpose on Samos Island, which was Greek.

"We managed to run the gauntlet successfully, and were congratulating ourselves on having come safely through a pretty thick time, when the captain decided to return the same way for further observations, instead of returning round the island on the other side. The fire on the return journey was hotter than ever, chiefly from guns which must have been somewhere about the size of our thirteen-pounders. On this journey it was the fast-gathering darkness alone, I am certain, that saved us. To add piquancy to this return trip we were fired on several times by Greeks, who were evidently under the impression that we were some enemy craft trying to steal through the Straits. Then the 'shorts' from both sides were splashing perilously near us at times. But in spite of it all we came through safely, M.L.s have a wonderful knack of coming through at times!"

★★★★★★★★★★★★★

These stories, then, must suffice for the present of the M.L.s on the various Mediterranean patrols. Let us hope, however, that someone who has served on them will write their history more fully. We should like to have the full details of the famous blockade of Smyrna, which, as no other vessels had a shallow enough draught for inshore work here, was audaciously undertaken by three motor-boats, and successfully accomplished too. There must be many more stories also, full of interest and excitement, of the listening patrol on the Otranto-Albania barrage; of adventures along the Bulgarian coast and searching for enemy submarine lairs among the numerous rocky islands of the Ægean Sea; all part of the great game played by the M.L.s in frustrating the work of the U-boat pirates of the "Mittelmeer."

144

CHAPTER 13

Two Hospitals

1: LE CHÂTEAU ANONYME AND THE LITTLE BLUE SISTER

(Le Château Anonyme here described was the Quaker Hospital at Petit Synthe, between Dunkirk and Calais, which was conducted by the Friends Ambulance Unit.)

Le Château Anonyme had all the romantic associations of France of the Second Empire—at about which period it must have originally been built—and upon the beautiful summer evening when first I saw it but little effort of the imagination was needed to eliminate the present and set it back a few decades, and to people its old-world setting with crinolined ladies and their bewhiskered swains.

It was not a castle, in spite of its name—a word having a broader meaning in France, where almost every country house is called a *château*,—and it was more quaint and interesting than beautiful, as we understand the beauty of houses in England.

It was a typical French country house of the better class: a tall grey building, with a porticoed entrance, shuttered windows, a rather elaborate coping meeting in a gable, and wide spreading steps leading to the garden at the back from a large conservatory. A house which, perhaps, in itself would not have called for any special admiration apart from its gardens and grounds. These were some of the finest I have ever seen in France, even in peace time. It was not their size, some twenty acres at the outside, but the general arrangement that was noticeable, and the use of the surrounding woods that had been left on all sides wild, and which acted as a perfect frame for a beautiful picture. The wood was the estate, and stood out as a conspicuous landmark from the flat, uninteresting country between Dunkirk and Calais.

It lay a little off the main Calais road, whence the wayfarer could see nothing of the house, but merely looked upon the circle of trees as a pleasant break in a flat, monotonous country. I had often noticed that wood from the sea, but never knew till I went to hospital that it contained so fair a heart.

When I arrived on that summer evening there were certain formalities to go through, which, for a service hospital, were delightfully informal, and in a short time I found I was apparently at liberty either to sit on my bed in the ward or go out and explore the grounds. The fact that I was a "walking case," and the few glimpses I had caught through the trees as the car brought me up the drive, naturally decided me on the latter course, so I set out.

The main gardens I found to be at the side of the house, and charmingly broken up with hedges, old brick walls, and groves leading to shady seats or arbours. The beds were a blaze of colour and nearly all enclosed in neat box borders. Scattered about here and there were statues and huge stoneware vases, a style of adornment of which the French are fond.

At the back of the house, in a grove of trees, was the lake—"*le lagoon*,"—a cool and still stretch of water out of which flowed a small stream, or moat, which surrounded the house on three sides, and which was spanned by one stone and three rustic wooden bridges. In one corner of the grounds was the stabling, a range of buildings really more picturesque than the house itself, because not so tall, with its old paved yard with the mossy borders between the stones, a sign of long disuse, but which lent additional charm to the place. For some reason the ambulance cars did not use this yard—or at least I saw no signs of it.

Surrounding the house and gardens and beyond the moat was the wood, perhaps the chief charm of the place. It was in its wild state, yet it still showed signs of use. Pathways through the trees there were plenty, and here and there one would come upon the elaborate vases, almost monumental in some places, and statues of gods and wood nymphs abounded. Still more numerous were the summer-houses. These met you everywhere as you walked through the trees, in all styles of brick and stone, one or two as large as small cottages. Why they wanted so many I could never quite understand. But the French are a romantic people!

I have described Le Château Anonyme and its grounds as they first appeared to me, when possibly I saw them through spectacles tinted with a certain amount of imagination and romance at the close of a summer day, a glamour which is sometimes dispelled later. In the

BOARDING A DUTCHMAN

present instance this was true to a certain extent, though the romantic possibilities of the place always lingered, and still remain in my mind.

We were not the sole occupants of the *château*, for one side of it—a wing obviously erected at a later date to the main building—was still used as a private lunatic asylum, into which the whole premises had been turned a few years before the war. We used to see the patients about; they seemed quite harmless; old men for the most part. They did not interfere with us at all, but eyed us with a great deal of curiosity. There was one old fellow, who might have been an old soldier, evidently an ardent supporter of the *Entente Cordiale*, who, whenever he saw an Englishman pass, used to get up and start singing "God Save the King" in very broken English; and as he saw an Englishman, on the average, about every two minutes, his life must have been the one grand sweet song of which the poet speaks.

The use to which the place was now put naturally altered it much, though it was always possible to escape from modern environment and wander in the woods and smoke a pipe in one of the many summer-houses, by adopting the "Nelson touch" when you came to a notice by the moat bridge saying that the woods were out of bounds for patients, and reading it with your blind eye. *Why* the woods were out of bounds I don't quite know, but I think it was a fairly nominal restriction, at least for officers, as I was never stopped, and used to go there quite openly.

The main house not being large enough for the hospital use, several additional wards had been made by the erection of huts in the garden, and into one of these it was my good fortune to be put. We were very happy in our little wooden home among the trees close to the lagoon; and it was pleasant to be able to lie in bed and listen to the air-raids going on over Dunkirk, with the ghastly voice of Mournful Mary echoing in the distance, knowing that you were more or less out of the danger zone and there was no need to "clear harbour" or spend half the night in a dug-out.

I was lucky in that I could spend practically all day doing what I liked. My trouble was a bad throat, irritated, so the doctor said, by the smoke, and possibly gas too, at Zeebrugge and Ostend; and as long as I was there at the doctor's rounds I could please myself as to what I did, and consequently spent many lazy hours in a deck-chair with a book beneath the trees by the lagoon, enjoyed the forbidden fruits of exploration in the numerous summer-houses in the woods, or went for voyages, not without danger, upon the lagoon itself in a leaking home-made boat I discovered tied to a board upon which was a notice forbidding patients to use it.

It was an extraordinary craft, built on the crab principle, for it went just as well sideways as ahead. It was nearly square, with one end a bit tapered off, and leaked badly. This amusement soon palled, however; it was too much in the nature of a busman's holiday, and I preferred the woods. One of the summer-houses there appealed strongly to my imagination. It was in a very lonely corner, dark even in the day-time, and must have been an eerie place at night, though I was never able to visit it then, as we were "tucked up" at eight, whatever our ailments. This summer-house was a brick building of two rooms, approached through a shady and winding walk, the very place for a lover's meeting or a deed of darkness.

I climbed in through a window. It contained a decrepit wicker couch, two broken chairs, and a small table. Here were signs, at least, of human habitation in bygone days, for the dust of years was over all. It cried aloud for a story, some romantic tale that would endow the place with a living interest. Perhaps it had one; who knows?

Among all the nurses at this war hospital, I think the Little Blue Sister (as we called her) was most loved of all. I know she was in our ward, where she happened to be on day duty. She got her name from her dress, as may be imagined, for she always dressed in darker blue instead of the usual "nurse's grey."

She was small and pretty, without being doll-like. Her smile seemed to brighten the ward when she entered, and her sympathy and tenderness were unbounded. But I think it was in her tact that she excelled. She made every man feel that *he* was her special favourite and the one she liked just a little better than all the rest, and this she was skilful enough (though I think it was unconscious rather than a studied pose) to do without causing jealousy. It did me good to watch her as she went round the beds, dressing a wound here, giving medicine there, and a smile and a word for those who needed neither.

She seemed to embody the spirit of that *château* hospital, and we all loved her. I know *I* did, for she also seemed to embody the spirit of English womanhood that so unselfishly went to France to nurse and care for Britain's sons wounded and sick in a foreign land.

So here's our love and gratitude to you, Little Blue Sister, and to all you other blue or grey sisters that nursed back to health or soothed the last hours of all your brothers, also children of old Mother England, that great family that went out to fight and work for her when she was in need of strong arms and brave hearts in her hour of peril.

2: R.N. Hospital and the Mutton-Fisted *Matloe*

It was to my genuine regret that I learned at the end of a week that I was to be transferred from the *château* in the woods in France to a Service hospital in England.

I do not quite know what it is about Service hospitals that makes them unpopular, but I have never yet met a man who ever looked back without something akin to horror to his sojourn in one. It is impossible to point to any one thing as the cause of this. One is well looked after and has plenty of attention, almost too much of it; the doctors are skilful, the nurses competent and kind, and yet there is an indefinable something that makes a Service hospital what it is. There is *too* much Service about it all; but I think one of the sisters at Dunkirk got nearest to the mark when she said in a letter:

I'm sorry you don't like your new quarters so well as over here. I have always heard the same about Service hospitals. Personally, I don't think there is enough 'mothering' of the men there.

When you come to think it out, this is a pretty good summing up, all the more true, perhaps, because unconventional. At our *château* in France, we all felt like members of a large family, but in the Service hospital we felt like parts of a big machine.

At Dunkirk even the methods of curing complaints were more or less homely. In the case of a bad throat, they merely used the old-fashioned, if unpleasant, paint-brush and gargle, but these would not do at an R.N. hospital at all. All sorts of complicated contrivances for squirting vile liquids down the throat, weird sort of inhalers that almost suffocated you, and extraordinary implements that nearly tore the root of your tongue out under the pretence of getting lumps of your throat to examine under the microscope, were in use here. Almost every day a fresh torture was put in practice. I think there must have been a special staff that spent all their time adapting implements from the Spanish Inquisition to modern use.

Anyone who spoke after lights out was in danger of death, hell-fire, shooting-at-dawn, or any other such punishment as might be deemed necessary by the Lords Commissioners of the Admiralty.

No greater contrast could be found, in short, to my late surroundings. A huge and somewhat barrack-like pile of buildings in place of a *château* and huts; severely conventional grounds to walk in in place of old-world gardens and woods; and a general atmosphere of take-care-you-don't-break-any-rules instead of the freedom we enjoyed on the other side. It is true that walking cases were allowed out in the town between two and five every afternoon if they cared to go; but the fact that you had to get back by a stated time and be "checked off" at starting and returning by the policeman at the gate, and if you were late had your name taken like a truant schoolboy, made this "freedom" irksome.

There is no need to indulge in personalities about this hospital; if one did so a separate chapter would have to be written, for there were many types among the thousand or so gathered under this roof. Those who know the place I write about will remember the surgeon who had earned for himself the somewhat unsavoury sobriquet of "Crippen" owing to his liking for the knife; and the waiter, once a valet to Lord Someone-or-other, I believe, who, when he brought you your tray in his most stately manner, would remove the cover with a wide flourish and announce in a grandiloquent tone, "A little fish, sir," as if he were conveying the news of some epoch-making discovery to you.

But of all the characters here, the one that interested me most was one we called "the mutton-fisted *matloe*" It was the unlucky fate of the man in the next bed to mine to come under his ministrations. He was a fat man, with a somewhat porcine type of features, and with hands like twin legs of mutton, which stood him well in his hour of knead—only his kneaded men instead of dough.

Before he joined the navy as a sick-berth rating, he had been a professional footballer's trainer, I was told, and his job here was massage. This duty he certainly carried out thoroughly, and I used to watch with horror and sympathy as he did his fell work upon my next-bed neighbour.

First of all, he would prepare the victim for the sacrifice by stripping him of his pyjamas, and then bare his own brawny arms for the one-sided battle. He would then turn over his prey upon his stomach, and start off the action by giving him a couple of resounding smacks in the small of the back, which echoed through the whole ward. This he playfully termed "waking up the liver." Ye gods, it would wake up one who was dead almost, let alone a liver! Then before the victim had time to regain his breath, off the M.F.M. would start again, warming to the fray as he went on. Smack, pinch, rub, bang, and smack again, in endless succession, till the wretched patient was reduced to a state of pulp and horrid blasphemy.

Then the M.F.M. would re-robe his victim, roll down his own

shirt sleeves, and march out of the ward with the self-satisfied smile of one who has combined duty with pleasure.

What a contrast to the smile and tender ministrations of the Little Blue Sister!

CHAPTER 14

The Silent Coast

These impressions of the Belgian Coast after the Germans had been driven out of it in the late autumn of 1918 were all written at the time. I think it will be more interesting if I give them here just as they were jotted down in my notebook at the various places visited either in the course of duty or curiosity, than to re-write them.

On Shore: The Belgian Coast.

The thing that strikes me most after a couple of years of very lively patrol up and down the Flanders Coast is the strange silence that now hangs over it. To look at, there is no difference about it now from a year ago, and we know that it is still thick with guns all the way from Zeebrugge to Nieuport; but these guns, once so active in spitting hate at us, will now never again speak at the command of a German, and probably never again at all, since most of them are smashed beyond repair. I do not know the exact figures, but I believe there are supposed to be about two thousand guns, large and small, along this few miles of coast.

Even at the last big bombardment most of them were silent: they had already been broken in view of the speedy evacuation. This bombardment was a wonderful thing. For forty-eight hours the monitors kept up an almost incessant rain of shells on the enemy positions, while we covered our ships with a smoke-screen. Only at the last did the Huns reply, and then I heard they had rushed a few big guns back by rail. The last phase of this strafing was the finest sight of all. My own boat was smoking one of the eighteen-inch monitors, so we had a grand view of the advance inshore along towards the Hun positions made by another batch of monitors and destroyers, accompanied by the ubiquitous M.L.s. It was like having a front seat at a naval battle a few miles away.

This was the end of the enemy opposition, save for the incident of the famous "Dummy Run" up the coast. We were in this, and it was the best joke of the war played on the Hun. It was the last brilliant stroke of Admiral Keyes' wonderful work on the Belgian coast. The idea was simple, one of those simple but effective ideas that a great mind thinks of at times. Roughly it was this. Every available ship should assemble off Dunkirk and advance up the coast towards the enemy position and make a feint landing to cut off the Hun retreat. We set off; it was a great sight. Monitors, destroyers, "P" boats, trawlers, drifters, motor lighters, M.L.s, and even ammunition barges took part. It was the weirdest collection of ships I have ever seen; but from the air it must have looked a formidable fleet.

It had the desired effect; it put the Hun in a panic, for as we closed inshore his airmen reported a large force about to attempt a landing, and two divisions of German troops were hastily hurried back from the front line to repel this supposed attack. This was just what was wanted, for the army, pushing at the same time, found less resistance and gained much ground by this trick. Not a shot was fired at us (their big guns were all dismantled by this time), so giving the astonished and panic-stricken Hun the "soldiers' farewell," we put out to sea again and went home to tea. We had about as much thought of making a landing then as we had of trying to capture the Goodwin Sands, but the enemy thought otherwise, as we intended, he should. I expect the Berlin papers the next day had wonderful accounts of the frustrated landing of the British Navy on "*der Flanderns Küste*," which was repelled by "our brave troops"!

Now that I have been ashore and explored all this coast on foot, I can imagine what a horrible massacre a landing here would have been. The whole of the sloping banks of the sand dunes are a network of thick barbed-wire. The opening in these dunes are not many, and these are very ingeniously netted in a zig-zag fashion: hard to manoeuvre in daylight with no opposition, but at night with a foe to encounter they would be veritable death-traps. All strands of the barbed-wire were twisted into three or four thicknesses before they were put up to render them extra strong. Every hundred yards or so are guns cunningly concealed, which could sweep the beach like a hail-storm. Behind the dunes are double rows of trenches and more barbed wire. There is no doubt that the enemy feared such a landing, and he had certainly left nothing to chance.

These trenches are very interesting, and I have spent hours exploring them. Some of the dugouts are filthy, and others seem very comfortable and contain some fine furniture; all smashed to pieces, though. Broken searchlights are quite frequent: usually near the anti-aircraft guns.

I came across a very pathetic sight in my wanderings today. I was exploring the dunes behind the trenches, and in a little hollow between two sandhills I discovered a lonely grave. At the head, on a small wooden cross, was written "*Ein junger englischer Flugmann*" ("A young English flying-man"). That was all: no name, no date or anything else to give a clue to the one who lay beneath. Here he had slept alone in the midst of his foes, perhaps for years. I wish I could have found some clue to his identity, so that I could have written to the poor boy's people and told them of his last resting-place.

The Belgian Coast at night now is even more impressive. No bark of anti-aircraft gun to break the calm, and no searchlight beams sweeping the sky. The voice of War has taken its strident notes to other fields, and left to these now lonely sandhills the silence of Peace—the stillness of Victory, perhaps we can call it; but over all there seems to hang the silence of Death, exemplified by that lonely grave on the dunes.

I can't get that picture out of my mind tonight, somehow.

On H.M.S. *Vindictive.*

The Germans have taken good care that she was left a hulk. Anything more completely gutted I cannot imagine; everything that is not actually under water that could be removed has been taken. Her funnels are gone, her bridge is gone; in fact, as I sit on a piece of twisted iron-work on her upper deck writing this and look astern, I might almost be on a huge barge. There is literally nothing on her deck but the conning-tower and part of the capstan, which they have been unable to shift, and a few odd pieces of iron-work also too solid to move. Everything else is gone, as if a giant scythe had swept all away as a reaper cuts corn.

Descending to the mess deck, which can be reached at low water, though even then it is necessary to wear sea-boots if you would explore it thoroughly, the same complete desolation meets the eye; there is practically nothing but the iron bulkheads and the ship's sides. Every scrap of metal, and all fittings that could be moved or forced, are gone. Brass seems to have been sought after most; even the smallest pieces have been wrenched away. The only piece of brass left on these two decks is the top of a temperature tube to the magazine, but even this bears signs of a struggle; the screw-heads are broken, and there are many marks of a cold chisel; apparently it was tough enough to withstand all assaults, though it is obvious that strenuous efforts have been made to remove it.

On the deck below, where the engines are, it is impossible to go, even at low water, and here is certainly the only remaining metal of any value, for even divers could not salve the twisted mass that was left here after her bottom was blown out on her famous entry into the harbour. Great masses of metal can be seen in hopeless confusion below the water, if one descends as far into the depths as it is possible to get.

It is a horrible but a fascinating sight, this inferno of metallic contortions; there is something almost living in the great twisted tubes that seem to curl round everything like huge slimy snakes crushing their prey. Seen through the green water in the dim light that comes down from above, it wants but a little stretch of the imagination to see some sinuous movement in them as they wind over the tangled mass beneath them. Even as I watched I saw a movement in the water, as a crab crawled slowly out of a broken pipe and made its tortuous way over a condenser to disappear into the darkness, whence arise, from far below, strange noises as the tide ebbs and flows: gurglings and bubblings that make a weird and ghostly echo in the desolation of the empty ship.

Great shell-holes are gaping on all sides, and tell of the terrible pounding she got before her mission was completed; and it is wonderful to think that anyone on board could have lived until the rescue motor launch came up and took off her crew.

A large part of the after-deck, the port-holes, and most of the large shell-holes too, have been covered with barbed-wire by the Germans, who had placed machine-guns on board. The gun-crews lived here also, for up by the fore-peak their straw mattresses are still lying about. There are signs, too, that the cells have been used for sleeping purposes.

The ship is not alongside the pier, as has been stated; her bows are some twenty feet away, and her hull is at an angle of about thirty degrees. The Germans are supposed to have slewed her round from her original position to a certain extent, but even now she is still quite a useful obstruction, in spite of the Hun's kindness in moving her before we captured the place, thus saving us the trouble.

If she can ever be refloated is a problem; she can't have any bottom left to speak of, and it seems to me she would break her back were any attempt made to move her. Still, I am no salvage expert, and may

OFT IN DANGER, M.L.s WARNING A SAILING SHIP ON THE EDGE OF A MINEFIELD.

be quite wrong. Personally, I hope she *can* be floated and brought to England. She deserves an honourable ending, if any ship ever did.

There have been clumsy German lies in plenty throughout the war, but none so clumsy, I think, as one which was told me by a Belgian in Ostend. On the morning after we had put the *Vindictive* in, the Germans spread the report that there had been a great naval battle, and that they had captured a British cruiser and towed her in as a prize!

Anyhow, the "prize" came into harbour with the British colours flying, and now, after five months, as an eyesore and a perpetual insult to the Hun, the White Ensign once more flies proudly over the old ship.

At Ostend.

It gives you a funny feeling when you see the next M.L. to yours go up after striking a mine, when you are but a few hundred yards away. It makes you think "There, but for the luck of war, goes my M.L."

Nor does it make you any more cheerful to see a small monitor and a minesweeper follow suit a few hours after.

The scene outside Ostend harbour, the day of the evacuation, was an extraordinary one at low water. To say that the mines were showing above the surface like gooseberries is no exaggeration. They did, and at one time I counted between thirty and forty of the horned devils. It was our job to sink them. They were so thick that we eventually took to our dinghies and sank them with rifle-fire from there; there was less chance of striking a half-submerged one while you were engaged with another, as M.L. 561 did. By an extraordinary chance the only man to be killed was the C.O. (poor old Purvis), who was forward at the time by the gun potting at a mine. The rest on board had miraculous escapes and got off with bruises and shock, for the M.L. did not sink at once, by some wonderful chance; she actually kept afloat for an hour, though all the forepart as far as the chart-house was blown away.

It was her frailty that saved her; she simply *tore* away; a tougher boat would have gone altogether.

Naturally, the most conspicuous thing to be seen as we entered Ostend harbour was the *Vindictive*. No need to describe her again; I have already done so in these notes. It recalls, however, still another extraordinary Hun lie I heard from a Belgian. He told me that the morning after the raid the Germans took the funnels off so that they could not be seen from the town, and kept all Belgians from going

158

anywhere near the harbour, and then told the inhabitants that the ship was really *outside* the eastern pier. This, however, I don't believe; even a German could hardly invent so clumsy a lie, to say nothing of the no small task of taking down the funnels before daylight! Besides, it contradicts the story that I also heard in Ostend that some Belgians who cheered when they saw the *Vindictive* inside the harbour were imprisoned. I think the story I mentioned in the notes on the *Vindictive* is true, though; it is so typically Teutonic.

The Germans have done their very best to block the harbour and ruin the docks. Right at the harbour mouth, close to the *Vindictive*, they have sunk a trawler and a large paddle steamer, while farther up are two huge dredgers. These look very weird, being piled one on top of the other. All the lock gates are broken, with craft of various sorts sunk in the entrances to docks or cutting-s. I am glad to see that in one dry dock there is the wreck of a U-boat smashed up by bombs.

The chief thing that has struck me about Ostend is the state of the town. I came here expecting to see a place almost in ruins, but was surprised to find how little damage has been done; save for a house here and there that has been demolished by a bomb or a stray shell, the place presents more or less a normal appearance as far as the buildings go. It is nothing like as knocked about as Dunkirk.

The railway station is the great exception. This is a complete and absolute ruin. I don't think I have ever seen a building more completely demolished. Great iron girders lie about on the ground in twisted heaps, or rear themselves in gaunt and fantastic shapes above great masses of fallen masonry. There is not a window left anywhere, of course, and very few walls; while in one place—I think it must have been the main hall of the station—about half a dozen great gilded pillars hang from the roof into nothingness; the bases have all been blown away. It is a most weird effect to see these long thick golden poles suspended from the ceiling, all swaying from the wind that sweeps through the gaps in the walls.

This destruction is a combined effort; a great deal of it has been done by bombs. Great circular holes in the roof going down each story till the cellar is reached, like a huge well without sides, tell their own tale. It must have been pretty well demolished from sea and air before the enemy exploded a few final charges with the idea of doing as much damage as he could before he left.

All along the front are concrete emplacements with the larger guns smashed and the smaller ones removed, and at frequent intervals, especially at the slopes that lead to the beach, are pieces of railway lines about six feet in length set in concrete at an angle of some 45 degrees to act as obstructions in the event of a landing in tanks, The Hun seems to have had the wind up pretty badly over landings.

No Belgians have been allowed on the front since 1914, and they are all flocking to it now as a novelty. We met a couple of *burgomasters* taking the air there this afternoon. At least I think they must have been *burgomasters*, they looked so respectable. They wore frock-coats and top hats.

The absence of animal life to be seen in the streets is very noticeable. I have seen practically no horses, and not a sign of either a dog or cat—sausages by now, I suppose, after four years of German occupation.

The prices here are steep, and you can only buy German goods in the shops. The poorest cigarettes cost threepence each. I got two German shrapnel helmets from a small boy in exchange for a packet of ten Gold Flake.

Eighteen *francs* for three glasses of beer is what I was charged today. It's a fine and effective method, though, to make a place "dry": a hint to the prohibitionists!

On The Mole.

No greater contrast could be imagined than the two approaches to Zeebrugge Mole that I have made this year, the first at the night attack in April last with the *Vindictive*, when the harbour was blocked, and the second shortly after we had recaptured the place. The former I need not describe again, but the latter will live in my memory quite as long.

It was a beautiful autumn morning that we went along the coast from Ostend; a slight haze hung over the water, and out of this the long grey line that was our first view of the Mole gradually took shape. Almost the first thing we saw was the break in the viaduct made by the submarine that blew herself up on the night of the attack, although the lighthouse at the sea end had been visible for some time; but it was not until we got closer that we saw that the lamp was completely wrecked.

The tops of buildings and gun emplacements next took the interest, many of the latter with their guns still pointing seaward, formidable looking yet, till a closer view showed the damage that had been done to them, thrown from their original mountings in some cases, or with barrels split and broken in others.

As we went round the end of the Mole a sunken ship came suddenly into view dead ahead. It was the wreck of the *Brussels*—Captain Fryatt's ship—which was used by the Germans as a depot ship before she was sunk. The lighthouse is on a stone pier about a hundred yards long, jutting out from the Mole proper, which is some three hundred feet wide and over a mile in length, and it was to the middle of the main part that we made our boat fast and climbed up on to the quay. The first M.L.s that went into Zeebrugge a few days before found that all the mooring bollards were wired, so that any ship that tied up would blow up as well. These had to be carefully disconnected before it was safe to moor; a delicate and ticklish job.

There is so much on the Mole that it is as impossible to describe it fully in a notebook as it is to explore it thoroughly at one visit; and although since then I have seen more of it, I will try and put down here my first impressions on that morning. Beginning at the sea end the lighthouse claims first attention, and to get to this one has to pass along the parapet on the sea-wall by many of the emplacements with their broken guns of various calibre, most of them damaged, of course, by the Germans themselves, although some were certainly put out of action by our ships or our airmen. There is little to see at the lighthouse; the stone tower is intact save at the top, where it has suffered in the complete destruction of the large lamp that now remains but a mass of wreckage, due probably to both our own and the enemy's efforts.

Powerful searchlights still remain along the seawall, smashed beyond repair, some of these fitted with what was once ingenious machinery for raising and lowering them; while ammunition hoists from the magazines below in the foundations are frequent.

Destruction of war material before a retreat is, of course, understandable, and it is not until you go into the living quarters, half concrete buildings and half dug-outs, that you realise the true nature of the Hun. Here is wanton destruction run riot. Signs of a hasty leaving are apparent. The litter is beyond description; broken furniture is strewn all round, bedding is torn and scattered about, there is hardly an unbroken piece of crockery left, and, although there are signs of quite recent habitation, filth abounds everywhere. In the officers' quarters there is some beautiful furniture, obviously smashed to matchwood intentionally; it seems that the Hun in his anger at having to leave determined that those who turned him out should not benefit by what he left, which, incidentally, was probably stolen in the first place.

There are numerous stores of all kinds, brick, concrete, and wooden buildings, and of these the same tale of destruction can be told, though the buildings themselves are not a great deal damaged. It is quite obvious that the Germans meant to keep the Mole for all time; the buildings that have been put up are very solid for the most part, and some are even still uncompleted. They had been at work here up to the last, for their gear and tools are still lying about. On one concrete wall they have moulded an inscription commemorating their capture of the place in 1914. A few lines added to this in English would complete the story. (I regret that it is no longer decipherable; too many indignant people, English, French, or Belgian, whose views differed from those expressed on this tablet, have destroyed it.)

Going towards the land end of the Mole, we next came to the seaplane sheds, in one of which there is still an enemy machine, which looks fairly complete at a distance, though it is really broken in every essential part and the engines smashed. Beyond these sheds is the railway station, quite as large as any average English one, with two roofed platforms, goods sidings, and the usual buildings. It is built as a terminus, though a line runs beyond the length of the Mole to the sea end, and there is also a smaller gauge line used for light trucks to various parts.

Following the line shorewards, we came to the viaduct that connects (or connected) the Mole with the land, and about a third of the way along this is the gap, some forty feet across. It is a wonderful sight. I heard the explosion, but I did not realise the extent of the damage until I saw this gap. Great wooden piles have been torn up like matches, while ironwork and railway lines are twisted like tangled rope. The Germans had put a temporary bridge over it (which they destroyed before they went), but for any purposes of heavy transport the viaduct has been useless since April.

As is only to be expected in a place that has been in German occupation for four years, notices, painted on boards chiefly, abound everywhere, and on most of these you are "*verboten*" to do something or other. No German is ever really happy unless he is being "*verboten*." The best motto in English for those who explore the Mole is "'Ware wire"; it may be a booby-trap; in fact, one needs to go very carefully about things at first and think twice before touching anything, however innocent it may look. At frequent intervals all over the Mole hang great iron gongs as alarm signals in case of attack, and by one I saw a notice giving the different Morse letters for air, land, or sea attacks or bombardments. The gong-ringers' jobs can have been no sinecure here for the past twelve months.

I have found quite an interesting collection of literature in the dug-outs on the Mole, both in prose and verse. All this would be very useful as an appendix to a longer account of the place than these few notes. One little sixteen-page booklet especially interests me (though I can read only a few words of it). It is called "*Das Lied von der Mole in Zeebrugge*." This "song" was written by a German sailor; it is probably quite humorous according to our standards, though probably deadly serious according to German ones. If the Scotch "joke with difficulty," it must be a veritable torture to a German. Although this "song" must be worth reading, I should like better still to hear what "swan song" the Huns sang as they were driven from the Mole to the echo of British naval guns.

The story of the snakes here I find is quite true; though if you tell people that you "saw snakes" on Zeebrugge Mole they are apt to be personal and cast unkind doubts upon your sobriety. I went into a dug-out this morning, and in the semi-darkness a hissing greeted me. I flashed an electric torch down, and there was a snake "sitting on its hind-legs" cursing me roundly. Trousers are not suitable for snake-charming, so I went out and found a man with leather sea-boots on, and I held the torch while he killed it with a stick.

Since then, I have seen about half a dozen snakes here, some alive and some dead, and also discovered the explanation of their presence on the Mole when I came upon a reptile house with all the glass in the sides smashed, obviously done by intention. The Hun is a pleasant fellow, even in his pets.

There was quite an excitement here last night—a spy hunt. Word came through, how or where from I don't know, that there was a German spy in hiding somewhere on the Mole. This information, coming on top of the definite news that two British and one French sentry had been shot dead somewhere ashore, caused the S.N.O. to organise a search of the Mole. This started about ten o'clock; there was no moon, and it was pitch dark. All ships had been warned that no one, except those in the search-party, was to be allowed ashore and we all had orders to fire at anything moving we saw ahead. We began down at the sea end of the Mole and worked shore wards. It was a strange task this poking about in dug-outs and dark buildings.

We did our best to keep together, but I consider it little short of a miracle that none of us got shot that night. We challenged all shadows, flashed torches here and there, and even fired shots at suspicious objects. The Mole is a perfect nest of hiding-places at night, and I think twenty spies could conceal themselves there more or less with impunity. We spent a couple of hours in this hunt, but caught no quarry. Personally, I don't believe there was any quarry to catch. A spy would either have to swim to the Mole or come by boat, since the viaduct was broken. We saw no boat, and if he swam, well, he deserved to get away after such a deed on this chill October night. Even if a spy had got here, he would not have found out much; he would not want to learn anything about the Mole, since the Germans knew that already, and as our ships had armed sentries on the quayside all night there was not much chance of gleaning any information in the darkness, in this direction.

But I enjoyed this spy hunt; it was another exciting incident in an exciting time. Even the prosaic job of getting meals here has an excitement of its own. Our breakfast this morning was caught with a hand grenade. The men found a store of them, and all day bangs have been going on in the harbour. The method is simple; you release the safety catch, throw the grenade into the water, and after the explosion go out in the dinghy and pick up the dead fish that are floating on the surface.

In Zeebrugge Harbour.

I'm afraid these notes will contain a good many mentions of fresh German lies being brought home to them, and an examination of Zeebrugge harbour exposed still another one. That is, their statement to the effect that the British raid here on April 23 last had been a failure, and that the port was still open. The *harbour* may have been, taking that part enclosed by the semi-circular Mole and the barrage of mined nets to the shore as the harbour, but the vital part, the canal to Bruges, was certainly not.

The *Intrepid* is well up and across the mouth of the entrance just before you come to the lock gates, the *Iphigenia* is only a little behind also across the canal, while the *Thetis*, though she is not actually in the canal, is lying just outside, and against her hull a very fine sand-bank has formed, so she still did good work where she is, though she did not reach her main objective as the other two did.

No ship of any size can get past the two blockships that are in the canal; an M.L. can just manage it, but for a destroyer or a modern submarine it would be quite impossible. This was proved by a number of ships being found in Bruges docks; the canal to Ostend is too narrow to get big ships up, so it meant either getting them to the sea up the Bruges canal to Zeebrugge or staying where they were. In this case it meant the latter.

The British blockships are not the only obstructions now in Zeebrugge harbour. Close to them the Germans have sunk two trawlers to try and block the fairway even more effectually still for our benefit, and all along the Mole quayside obstructions have been placed. Here the Hun has put anything he can; trawlers, dredgers, and boats of all sorts have been sunk, some even on top of each other, and, not content with this, he has toppled over railway trucks and carriages. Huge cranes have been smashed and hurled over the edge, and even those cranes that have resisted his efforts he has broken up somehow. One looks very like a huge camel kneeling down looking over the edge into the water.

At low tide the quayside of the Mole presents a very extraordinary appearance. Woe betide any M.L. who enters harbour at high water for the first time and moors up without asking any questions; the chances are that at low tide it will be high and dry on top of a guard's van!

I see that the huge bomb-proof roof that is built out over the quay at one place for U-boats to shelter under has belied its name, for one end of it is badly smashed up by a bomb.

There are many marks on the Mole left by our air-craft or our monitors, and in some places, I have found large pieces of shell from the big guns of the latter.

The big gates in the Bruges canal have been broken by the Germans before they left. Just beyond these are two huge shelters built over a cutting from the canal proper for submarine shelters. These seem to be undamaged, though I have not yet examined them closely.

The Bruges canal is as straight as a die for miles, and at the end the belfry and the tower of Notre Dame Cathedral can be clearly seen.

Altogether, Zeebrugge harbour is in a nasty mess just now. Even out in the middle there are obstructions of sorts. This morning we broke a blade of our propeller on something; what, I don't know, and don't suppose I ever shall.

The Land Batteries.

Of all the scenes of destruction in which this coast abounds, I think the worst is to be seen during a visit to the shore batteries that lie behind Ostend and Zeebrugge.

165

America has declared war. M.L.s on patrol off the Newarp Lightship, getting the news by Morse from a passing destroyer.

The one that impressed me most is the one I have seen today—the Tirpitz Battery—a few miles out of Ostend. It has five 11-inch guns, or rather now possesses the shattered remains of such guns. Four of them have been wrecked pretty much in the same way. The breeches have been jammed and broken, great rocks or chunks of iron rammed down the muzzles till they split, and a charge put underneath to blow them off their carriages, and they now lie in their pits like giant snakes outstretched in their death agony amidst the confusion and wreckage around them. The solid concrete emplacements are torn and split, and the roofs of the adjoining dug-outs and magazines blown off. In the latter are vast quantities of shells, but I noticed most of the brass cases containing the charges have been taken away by the enemy. Brass is too precious for him to leave lying about. Thousands of sticks of melinite of varying lengths are strewn about everywhere. It only wants a match, and there would be a victory bonfire *de luxe*!

The fifth gun is smashed in an entirely different way from the others. It has obviously been hit by an explosive that came from the outside and not inside the emplacement; either it was destroyed by a bomb thrown by the Germans themselves, which is a little unlikely, as so big a charge as has evidently been used would be too dangerous to throw from anywhere near enough to get an accurate aim. The far more likely cause of this difference of destruction is that this gun was not destroyed by the Germans themselves at all, but either by a bomb from the air or, more likely, a shell from one of our monitors during a coastal bombardment.

There are many signs about this battery that give colour to this theory, especially in the trenches that surround it, where the ground is torn up at frequent intervals, and in the fields skirting the defences, where the shell-holes are even more noticeable still. It says much for the monitors' shooting.

Yesterday we went to the Kaiser Wilhelm Battery at Knocke, towards the Dutch frontier from Zeebrugge.

We landed from the M.L in our dinghy, and got quite a civic reception. The *burgomaster* came down to the beach to receive us in state, accompanied by what was left of the population. It was not a very dignified landing, I'm afraid, for owing to the shelving beach we had to "off boots" and wade ashore.

I think the *burgomaster* loves me. He hugged me most affectionately and kissed me on both cheeks. He said we were the first English to come to the place since 1914. He was also the keeper of the chief hotel, and would not be content till he had taken us there and opened a special bottle of umpteen-umpteen vintage in our honour. Quite a crowd collected as we came out, and cheered us as we walked away. It was certainly a crowded minute or so of glory.

The Kaiser Wilhelm Battery, to which many willing volunteers conducted us, is smaller than the Tirpitz and has only three guns, but they are 12-inch. Here is the same scene of destruction, and there is nothing left but scrap metal. This battery is in the middle of the dunes. It must have been a mighty task to get these guns over the sands. They are all in concrete pits that are built in depressions in the sand-hills, a task which in itself must have been considerable. It cannot be too easy to build such solid structures on a sandy bottom.

There was one huge pit that was full of water, though not a sign of gun or emplacement could be seen. A Belgian who was there said that a gun was at the bottom, but I doubt it; more likely that it had been prepared for a foundation to be built for a new gun, then for some reason or another the idea had been given up.

We had a great send-off as we embarked to the M.L. that was lying at anchor off-shore waiting for us. We were certainly the heroes of the war to the people at Knocke.

The Loogenbaum Battery near Ostend had a surprise for us. It is the battery where the single huge long-range gun is, and we got there expecting to find it broken up like the rest, but to our astonishment it was undamaged as far as we could see. This battery was evidently one of the last to be evacuated, and there could not have been time for the elaborate plans of destruction to be carried out here as in the other places. What had been done was fairly obvious; the gun had been depressed to its extreme limit and fired into the concrete of the pit in the hope that the recoil would smash up everything, gun and all; but the concrete could not stand the test, it had given way too easily, and the charge burst in the earth more or less harmlessly, leaving the gun undamaged. I'm glad in a way that we had captured this gun intact, but I should have liked to have seen our people break it up or, better still, turn it on the retreating Hun.

I owed this gun a grudge, for it was the one that nearly killed me at Dunkirk.

CHAPTER 15

U-Boat Avenue

The sight of the long double line of surrendered U-boats which stretched for about half a mile in the River Stour at Harwich was one of the most impressive I have ever seen. Over a hundred boats were there at one time, moored in trots of four at a buoy, which gave them an appearance of a street, especially at night, when each boat carried a riding light, and lines diverging to what seemed almost the far distance made this impression doubly real.

This avenue seemed to signify the sacrifice of a nation, when one thought of the millions that had been spent in their construction, and the hope that had been fostered in the hearts of the German people, fed on the stories of how these boats would soon reduce arrogant Britain to her knees and gain for Germany a victorious peace—and then this ignominious end. Here they lay, as tame and harmless as a string of dumb barges, or perhaps a better simile would be like a collection of sharks whose teeth had been withdrawn; evil creatures who, by bloody murder, hoped to wrest the trident from the hand of Britannia, but now held captive by its power. A fitting conclusion to their ill-favoured boasts.

Of all Germany's war blunders the greatest, perhaps, has been her inability to understand the psychology of other nations, and never has this been shown clearer than in her imaginings that "frightfulness" at sea could ever have a lasting effect. She could not understand how for every British sailor murdered two more arose ready to take his place and to avenge him. I am not trying to minimise the submarine menace, for at one time it was a very real one, till measures could be adopted to combat it; but I think it was the wonderful motto "Carry on" that was the real reason that made the submarine campaign an ultimate failure. One cannot speak too highly of the pluck and grit of the mercantile marine for the part they played and for the way they carried on, with a very small armament in some cases, and others with none at all, and went about their business on the high seas as calmly and as methodically as if no under-sea foes were waiting to sink them at the first opportunity.

So, if these captured U-boats symbolised the sacrifice of one nation, they typified the triumph of another.

The actual surrender was an equally impressive sight. A flotilla of some twenty U-boats, accompanied by a German cruiser, were the first to arrive; these were met some few miles out to sea by our ships. Here the British crews were put aboard, and the surrender taken; every U-boat entered Harwich flying the White Ensign above the German flag.

They came up the harbour to their moorings in dead silence. Not a cheer was raised from the crowds that watched to break the grim stillness that witnessed, this piece of history—these sea-monsters that were to have defeated the British Navy now throwing up the sponge without striking a last blow, and passing, for ever dishonoured, to their eternal shame.

I never thought at one time to have the deck of my M.L. crowded with German sailors, but it was this day, when we took them off the U-boats back to their own ship. It was interesting to study them. They seemed to vary a good deal both in appearance and manner. One crew we took off looked the most bloodthirsty gang of unshaven ruffians I ever hope to meet, but other lots did not seem such bad fellows—that is, for Huns. Most of them did not show much sign of feeling their position, some even seemed relieved that it was all over, which they very probably were, for life on a U-boat, hunted and harried for almost every hour of the twenty-four, must have been a nerve-racking job, especially towards the end, when our anti-submarine defences got one too many for them.

The German officers were fairly quiet for the most part, though some of them seemed inclined to talk, one even to be bombastic and talk largely of the next war and what their U-boats would do then: a pitiable and typically Hunnish attempt to bluster to the end. I asked him quietly what the Germans thought of Zeebrugge; he looked at me for a moment as if about to give vent to some further boasting remark, but, seeing the smiles of one or two who were standing around, he suddenly collapsed like a bubble, and beyond a muttered expression in German—of hate, I suppose—-he did not speak any more. Zeebrugge is evidently a very sore point in German naval circles. The fact that we could block their pet submarine harbour under their very noses is a thorn in their flesh that still festers.

The surrender of the German High Seas Fleet took place in one day, but not so that of the U-boats; these were given up in batches of from ten to twenty spread over an interval of about a month. The surrender of the first batch was intensely interesting, but the novelty soon wore off, till it became wearisome, especially when one batch kept us hanging about till 4 a.m. on a winter's night before the last boat came in, owing to adverse weather conditions.

All sorts and conditions of U-boats there were, very different in type and size, from the small U-9 to the huge, unwieldy-looking U-155, better known as the *Deutschland*. The latter is an extraordinary looking craft, at least twice as large as any other, with double the freeboard when on the surface. She could only carry about one thousand tons of cargo, and this fact, combined with the number of cabins, makes one think that it was built more as a passenger than a cargo boat. German agents were busy in America in those days.

Latterly the *Deutschland* had been converted into a fighting submarine and mounted two five-inch guns. There were other U-boats with histories. U-9, already mentioned, was the one that sank the three British cruisers, *Crecy*, *Aboukir*, and *Hogue*, in the early part of the war. U-53 was another that also visited the States; and U-55 was the notorious boat that sank the *Belgian Prince*, taking the survivors on board and afterwards submerging with about thirty of them *on the deck*. Surely one of the foulest crimes in naval annals—even those of Germany.

There are three classes of U-boats taken as a general rule, though even these differ in their own class. There are the U-boats, or ordinary submarines; the UB-boats with special electric motors for operations from the Belgian coast bases of Zeebrugge and Ostend; and the UC-boats, which are minelayers.

With very few exceptions the state of the surrendered submarines was filthy, and little care seemed to have been taken in their upkeep for some time; ever since the mutiny at Kiel, probably. In some of the later boats the accommodation was good, especially that for the officers, whose quarters were panelled and fitted up very comfortably, in some cases almost luxuriously, considering the small space available. The life on the smaller boats, however, such as U-9 must have been a veritable "dog's life"; everything was very small and cramped; the officers' quarters were muddled up with those of the men, and one could hardly move without falling over a torpedo tube or some machinery or other.

Six months duty with the U-boats made one pretty familiar with them, and I don't think there was one of the hundred odd boats that were surrendered during my time at Harwich that I did not explore from stem to stern, usually at night, for it is slow work spending a night on guard duty up at the trots. Interest I found in plenty, and one shock. This was rather a weird experience. It was while I was exploring one of the larger UC-boats. For some freakish reason I had squeezed myself right up to the bows where the minelaying tubes are. This was a difficult task, as the tubes are big things and there is precious little space left to get by. My electric torch was getting so dim that I found it easier to use matches in my crawlings and grope the greater part of the way.

I had just reached the narrow space between the last two tubes when, on putting my hand out, I touched a boot. Horrors, was this a dead Hun? I struck a match; yes, there was no doubt about it; there were two feet and legs sticking out from the darkness cast by the shadow of the tube. The body must have been well wedged in and put there by force, for the feet were pointing upward at quite a sharp angle. The match burned my fingers, and I felt for another, but to my disgust I found I had used the last. I tried my feeble torch, but could see nothing but the two legs, The boots seemed to be some sort of sea-boots and very large.

It was a weird situation to be in: alone in a deserted U-boat at two in the morning with what was apparently a dead German.

I did not relish groping about with my hands to try and discover more, so I backed out from my cramped position and made my way back to the M.L. Here I got some fresh matches, a candle, and a new torch, and, telling the man on watch to come with me, went back again to try and solve this mystery. This we did with the increased light. There were certainly two legs and feet sticking out, and on pulling these we brought the "body" into view. It proved to be one of the large diving suits fitted with the oxygen apparatus; at least they looked like diving suits, but I think they were meant to be used in a last desperate effort of escape should the boat be sunk; really for the opposite purpose to diving. There were a good many about on the submarines, though how this one had got jammed up among the minelaying tubes is more than I can say.

The legs, half inflated, certainly looked very real, and in a bad light enough to give one a horrible shock under conditions that were sufficiently eerie in the ordinary way. A deserted U-boat, haunted by horrible memories at which one can only guess, is a ghostly place to explore alone at the dead of night.

CHAPTER 16

The Scroll of Emmel

(This ancient scroll was found in *a,d.* 3000 by a diver at Southampton docks. It throws some vivid sidelights on the habits of that strange tribe the Emmelites, who flourished during the European War 1914–1918. Unfortunately, portions of it are indecipherable on account of the water damaging the parchment, and it is to be regretted that up to the present not the slightest clue has been discovered to help solve the impenetrable secret as to the identity of the mysterious ship, the *Herm*, referred to by the writer.)

1. Now numerous officers of the king's ships came unto a certain scribe saying, Verily, *it is* meet that you should take your quill and write upon parchment the truth concerning certain things.

2. And the chief of these things, is it not the wonderful ways of the ship called *Herm* and those who do make of this ship an habitation.

3. And so it came about that I, Emmel, a scribe of the Emmelites, have here set down divers things concerning *that* which befell the officers of the king's ships, who upon occasions were gathered around the ship called *Herm*, either for *the* instruction of their minds or *to do* with the mending of their boats from the scars of war.

(The scroll is here indecipherable.) . . . and so, it befell that the *Herm* came *unto* her moorings in the dockyard of the king at Hampton in the South country.

21. Of the state of her when she arrived it is best unwritten, for was she not manned by many more living things than authorised by the king, his regulations; which, until the fumes of smoke had driven *them* forth, did mortify the flesh exceeding sore.

22. And the Room of Guns, was it not like unto a Garden of Bears, where eighty and eight had to be in the place *meant* for eight, and were not the times of eating like *unto* a fierce battle which wageth unceasingly?

23. Yet still the ship called *Herm* was *dear* to the young officers of the king's ships, as many found as they fell to examine their monies when the accompts for their bills of messing had been deducted. And who knew for what he had been charged, or why; verily, not even the most wise knew this thing that was *put* across him.

24. And certain officers of the king were attached to the *Herm*; but to this ship no other man was ever attached; for all rejoiced exceedingly when *their* time came to depart.

25. And these officers who were attached to the *Herm* did look with scorn upon the others who were there for a passing time, for the ship's officers took themselves to be *big* bugs.

26. Now the first captain of this ship called *Herm* was one the son of Dick. Other names and many was he also called by those under him, though it is not meet that these names be written *upon* this scroll, for might it not fall perchance into the hands of womenkind, yea, *even* into the hands of damsels, the daughters of womenkind, whereupon would they not be exceeding shocked?

27. Albeit these names were many *and* fruity.

28. Now this captain was not a sailor, even though he wore the robes of an officer of the king, his navy, and many were the mistakes he made and much secret merriment did he cause thereby.

29. Nevertheless did he hold the *whip* hand, which he did use to the undoing of those he did not love; wherefore he himself was not loved with a very deep *or* lasting adoration.

30. Now it befell that the first lieutenant of the ship called *Herm* was *of the tribe* of the Baronites, and he did love the damsels.

31. Yea verily, had they even faces like *unto* torn-up roads, did he still love them.

32. Albeit he was on in years did he still love the young damsels with a love exceeding *that of a* father.

33. Now it passed that in the town of Hampton in the South there was a circus (or hippodrome) for the conducting of games *and sports* to amuse the populace. And it oft-times chanced that at the door whence the damsels of the circus were wont to emerge, there did foregather numbers of young officers hoping to gaze upon the beauties *of these* damsels.

34. But when the Baronite discovered this thing (some have it by hearsay, and others say that it was *from* observation), he did wax exceeding wrath, saying, "Shall my young men thus be tempted from *their* duty?" And straightway he went and wrote upon the tablets of

THE PILLAR OF CLOUD BY DAY

THE PILLAR OF FIRE BY NIGHT

OFF THE TYNE COUNTRY.

the ship.

35. And this is what he wrote, saying, "It shall be forbidden for officers of the king, his Navy, to await the damsels *by the door* of the circus."

36. And I, Emmel, a scribe of the Emmelites, wonder, with others, if it were to save the junior officers *from the* lures of the damsels that he did this thing, or that the coast it might be clear for himself.

37. But our wonder was not of a great depth; nor were our understandings taxed sore to solve this riddle.

38. Now it befell that upon a certain evening the Baronite met a damsel of the circus . . .

(Here the scroll is indecipherable.)

. . . that a certain ship of the Emmelites came to the *Herm* for the repairing of her scars of war after many winters on the high seas and times of stress off the coasts *of the* Gauls.

77. And the officer in charge of this seafaring vessel found that the officers of the Herm to have waxed fat and flourishing, albeit that many changes had taken place in the personnel *of the ship* since he had been away.

78. But it is the aim of me, Emmel, a scribe of the Emmelites, to render a fair telling upon this scroll, so it must be recorded that certain of the officers of the *Herm* were good men and true *and* sportsmen, and did treat the officers that came back from the sea with justice, and offered to them the hand of friendship.

79. But there were others who thought themselves to be even bigger bugs *than ever* (and some of these were men young and lusty), and did hang on to their jobs, safe and cushie, like even unto the barnacles that clung to the keel of the *Herm* and moored her safely to the quayside. And it came to pass that it was these men that did treat with scorn those who were fools enough to go upon the far waters.

80. And these *big* bugs did laugh at danger, for was it not yet a great distance *from them.*

81. But let it be recorded that they were not afraid of water, and often did they face it *with spirit.* Yea verily, did they have their rough nights with the strong waters.

82. Nor were they afraid even to *face powder*, as the damsels of the circus could testify.

83. And the refitting of the king, his vessels, at the depot ship called *Herm, it was* a wonderful thing, and it befell that . . .

(Here the scroll is indecipherable)]

. . . and the officer of the refitting ship did come to his cabin at a time when the *craftsmen* of the *Herm* were *about* their business.

101. And he stood awhile by the hatch leading to the *great* engines to watch the slumber of a craftsman. As a babe he reposed, innocent and free from worry.

102. Deeming it to be a *shame* to awaken *him*, the officer of the ship did pass down to hatch of the place of cooking unto the ward-room; but to pause again *in wonder*.

103. For it happened that in the sleeping cabin he beheld three craftsmen; and albeit it was the full working hours and not *those* of standoff, he saw that one *was* reclining *even* upon his own bunk, and the two remaining were seated upon the deck *of the* cabin all offering up a sacrifice to the goddess Nicotine.

104. And even as the officer watched their worship, he did hear the craftsman upon the bed say unto them, *his fellows*: "Lo, before I came to be a craftsman at the *Herm*, I had a *soft job*."

105. And the officer went on his way wondering upon this, and what *craft* the man could have been; perchance the vendor of scrolls, or programmes, at the crowning of kings,

106. Albeit before he departed the officer did speak a few *well-cho-sen* words unto these craftsmen saying what manner *of men* he deemed them to be.

107. Wherefore this officer was not loved by these craftsmen for the bitterness *that* was upon his tongue, for his words they were *to the point*, seeing that all three craftsmen were young men who, albeit they wore the uniform of the king, would not do his work, *even* in safety.

108. And so the life of the *Herm* it did proceed in even tenor, in spite of certain *horrid persons* who did dare to criticise or jest upon it.

109. And he of the tribe of the Baronites did still love the ladies, even as did his satellite.

110. And when the refitting was *supposed* to be complete . . .

(Here the scroll is indecipherable.)

. . . and was glad to shake the waters of this *place* from his keel to go once more upon the high seas.

(Here the first scroll ends with a note as to the existence of a second one dealing more with personalities; but this has not yet been recovered by the divers, who are still at work in the dock searching for it.)

CHAPTER 17

The Freedom of the Seize

AN EPISODE IN NAVAL CRIMINOLOGY

The system of paying off an M.L. seems to be in inverse ratio to commissioning. For whereas in the latter case all kinds of weird and wonderful things are dumped down upon the deck apparently without rhyme or reason, in the former case mysterious persons you have never seen before appear seemingly from nowhere and lay violent hands upon everything within reach—a sort of Freedom of the Seize—and proceed to strew the deck and the quayside with your gear, till a casual observer might easily imagine that an itinerant marine-store dealer had called upon you and had left a few samples for your inspection.

Things that have never seen the light since the boat was commissioned appear now from the depths to blink at the unaccustomed daylight, such as the patent folding and (very) collapsible canvas bath in its thin wooden framework, which only an enthusiast in tubbing ever had pluck enough to use, most preferring the homely, but far more serviceable, method of putting a grating in place of the bilge-board and using a sponge.

All your gear is ruthlessly torn away from its resting-places and spread out for the inspection of quayside loungers in stand-easy times, who look upon the collection in the light of a naval museum. Occasionally a petty officer with a list is seen dimly through the debris, but neither he nor those engaged in seizing your gear and throwing it about worry much about a mere C.O. When this process has been going on for an hour or two the things are carted away, presumably to some shed or other, but they pass beyond your ken.

Then people are surprised that things are missing.

I cannot help thinking that a great lack of that rare misnamed commodity known as common-sense is shown in paying off an M.L. Let me quote an instance. For some reason—I don't know why, and I don't suppose anyone else does either—two glass tumblers are supplied with the original hull fittings of the boat, quite apart from the ones issued with your mess-traps from the victualling stores. These are supposed to be, I think, for use in the after-cabin. In my own boat these were not to be found when she paid off, a fact scarcely surprising after a three years' commission, most of which was spent with the Dover patrol, which included night patrols, and various "stunts" on the Belgian coast under fire a good part of the time. Any one night in the winter-time off Dunkirk was enough for two hundred tumblers to go the way of all glass on M.L.s, let alone two. This I ventured to point out in explanation of what possibly may have been their fate; but no, they were missing, and they must be charged against me. The first black mark in my naval career.

However, this offence, serious as it was, sank into complete insignificance when compared to my second and great crime; one which I feel has besmirched my fair name for ever in the annals of the Navy, and put my memory perpetually under a cloud. I had lost a pickle-fork!

No landsman can hope to understand the enormity of this sin, which, it seems, is the blackest and most damnable of all naval crimes. Had I lost the starboard engine, the binnacle, the mast, the dinghy, or the 2½-pounder gun, I do not think anyone would have worried in the least; such minor things can apparently be lost with impunity. But not a pickle-fork.

A solemn and perfectly polite petty-officer waited upon me in my cabin when this delinquency was discovered, and asked me what I had done with my pickle-fork. I said I had not the least idea. He scowled, and said I must come and see the officer in charge of the stores. I think he would have liked me put in irons. Accordingly, I was taken on deck, through the debris on the quayside, amidst curious eyes (for I think my crime was known by now), to an office ashore, which made me feel like a notorious murderer passing through the crowd to the court.

Again, I was given a chance before the officer to clear myself. Where was my pickle-fork? I did not know. This fact was solemnly entered into a huge book, a record, I suspect, of the more serious crimes in the navy. This statement I had to sign, and no doubt my Lords of the Admiralty are still considering what dire punishment they can mete out to me for my unpardonable transgression.

I will say that I was given every chance and help to have this blot taken from my clean sheet. A special working-party was despatched to search among the debris on the deck and the quay for the lost pickle-fork. But it was unavailing—it was never found. One budding Sherlock Holmes reported that he had discovered in the ward-room cupboard a half-empty bottle of pickles, and although he had searched the area thoroughly this valuable clue had led to nothing. Looking for a ship's whaler adrift on the Atlantic Ocean without any known bearing of its position would have been an easy task compared to trying to find a pickle-fork among the heterogeneous mass of articles strewn about after paying off an M.L.

So, I left the "court" a disgraced man, and I felt lucky to be free and alive.

I believe that if a naval officer won the V.C, the D.S.O., and the D.S.C, but lost *two* pickle-forks, he would be publicly degraded, all his medals stripped off his breast, and dismissed the service with disgrace.

Anyone who has read the Articles of War must have noticed the severe penalties that *can* be meted out for trivial offences, such as "Any man who is found to have a bootlace undone on the quarter-deck shall be punished by Death—or any other such punishment as may be deemed necessary."

I expect by the next war a special clause will be inserted with regard to lost pickle-forks, without, of course, the amendment to the sentence that is added.

On thinking over this episode, I have come to the conclusion that there must be something symbolical in the whole affair. Doubtless in the official mind the pickle-fork must represent the trident of Britannia, which if lost means that she loses the command of the sea, and the pickle-forks supplied to M.L.s should be guarded most jealously for this reason. So next time I go into action in an M.L. I shall nail my colours to the mast, and, with a firm grasp of my pickle-fork, wave defiance to my enemies.

Only, I wish the King's Regulations would make this a little clearer.

CHAPTER 18

"Sic Transit . . ."

When you commissioned a boat in September 1916, and have been in command of her the whole time until she paid off in May 1919—as was my case with M.L. 314,—one cannot see her taken down to the "knacker's yard" in Hamble River to be "laid to rest" with some two hundred other M.L.s without a pang of genuine regret; at least I could not.

I have no intention of writing a maudlin screed, with a pathetic "It's only an M.L." sort of tone about it, but I can truthfully say I left the old boat with a touch of sadness. As I stood on her deck for the last time, when she was moored up in the trot with half a dozen other deserted boats, I spent a few moments gazing into the mirrors of memory, where passed in rapid review vivid pictures of all I had gone through on this same boat since I first went aboard her in the pocket at Portsmouth harbour two years and nine months ago.

I saw our maiden voyage to Great Yarmouth; the strenuous winter days and nights in the North Sea, and the pleasant hours of summer, ere the mirror flashed me down south again to the Dover Patrol. For a little I lingered gazing on these animated visions, till the scene passed to Dunkirk and the unforgettable years I spent there. Bright flashes in the darkness illumined the mirror as I saw the air-raids once again in all their horrible splendour; and when that passed into a white mist that enveloped all, I knew I was looking again at those exciting bombardments of the Belgian coast, when, enclosed in fog of our own making, we smoked inshore for the monitors to fire over our heads.

Then came the ever-memorable night of the Zeebrugge-Ostend raid. Amidst the fog in the darkness, I could almost hear the roar of the guns at every flash I saw, and the mighty explosion, brightest and loudest of all, as the submarine blew up the Mole viaduct. This was a very real picture. This passing gave place to the day patrols off the coast and the nerve-racking night work in the Zuidcoote Pass, when nothing but the M.L. patrol lay between the enemy and our fleet in Dunkirk Roads. Then back to our own shores once more to the surrender of the German submarines at Harwich, interesting if not so exciting as the former scenes, and so on, to our last voyage to Southampton to pay off; and last of all, a scene that brought me back to the present once more—the last picture of all as we lay "at rest" in Hamble River,

It was a good bit to have gone through in the same little ship. She had borne me safely through many perils and had been my only home during those strenuous days, so perhaps a touch of a sailor's love for his craft can be understood creeping in at leaving her to an unknown fate—probably the shipbreakers' yard.

There was something a little pathetic, I think, in seeing over two hundred M.L.s all lying up here in idleness, boats, which a short time ago were so full of life and virility, now silent, still, and deserted. As one looked around familiar numbers caught the eye, boats in whose company this or that adventure had been passed; and now, like grey ghosts of former time, these veterans—for an M.L. is quite a veteran in two years—were spending the evenings of their short but eventful days in this peaceful anchorage, perhaps telling each other in M.L. fashion of all they had passed through since they last met in the Tidal Basin at Portsmouth Harbour, new and raw recruits to the navy, ere they scattered to their various patrols round our coasts.

Well, it is all over now, this "Great Adventure" of M.L. life, and we go back to become civilians once more, a little regretfully perhaps, with the storehouses of our minds filled with vivid recollections of the Little Grey Patrol and all that befell us in those days, when we went forth to a new life, and, learning wisdom by experience, carried on with our jobs to the best of our several abilities, gaining a sporting tolerance for our early failures, a generous appreciation of our desire to do our best, and, I venture to hope, some little credit for our subsequent successes.

We had our growls—one sailor's habit we soon acquired; we had our grievances, real and imaginary, and were content to take a little smooth with a good deal of rough. But we had our good times too; and should there ever come a day when Britain wants us again, I trust she will find us all ready.

And so, for the last time I ring the engine-room telegraphs to "Stop," and leave the bridge of my M.L.

The Cinderellas of the Fleet

By William Washburn Nutting

PREFACE

This little book does not pretend to be a history of anti-submarine warfare. Neither is it a scientific treatise on the instruments and methods used in this the newest phase of naval fighting. On the other hand, I am afraid there is all too little in it of the romantic personal element, in which a war fought largely by kid reservists in small boats is bound to be rich. It is the story of an idea and how it grew in the face of indifference and ridicule to a success as unexpected by the regular Navy as it was by the average layman. It is the story of the Submarine Chasers.

Without wishing to underrate the part played in the war by the high-seas fleets of Great Britain and our own country, we may say that their part was largely a potential one. The actual work of strafing the U-boat, which was the big job of the war, was done by the scrubs— the destroyers, the yachts, the trawlers, the drifters, the motor craft, that Rudyard Kipling so aptly dubbed "The Fringes of the Fleet."

When the war cloud burst over Europe the submarine was the big, new, practically untried instrument of naval warfare, to which the Germans, foiled in their attempt to terminate the conflict in a single, rapid thrust, looked to isolate England and to bring down the mighty British Fleet, bit by bit, to the level of their own. No weapon had yet been devised to counter it nor any successful method of fighting it evolved. Its success was appalling and to make matters worse, it seemed to evolve and multiply much more rapidly than the means and methods of combatting it.

But gradually, out of the chaos and the experience dearly bought with countless lives and scores of ships, there was evolved a method of defence against the submarine and then a method of aggressive warfare, with specially designed boats and numerous and elaborate instruments for apprehending and destroying the tin shark.

Possibly we are still a little too close to the war to pick out of the welter of unheard-of things and stupefying events those which were really important, but as time goes on the last five years gradually will resolve themselves into a few salient, outstanding facts, just as wars always have done since the beginning of time. To many people the scrap between the *Monitor* and the *Merrimac* is the only thing that happened on the water during the Civil War, although at the time, I dare say, it received no more than passing notice. To the generations to come, the big things in the World War, so far as the naval part of it is concerned, will not be the Battle of Jutland, nor the Gallipoli fiasco, nor the few other engagements in which capital ships took part, but rather the spectacular, though long-drawn struggle between the comparatively new submarine and the even newer means of combatting it—the Submarine Chaser and its deadly depth bomb.

The Chaser is essentially an American product as was the British "M.L.," its predecessor. The idea originated here and the boats, as well as their motors and much of their ingenious equipment, were built in this country. And now that they have made good, we're proud of them. Everybody who knows what they did is proud of them. Even the regular Navy shows marked signs of pride in her precocious step-children, and those of us who talked motor boats from the time the war began are trying hard to suppress a very real and a very human impulse to say: "We told you so." For the Submarine Chasers, the Cinderellas of the Fleet, have come home with a service record unsurpassed by any class of ships in the navy.

For a year, flung far along the Allied coast lines and our own, these little vessels carried tirelessly on—convoying merchant ships, hunting the submarine with their uncanny detection apparatus, dropping the deadly depth bomb when they found him, exploding mines, fighting ahead of the fleets and performing a thousand drudgeries as well, too menial for their bigger sisters. And then, many of them in the dead of winter, they came home across three thousand miles of ocean, bearing proudly the scars of Durazzo and with a record of 40% of all the submarines destroyed by American vessels.

Nobody, not even the visionary gentlemen who first began to play with the idea, could have predicted the remarkable success attained by the Submarine Chasers. Nobody except a handful of small boat enthusiasts would have believed it possible for them to live out some of the dirtiest weather that ever flayed the Western Ocean. And but few, even after the job was finished, seemed to appreciate the fact that the Chasers more than any other one thing sealed the fate of the German submarine.

But they did more than that, for through their performance over countless weary, rolling miles of sea, they have given us a fund of valuable data on the possibilities of small boats and their power plants that we never should have gathered in many a lazy year of peace.

Yes, we're proud of them now and of the kid reservists who commanded them and of the gobs who manned them. The little vessels that were damned and ridiculed by the majority of battle-wagon men from the time their design was first noised about, made good—gloriously made good. They have written a story that will live along with the classics of naval history to fire the imagination of the youth of generations to come.

William Washburn Nutting.

New York City,
September. 1919.

DEDICATED
TO
THE BLACK GANG

The British M. L.'s

THE M. L.'s—THEIR ORIGIN AND THEIR DUTIES

I have always thought of the world as divided into two classes of people: those who are interested in boats, and—well, just plain folks.

So far as America is concerned, the "just plain folks" have been somewhat in the ascendency since the days when the New Bedford whalers and the famous Yankee clipper ships made the American ensign a thing well known and respected on all the seven seas. Of late years there hasn't been much to keep alive in our people a love of the sea or much to which we could point with pride to refute the taunt of the lime-juicer that we have forsaken the sea and become a soft, land-loving nation—not much besides our Navy and always our Gloucester fishing fleet.

But the war has changed all that. Not only has it put us back on something like a decent footing as a maritime nation, but it has added a brilliant chapter to our naval history as well. It has brought back thousands of men to the sea, and it has instilled in other thousands a new interest in things nautical.

Let us take it for granted then that whoever finds himself in possession of this book is interested in boats, that he speaks the language, and that he wants in one volume as much information as he can get about the particular kind of boat that, developed by the war, did as much as any other instrumentality in bringing it to a successful conclusion.

No weapon, no policy, no idea developed under the stimulus of war returned a fuller measure of what it was intended to do than did the Submarine Chasers. No program was carried through to a successful conclusion with less waste, less confusion, less blundering than the seemingly impossible feat of building and powering in a year's time four hundred and fifty 110-foot boats in forty different places all over the country. And no individual or organisation is more entitled to the gratitude of the nation at large than the company that built, with-

The Movies in the Mediterranean

out hint of profiteering, the hundreds of engines with which these boats were powered. But the really remarkable thing about the whole program is that it was accomplished for the most part in the existing boat-building yards of the country without deflecting labour or material from the shipyards or delaying in the slightest the production of merchant and naval vessels or their propelling machinery.

Another remarkable and typically American accomplishment was the building of the earlier patrol boats for England—the five hundred and fifty 80-footers, known as the M. L.'s, which did such varied and valiant service during the later years of the war. These boats were the forerunners of our own Chasers and it was upon the results of their performance, to some extent, that our boats were designed. For this reason, I have decided to tell something of the M. L.'s and what they did for England before continuing with the story of the Chasers.

THE BRITISH M. L.'s

Back in 1914 America, the big, more-or-less neutral bystander, startled and fascinated by what was happening on the other side of the Atlantic, began to develop an interest in the scrap and to shout suggestions to John Bull. John, fat and somewhat out of training, was taking a lot of punishment on those self-same waves that he had been ruling for so long.

These suggestions were numerous and many of them proved of service, but the best of them was this: "Why don't you go after the pirates with a fleet of fast motor boats?"

Probably John Bull already had been thinking along this line himself for he had mobilised his trawlers and his yachts and his motor craft early in the war, but at any rate his boat yards could not turn out a job of this size. Standardised Chasers might be all right and they might not, but other definite things were needed and his shipyards were having all they could handle to produce these things without experimenting with something doubtful.

By the spring of 1915 the submarine situation had become so grave that the Lords of the Admiralty decided that something had to be done and done quickly. From the frequent and audacious sinkings, some of them at the very mouths of English harbours, and the toll already taken from the British fleet itself, it was plain that a large and powerful Navy was not the solution of the problem. Neither were the thousands of trawlers, and other auxiliary craft patrolling the waters of the British Isles, able to check the growing menace.

AN M. L. STRIKES HEAVY WEATHER IN THE STRAITS OF GIBRALTAR.

A GROUP OF M. L.'S ON THE WAYS READY FOR LAUNCHING.

It was not long after this that a steamship arrived in New York harbour bearing a commission of prominent British engineers on a quest for boats, and they frankly solicited the co-operation and advice of those whose experience might be of service. America, through John P. Holland, had given to the world the most terrible of all the deadly implements of modern warfare and now America was called upon to devise a means for its destruction.

The very day of the arrival of the ship a message was received by the Standard Motor Construction Company and the plant was kept lighted that evening for the inspection of the engineer officers. The facilities of the company were carefully considered as well as the design of the motor and late in the night the visitors departed convinced of the possibilities of the plant for the production of engines in the quantities in which they were likely to be needed.

Subsequently members of the commission met the head of the Elco Works, a boat building organisation, with a record as old and as excellent as that of the Standard Motor Construction Company. Away back in 1893 this company had built a fleet of fifty electric launches for the Chicago World's Fair and from that time on had acquired a reputation for standardized boats. It seemed the logical yard to tackle the job.

Several days passed and then the commission expressed its readiness to place an order for fifty 75-foot boats if the whole lot could be delivered within a year's time. This was a task unprecedented in the history of boat building, but Mr. Eugene Riotte of the Standard Motor Construction Company and Mr. Henry Sutphen of the Elco Works decided that it could be done.

On April 9, 1915, the contract for fifty boats was signed and once actually started, the work progressed so rapidly that by the first of May the master or pattern boat, from which the others were to be standardized, was in frame at the Bayonne plant.

It was on this day that the *Lusitania* sailed on her last voyage and a week later the appalling news of her destruction rocked the world.

This probably was the cause of a cablegram from the Admiralty ordering five hundred additional Chasers, the whole lot to be delivered complete and in running order by November L5, 1916. Five hundred fifty boats in as many days! Eight miles of boats—think of it! There was romance in the idea—romance beyond the dreams of a Kipling or an H. G. Wells.

In order to appreciate the work that the M. L.'s have done in the war. let us look at the design and how it was arrived at.

The problem which was put up to Mr. Irwin Chase, the designer, was one which at first glance would seem impossible of solution. The first consideration was the speed, which was to be 19 knots minimum when fully loaded. The second consideration was the large cruising radius specified, to attain which the fuel capacity had to be over 2000 gallons, which meant a weight of 12,000 pounds for fuel alone. Besides this, it was necessary to allow for a deadweight of 20.000 pounds, the equivalent of the weight of the guns, ammunition, water and supplies—in other words, the weight over and above that of the boat and its power plant complete.

The next consideration was seaworthiness, for it was specified that the boat should be able to maintain station in any sort of weather. And finally, there was the problem of rapid construction which eliminated at the start any possibility of the use of such features as double planking and the like. A type of construction had to be decided on which would be within the limits of complete standardisation.

Further to limit the designer, the size had to be such that the boats could be carried on the decks of steamships and for this reason 75 feet at first was decided on as the length of the boats.

This set of conditions would seem to be absolutely incompatible. Never had there been a boat built which might offer suggestions and the speed-length ratio was so high that any existing data from the designs of torpedo boat destroyers was of no use whatever.

And so it was with an absolutely clean slate that Mr. Chase went to work. Several sets of lines were drawn up as quickly as possible from which models were made and in order to determine beyond a doubt which of these would best meet the requirements, a flying trip was made to the University of Michigan where they were towed in the experimental tank. There had to be a compromise between speed and seaworthiness and after elaborate tests in the basin, a model was decided upon which had fairly fine lines forward and a rather flat after underbody or run, but still with considerable underwater body or deadrise as the depth of the boat from the turn of the bilge to the keel is called.

One of the models was more symmetrical in shape with the V-sections carried clear to the stern, but while this might have proved a trifle easier especially when running before a sea, it was found impos-

M. L.'s awaiting their trial runs on the St. Lawrence.

Assembling the M. L.'s. Even the planking of these boats was standardised and cut to templates before shipping from the Bayonne plant.

sible to attain a speed of 19 knots with reasonable power on a length of 75 feet. The latter model, the so-called more seaworthy model of the two under discussion, was found more easily driven up to a speed of 15 knots but beyond this the advantage was all with the boat with the fiat run, especially when trimmed by the stern.

From the start the designer and the British Commission were determined to employ medium speed motors, for the boats were to be used day in and day out and they could not afford to risk a high speed machine in a decidedly heavy duty outfit. Twin Standard air-starting and reversing motors, rated at 220 horsepower each seemed the logical power plant.

The results of the tests were wired at once to the Admiralty, and these gentlemen, although they had specified a speed of 19 knots, were inclined to doubt that such a speed could be obtained on the calculated displacement and waterline length and with the power specified. The designer realized the conservative rating of the motors and their capacity for delivering considerably more than their rated horsepower, but it was not until the trials of the first boats were run off that the British representatives were convinced that this speed was possible.

It was calculated that the cruising radius at full speed with 2,000 gallons of gasoline would be 800 miles, although at 15 knots it would be possible to cover 1,000 miles and at 11 knots, 2,100 miles. When the order for 500 boats came in shortly after the completion of the first sample from which the rest were standardized, it was decided to lengthen out the boat from 75 to 80 feet. The body plan was kept the same but it was found that by loosening up the interior arrangement more comfortable quarters were obtained without the slightest reduction in speed.

Crowding 500 horsepower into even an 80-footer means that you're not going to be able to treat the crew very generously in the matter of living quarters with what space is left. Up forward, in a length of twenty feet, seven men lived and slept in a fo'c's'le considerably smaller than that of a Gloucester fisherman. The officers' quarters in the stern were divided into a ward room "where two can turn around and three becomes a crush" and a pretty decent sized stateroom with two bunks.

Stuck in between the engine room and the pretentious ward room was the galley, "stink hole of weird stenches that carry their message of strange forms of nutrition fore and aft and permeate the nostrils of all hands and especially of the cook." Lieut. Dawson says:

"I am afraid, that I cannot tell in restrained tones of that hole of iniquity in the galley, with its tintinnabulation of shifting pots and pans and burning concoctions flung in a heavy sea over paraffine burners."

THEIR RECEPTION IN ENGLAND

It was to be expected that there would be some criticism of such a type of boat when it arrived on the other side. Not only were the naval authorities unfamiliar with this sort of craft, being somewhat behind our own navy in experience with motor-driven boats, but the yachtsmen of the R. N.V. R., who for the most part commanded them, were equally inexperienced in the type. The Britisher had a constitutional leaning toward a model with greater draft for sea work and a pretty good leaning it is too, and there was not a little apprehension that the boats would behave badly and might actually capsize in a heavy sea. The motor they knew to some extent and besides, its sturdy, honest qualities were just those to appeal to the conservative British temperament.

Gradually whatever doubt there may have been at the start was dispelled by the remarkable performance of the boats. When they arrived, the submarine shifted the scene of his activities farther and farther out to sea and the M. L.'s gradually came to be called upon to perform much more strenuous work than anyone had anticipated when they were designed. For days on end, they maintained their station far out at sea—too far to be able to run for a harbour in case of dirty weather. Frequently they were forced to ride out storms which for cussedness and perseverance have our own brand beaten forty ways. The shallow North Sea is bad enough at any time, but in the winter, it is downright wicked.

But the M. L.'s made good. Not only in the actual work of patrolling for submarines but in countless other ways as well—sweeping for mines in the channels ahead of ships, convoying merchant vessels, towing the deadly Q type *paravane* for lurking subs, laying mines, cooperating with air craft—in the Channel, in the North Sea, in the Mediterranean, at the Dardanelles and in the Adriatic.

The ubiquitous M. L.'s did what the other ships could not do and did it well. Their work attracted the attention of the French and Italians, and large orders were placed for Standard motors and in many cases for completed boats which brought the total number of M. L.'s up to 720.

★★★★★★★★★★★★★★★★★★

In this connection it might be interesting to read what the skipper of one of the M. L.'s has to say about them. "Seven Pennant," writing in the *Yachting Monthly*, says:

"Our sympathetic friends and relations on shore have often expressed pity for the hardships of the winter of wet and cold, but no one outside the M. L.'s themselves have ever realized what is really the greatest hardship of all. It is summed up in the word motion. Reader, have you ever tried to do a continual course of Swedish exercises from, say. 4 a. m. until 6 p. m. with no interval for food? I take it you have not, but if you can try and imagine to yourself the bodily fatigue and vexation of spirit that would be produced by this form of penance and then add to it wind, bitter cold and, perhaps, nay probably, wet, you may glean some idea of the hardships expressed by this little two syllabled word.

"I might also have added a slight form of nausea common to many of us, but often not admitted. Motion—and we get it throughout most days of the winter—is the curse of our existence. It is present without respite, without pity for fatigue and aching bone and muscle, an enemy to rest, to rob us of food, and indeed of every amenity of life. This briefly is what the hardships of motion mean to us. An M. L. is never on an even keel, save on the very smoothest of days, days that during the year one can count on one hand. We ride over everything, and our very lives depend on this fact, for we are too fragile to 'go through' or take it really 'solid' It is due to this fact, too, that our brave little ships derive their wonderful seagoing capacity.

"In spite of all we hear to the contrary, how wonderful are the seagoing qualities of the M. L.'s. Never in my wildest dreams did I think a small vessel of their size could live in the seas I have seen them live in, and survive without the smallest hurt, the only anxiety being the engines, the failure of which might have meant disaster, and perhaps death. The longer I live and have my being in them the more I marvel at the boats and the more confidence I gain. How different it has turned out to that which I was led to expect in those early days of the service when we were all 'doing' our M. L. course at one of the bases. Speaking personally those were the days of expectant cold feet, and so much did I hear of the unseaworthiness and general futility of these little craft, that I dreaded the day when I should have to set out on one.

"Even our instructors used to inform us that with a following sea in the Solent it had been found impossible to steer an M. L., and that they had even tried towing 30 fathoms of a 1-inch rope astern, but

THE GUN CREW OF AN M. L. AND THEIR WICKED LITTLE 3-INCH GUN.

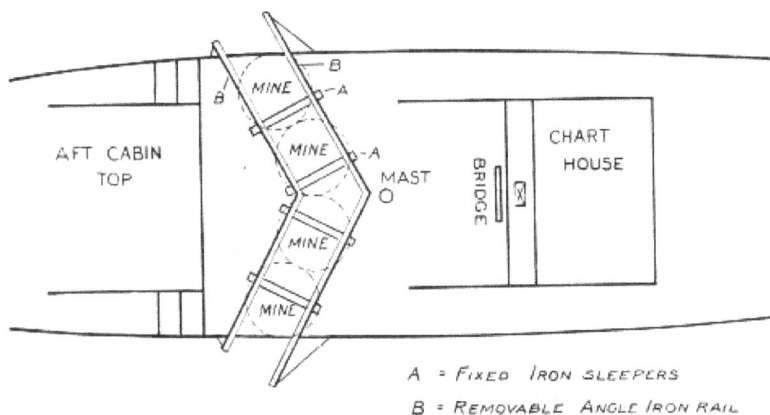

A = FIXED IRON SLEEPERS
B = REMOVABLE ANGLE IRON RAIL

METHOD OF CARRYING AND LAUNCHING MINES FROM THE DECK OF AN M. L.

apparently without avail. Then we heard a vessel had blown up going round the coast and that the crew had perished miserably in the flames as the burning petrol surrounded them as they swam. This and like harrowing tales were bandied round, but, looking back after this considerable lapse of time, I am inclined to think it was part ignorance and partly a case of bad workmen blaming their tools.

"We M. L. sailors are specialists. We do things and go out in weather that no sailor, accustomed to ordinary ships, would in his prudent senses attempt unless he had served with understanding in our ships. Some of the most fundamental axioms of seamanship we put aside. Do not the more knowing ones among us invariably clear from a crowded harbour quayside in a tideway by going astern? Provided she is handled astern and not ahead, in the hands of the artist the M. L. can be made to 'do anything except wait at table,' but who taught the knowing ones this now quite obvious principle but that most excellent of all teachers, practical experience? And indeed, it is this teacher that has taught us most of what we know. We have had to find our own way along a thorny path for the most part, with no one to advise us, and at first generally under the orders of someone who, through no fault of his own, had no more idea of what we could do than the man in the moon—in those days we had very little idea ourselves."

★★★★★★★★★★★★★★★★★★

Hunting Submarines

When used actually to hunt submarines, the little boats of the "Grey Patrol" operated in groups of four, one of which was the flagship. Sometimes they worked out of an important harbour a day at a time, but as often you'd find them 100 miles off shore, for days on end under conditions hitherto considered impossible, and with the small comfort of, say, some Scotch fishing village to return to. For the men stuck off out of touch with civilization for months, the simple everyday things of life took on a totally new significance and the thought of a week in London was a dream comparable only to the orthodox idea of heaven. No wonder the men whose lot it was to hunt the submarines aboard the "movies" became attached to their little ships and the motors that stood by them so gallantly.

In the work of U-boat strafing the M. L.'s worked frequently with seaplanes and blimps, the small dirigibles which were found to be even better than the planes for spotting the sub-sea fighters. The boats carried no wireless or telephones and depended upon the blinker and semaphore systems for intercommunication. In the event that a blimp

You are standing into a minefield

or seaplane spotted a sub the information was communicated to the patrol boats by means of smoke bombs.

The fighting equipment of the M. L. consisted of a short calibre 3-inch gun using a shell weighing in the neighbourhood of 13 pounds. It was a short gun with a long recoil and while the range was much less than that of a standard navy gun of the same bore, it required a smaller gun crew and was successful for these small quick-acting vessels on which the ability to shoot a large shell was more to be desired than range.

But more important than the deck gun was the depth bomb with which the little fighters put the fear of *Gott* into the biggest U-boats. This highly-revered shipmate known to our own gobs as the ashcan, contained 250 pounds of T. N. T. and could be set to explode at any predetermined depth. It was the depth bomb that sealed the fate of the submarine. With it, it was not necessary actually to hit the submerged target; merely to explode the can within 30 or 40 yards of the sub frequently was sufficient to cause the starting of a seam or the disarrangement of the storage battery or other interial mechanism.

In order to fight the submarine at close range the early boats carried what were known as lance bombs—14-pound bombs on the end of 4½-foot handles. These were designed to be thrown much as an athlete would throw a hammer and, needless to say, they were handled and treated with the utmost reverence. Later they were omitted from the equipment.

Loaded as the M. L.'s were with enough high explosive to blow a dreadnaught to kingdom come, it is not pleasant to think what would happen and what did happen occasionally when a shot found its mark. Lieut. Dawson says:

"Like Agag, we must go tenderly all our days and not bump too hard lest not only M. L. disappear like the conjuror's cat, in a loud explosion and a puff of smoke, but also most things within a quarter of a mile's radius."

All the M. L.'s carried portable directional hydrophones, which were sufficiently accurate to enable them to tell within about two degrees the direction of the approach of any sort of vessel and listeners became so proficient that they were able to determine whether the sounds heard were those of a turbine engine, a reciprocating engine, a paddle wheeler, an M. L., a submarine on the surface operating on her Diesel engine or a submarine submerged and driven by her electric motors. These sounds were entirely different and, in the confusion,

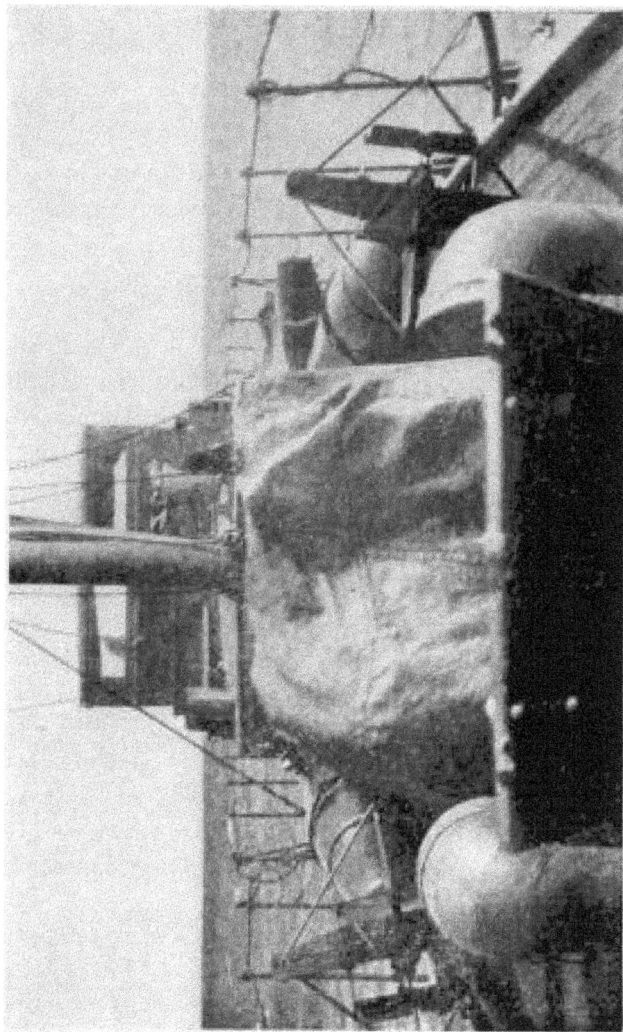

SEVERAL OF THE M. L.'s WERE FITTED WITH PARAVANES—THE ORDINARY TYPE FOR CUTTING MINES ADRIFT; THE DEADLY EXPLOSIVE "Q" TYPE FOR ANTI-SUBMARINE WORK. A PAIR OF THESE MOST INGENIOUS INSTRUMENTS ARE SHOWN ON EITHER SIDE OF THE DECK.

caused by several at the same time the listener was trained to eliminate everything but the sound of the submarine. Our own listening devices with which the Submarine Chasers were equipped, were somewhat more elaborate than those of the M. L.'s and will be described later.

MINE LAYING AND SWEEPING

Those who had occasion to traverse the war zone during the last two years of the war will remember the varied duties that the M. L.'s were called upon to perform and the remarkable gear with which many of them were equipped. Dubbed the "movies" because of their activity in a sea way, the ubiquitous M. L.'s earned the title in a better sense because of their never-ending activity in performing all sorts of nasty jobs for which they were never intended.

Probably one of the last duties one would expect an M. L. to perform is mine sweeping which was generally done by heavily built steel trawlers and paddle-wheelers. But many of the M. L.'s were called upon for this service because of their ability to sweep a channel much faster than the regular sweepers. Frequently they swept in flotillas of four in quarter line formation using the "kite" to hold the sweeping cable extended.

At other times the P.V. sweep was used, consisting of a pair of *paravanes* towed off the quarters. These *paravanes* or "otters" were much the same as those with which all merchant and naval vessels traversing the war zone were equipped in order to protect them from moored mines. When used for sweeping, the *paravanes* operated in practically the same way except that they were towed off the quarters instead of off the forefoot, thereby offering no protection to the boat from which they were towed. Extending out at an angle of approximately 45 degrees, the towing cable of the *paravane* encountered the mooring wire of the mine, deflecting it out to the *paravane* where it was cut by the steel knives in the head of the latter. After being cut adrift the mine was exploded by gun fire.

But the ordinary method was the "D" sweep. With this sweep the boats worked in pairs towing a cable one end of which was attached to either boat. The mines were caught by their mooring wires and if not pulled adrift from their mooring, were reeled in and disengaged by hand—a hazardous operation which has resulted in many a casualty.

When the M. L.'s were designed no one had the slightest idea that they would ever be called upon for the work of mine laying but in the latter months of the war many of them were so engaged. They were

Picking up a German Mine, bottom up for safety. If one of the horns were bent while in this position, the liquid from the glass phial could not cause a detonation.

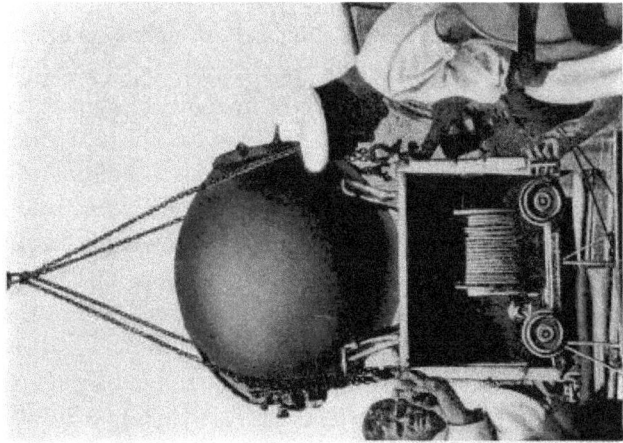

Laying a British Mine aboard an M.L. The sinker door has been removed showing reel on which mine mppring rope is wound

fitted with tracks capable of carrying two mines nested in their sinkers on either side, and their operation was something like this: three or four divisions of four would proceed to sea in single line formation having to cover possibly fifty miles before arriving at the mine field, which was indicated by a buoy. After bearings had been taken and the exact position determined, they would proceed in single line ahead until the senior officer's boat arrived at the buoy.

Then a signal would be hoisted calling for an eight-point turn which would bring the M. L.'s in line abreast at intervals of about ?5 feet. A rocket fired by the senior officer was the signal to start to lay, when the forward starboard mine would be dropped. Thirty seconds after the forward port mine went over, then the aft starboard one and then the last one from the port side. In this way a staggered formation was obtained and a flotilla of twenty boats would lay eighty mines in scarcely more than the time it takes to describe the operation.

The last M. L. carried several buoys which were dropped at the time the mines were laid to indicate the length of the field laid on that trip.

A Dangerous Game

We are indebted to Lieut. Morris P. Shea, R. N. V. R., for many interesting facts about the work of the M. L.'s. During the last eight months of the war, Lieut. Shea was in command of one of the M. L.'s working with the British Grand Fleet at Scapa Flow in the Orkney Islands. His work, with that of the other M. L.'s, consisted in patrolling, convoying, running torpedoes for the ships of the fleet and in fact almost any sort of a job which was beneath the dignity of the larger vessels. One of the motor launches was tied for several days to a pier operating its auxiliary engine, furnishing electric light for an air station on one of the islands and also furnishing current for a movie show to entertain the sailors of the Grand Fleet.

For a considerable time, Shea's M. L. was stationed in a little bay outside the entrance to Scapa Flow harbour where the British fleet, as well as some of the American battleships, lay at anchor. It was expected that sooner or later the Germans would endeavour to break through the nets at the entrance to this harbour. The risk was great but the stakes were high. In order to be prepared for such a raid, the M. L.'s were kept at five minutes' notice for weeks on end and were ordered to sea at any hour of the day or night—sometimes because suspicious craft were heard by the hydrophone listening stations on shore and at other times merely to keep them on the jump and prepared for the real thing.

An interesting stunt and a dangerous one in which Shea participated was pulled off shortly before the armistice was signed. A signal came for his M. L. No. —— to remain at anchor at a given point within shelter of a certain island and to carry out a prearranged program at eleven o'clock that evening. It was pitch dark. The orders were to proceed at full speed without lights and make for the entrance to Scapa Flow. It must be remembered that the war was very much on at this particular time and this was exactly what it was expected that some daring *unterseeboot* might attempt at any moment. His job then was to play submarine and endeavour to get as far as the boom without being noticed—scarcely an enviable position at a time when your friends are likely to shoot first and investigate afterward.

The islands round about were equipped with powerful searchlights with watching crews to look for and locate instantly any suspicious craft that might attempt to enter the prohibited area. Any such craft would also be heard by the hydrophone listening stations.

The orders were to proceed at full speed and not to stop until picked up by the searchlights or fired upon. This he did, zigzagging, stopping, going full speed astern, in order to elude the searching fingers of light that seemed every instant to be on the point of exposing him. Finally, a blinding shaft picked up the M. L. and in scarcely a second's time it was the centre of two score powerful beams like a brilliant gem in some weird, titanic stage setting. Then when the watchers discovered that they had not bagged a German, the lights went out and the M. L. returned to an extra late supper.

Such things as those were all in the day's work of the M. L. and many a time the similarity that these little craft bore to a submarine on the surface, accentuated by fog, darkness or the fevered imaginations of some high-strung gun crew, drew the fire of their own countrymen—and a brief line in the obituary column.

By all odds the most spectacular and genuinely heroic naval event of the war was the raid which resulted in the blocking of the mouth of the canal at Zeebrugge. This canal which connects Bruges with the coast had long been a base for German submarines. It was of the utmost importance to the Germans, obviating as it did the long run to and from Wilhelmshaven and the other home bases, and consequently it was so thoroughly fortified as to make it supposedly immune from attack. But here the German psychology was wrong again for the "conservative" British Admiralty planned or consented to let a group of its officers plan not only to attack Zeebrugge but actually to do the "impossible" stunt of closing the canal by sinking block ships across its entrance, under the concentrated fire of the land batteries.

It took many months to perfect the plan of attack and during this time the men, who had volunteered for what was explained meant a fifty-fifty chance with death, were trained to the highest pitch of efficiency in the parts they were to play in the "big show." and all communication with the outside world was cut off. After several false starts and long, tense, agonising days of waiting, the night of the attack came and just one hundred minutes after the firing of the first shot the flotilla withdrew, leaving the mole and its batteries a total wreck—and two concrete laden block ships sunk across the channel.

The raid was one of the most audacious of all time and its fortunate outcome was due largely to the work of the M. L.'s. Everyone knows of the splendid work done by Capt. Carpenter and the crew of the *Vindictive* as she lay in that inferno alongside the mole, but less loudly sung are the exploits of the little boats that placed the marking flares and made the smoke screen and stood by and removed the crews of the block ships after they had been sunk in the channel.

This tale of the work of the M. L.'s at Zeebrugge has been told admirably by Lieut. Gordon S. Maxwell. R. N.V. R., who was in command of one of them. His story, which appeared originally in the *Yachting Monthly* of London, follows:—

★★★★★★★★★★★★★★★★★

"On St. George's Day, 1918, Tradition was born to the Royal Naval Reserve. In the early hours of the now famous day the R. N. V. R., represented by a flotilla of motor launches, played an important part in a Naval engagement that thrilled the nations.

"Of the action in general I do not propose to deal, save so far as concerns the M. L.'s, for the former has already been described; but of the experience of the particular part played by the R. N. V. R. this, I think, is the first account to appear.

"The worst part of the whole affair was perhaps the waiting—the anticipation of the unknown. Before the action we had two abortive starts, both of which failed to materialise on account of the weather conditions. The ten days that elapsed were trying to the nerves, and we were glad when we had orders to leave harbour. Word quickly circulated that it was to be the real thing this time. The M. L.'s made a fine showing as they left Dover Harbour and formed up ahead. At "A" position, where the other forces joined up, we started in earnest. The destroyer *Warwick* with Vice-Admiral Keyes on board led, *Vindictive* came next with *Iris* and *Daffodil* in tow. Then came the blockships, *Thetis, Intrepid, Iphigenia, Brilliant* and *Sirius*. On each beam of the line were the M. L.'s and, outside, the destroyers. It was an imposing sight in the twilight. *Vindictive* seemed to loom up above everything else; she was a weird looking craft with no mast, tall funnels and boarding gangways swung up high upon her port side.

"At 'D' position *Brilliant* and *Sirius* left us for Ostend, while we continued our way to Zeebrugge, each ship going to its appointed station for the attack. As we neared our objective the Huns learned of our approach by aeroplane. Star shells began to go up. They were wonderful star shells, and lit up the sea like day. The last I saw of *Vindictive* that night was when the first star shell soared above her. There she was, like some grim phantom ship ploughing her way towards the dim outline of the Mole (our smoke screen had already begun), while close behind rounded the squat looking *Iris* and *Daffodil*, with all surrounded by M. L.'s and C. M. B.'s.

"The smoke began to thicken, till finally it blotted out everything in its fumes. Still, the relief when one of those brilliant star shells hit the water and went out was great, for while their light was shining it seemed that every ship approaching the enemy harbour must be an easy mark for the batteries, and it gave one a very "naked" feeling. Thicker and thicker grew the smoke as more floats were dropped. All sight of the Mole and the happenings on and inside it were blotted out from our sight if not from our cars, for we could still hear the guns' incessant roar and the greater single roar that seemed to rend the very night as the old submarine blew herself up to destroy the viaduct connecting the Mole with the shore.

"The action, from the attack on the Mole by *Vindictive* to the retirement, lasted exactly *One Hundred Minutes*. During those fatal moments history was made. It is indeed good to hear men say that had it not been for the smoke screen put up by the M. L.'s and C. M. B.'s and the rescue work of the former, the action could never have succeeded; in fact, could not have been attempted. In this the R.N. have acknowledged our part like sportsmen, and the R. N. V. R. are proud to have had the chance of proving themselves blood brothers to the R. N. One remark, overheard in the Burlington Hotel at Dover, shows how a new feeling towards us has been born. A group of R. N. officers, some from the blockships and some not, were overheard discussing the part played by the M. L.'s, and one said: 'Well, if I ever hear anyone call them Harry Tate's Navy after this, I'll punch his damned head.' And the rest answered in chorus. A casual incident, but one with much behind it. Not that we mind banter, for you will hear more jokes at the expense of M. L.'s on board M. L.'s than anywhere else—thank God for a sense of humour.

"I am saying little about the part played by the 'Hush Boats' (C. M. B.'s), not because their work was not as good as ours (in many ways it was far more wonderful, for, although they have double our speed, they are only half our length and practically open boats), but because I think it better that someone who was on one of the marvellous little boats should write up the 'stunt' from their point of view. Their personnel is, of course, a mixture of R. N., R. N. R., and R. N. V. R.

"The first two M. L.'s to get inside the Mole were those of Lieut. H. A. Littleton and Lieut. P. T. Deane, and these two boats constitute the keystone of what credit is due to the M. L.'s for their share in the action. The first of the blockships to enter was *Thetis*. Close on her quarter was an M. L. Next came *Intrepid*, with another M. L., and *Iphigenia* close behind. Of the other M. L.'s that were designed to enter the enemy harbour one was that of Lieut.-Commander Young, which was sunk before she got in.

"A very brisk fire was opened on the ships as they came round the end of the Mole through the gap between the barges and the boom to the shore. But the old cruisers plunged on to their objective—the blocking of the entrance to the Bruges Canal—at the same time answering the fire of the shore batteries with their guns. Then *Thetis* had the bad luck to fall foul of the net boom with her propeller, which left her at the mercy of the guns on shore, so her commander was forced to sink her where she was, where she would be an obstruction, though not in the spot intended. Heedless of the heavy fire from the shore,

Lieut. Littleton closed her in his M. L. and picked up the crew who were already in the boats. When all were aboard, he turned to leave the harbour, but just as he did so a shout was heard from behind and someone cried out that a boat-load was coming up from one of the other ships. A begrimed and hatless figure in a duffel coat said, 'Do you mind waiting a moment, I think there are some more men coming?'

"Littleton's answer surprised the captain: 'You priceless old thing, of course I won't wait for them.'

"The captain stared.

"'I'll go back for them,' added the 'Doctor,' and right back into that inferno of fire he took his M. L., got the crew aboard and turned once more to clear harbour, but stopped yet again to pick up a man who had fallen in the water. With a surplus crew of 60 odd, the M. L. found her way outside the Mole amidst the smoke and trail of shells, to arrive finally at Dover without mishaps save for a machine-gun bullet through her after hatch, and a piece of shrapnel through the roof of her bridge house—a wonderful achievement and a wonderful escape.

"To the number one, Lieut. Lefron Geddes, praise is due for his untiring efforts throughout the whole affair, and for seconding his skipper in the rescues and in the running of the ship under heavy fire, and bringing it safely out of the danger zone, while Lieut. Littleton was doing his best to make the wounded comfortable with the limited accommodation a motor launch affords.

"The rumour that the 'Doctor' put on a clean collar in the middle of the action because the 'damned smoke' had soiled the one he was wearing is, I believe, unfounded, but it is at least characteristic of Lieut. Littleton. He told me afterwards that he had no idea that the dishevelled figure was a hatless 'brass-hat.' He thought he was an A. B. I wonder how he would have looked under normal conditions on being called a 'priceless old thing' by a two-striper R. N. V. R.

"Meanwhile *Intrepid* and *Iphigenia* were making their way into the mouth of the Bruges Canal, followed by Lieut. Deane in his M. L. His achievement was possibly the most remarkable of any M. L. throughout the action, for he was instrumental in saving over a hundred men from *Intrepid* and *Iphigenia*. Curiously enough they managed to get inside the Mole with hardly a shot being fired at them, by using one of the blockships as a screen from the enemy guns. Still following close behind *Intrepid* and *Iphigenia*, Lieut. Deane managed to get his boat straight into the mouth of the Bruges Canal, where he waited alongside the western arm while the blockships swung into position, putting up an effective smoke screen which certainly hampered the shore batteries which had by this time transferred their attention from *Thetis* and were submitting the two ships in the mouth of the canal to a devastating fire.

"After the explosion which sank the blockships, Lieut. Deane closed them and took off the crew who were already in the boats casting off. These he got aboard, and he was just going to leave the harbour when his boat grounded on the sloping side of the canal, damaging her propellers. At the same moment he discovered a Carley float with one man on it, so he went ahead again and took off the occupant, which happened to be the captain of *Intrepid*. So intense was the fire all around that the M. L. was forced to back out to save time, and, as this had to be done with damaged propellers, it was certainly a wonderful piece of work, laden as the launch was. It must be remembered that all the while brilliant star shells made the scene as light as day.

"During the manoeuvre three men on the launch were killed, including the coxswain at the wheel. Slowly the C. O. brought his vessel round the stern of *Thetis*, where he managed to turn her and commence the perilous passage out of the harbour, passing the gap in the Mole, now clearly visible by the light of the star shells. It says much for the coolness and resource of Lieut. Deane that he conceived the daring plan of running his boat close along the Mole wall, thus rendering ineffective many of the larger German guns which could not be depressed sufficiently to bear upon him, although of course the manoeuvre did not prevent the heavy machine gun fire being directed on his boat.

"But just as the M. L. was clearing the harbour, in fact, as she was passing the last of the anchored barges which marked the entrance, a shell from the shore batteries burst over the dinghy and killed several men, and carried the deck pump away, while another hit the forecastle, killing three men and wounding several others.

"It is certainly a little less than a miracle that the boat managed to get to the open sea at all, for at this point the steering gear jammed, owing to somebody's coat getting entangled in the ware, and several valuable minutes elapsed at this vitally critical juncture before the cause could be discovered and the wires cleared, during which time the boat had to be steered by the engines alone.

"The behaviour of the Number One, Lieut. Keith Wright, throughout the action deserves the highest praise. Soon after the shell that killed the coxswain had hit the boat, the C. O. sent a message to him from the bridge and received a reply as though nothing had happened. Just as they were clearing harbour he sent again to him, saying that he was wanted on the bridge, but received the answer that Lieut. Wright was busy attending the wounded and could not come. Ever since they had left the Canal entrance Lieut. Wright had been lying on the floor of the Chart House, dangerously wounded and unable to move. He had given strict instructions to the messengers that this fact must be kept from the C. O. until they were clear, in case it might distract his attention from his work and thus add another danger to the boat, so already encompassed by perils.

"Subsequently Lieut. Deane managed to pick up *Warwick* and put the rescued crews aboard her, except one or two dead men and one man too seriously wounded to swim, whom he took direct to Deal Pier, where an ambulance had been summoned by wireless.

"That an M. L., whose full complement is ten men all told, should have been able to get out of harbour with over a hundred men on board, at night, would have been wonderful under peace-time conditions, but when we consider that the feat was performed amidst a tornado of gun fire, some idea of the achievement can be imagined, for by the time the *Vindictive* was clear of the Mole all the attention of the enemy was directed on the M. L.

"The first R. N. V. R. officer to be killed was the Senior M. L. Officer in the action, Lieut.-Commander Dawbarn Young, who was in command of the first M. L. to approach the Mole with the purpose of laying flares to guide the blockships in. This he was never destined to do, for when he was yet four hundred yards away his bridge was struck with three shells from a shore battery, killing the coxswain instantly and severely wounding Lieut.-Commander Young, Lieut. Lee and members of the crew.

"Although mortally wounded he stuck to his post and gave orders for the dinghy to be lowered. Lieut. G. F. Bowen, the first lieutenant of the ship, had perhaps what was one of the most marvellous escapes of the night; although standing on the bridge close to his C. O. and Lieut. Lee, he escaped without a scratch. Great credit is due to Lieut. Bowen for his coolness at this time, for with the M. L. still under heavy fire, with the help of the unwounded members of the crew he launched the dinghy and managed to get his C. O., who had now collapsed on the deck, into it. When all the rest were aboard, he wrenched off the ship's compass, passed it over, and from the Lewis gun emptied two trays into the already holed hull of the M. L., at the same time smashing her in several places under the water line with an axe, not leaving her until she was settling down by the head. The plight of nine men, many of whom were wounded, in a little tin dinghy in such an inferno could hardly be worse, but they stuck gamely to it. Lieut. Bowen and the chief motor mechanic were the only men in a fit state to row; all the rest were either badly wounded or prostrated with shock.

"The circumstances in which Lieut. Lee happened to be on board the M. L. are interesting. He had just arrived at Dover for the 'stunt', to find to his disappointment that his boat was not ready to sail, owing to some important repairs being necessary. Rather than miss the action he obtained permission to go on Lieut.-Commander Young's M. L. as a spare officer. Even now, while they were in the dinghy, Lieut. Lee, though unable to row, refused to be a passenger in spite of his wounds, but held the compass between his knees and with his uninjured hand managed to work an electric torch and set the course.

"For about half an hour they toiled on, heading away from the Mole with a strong easterly tide. Three C. M. B.'s dashed by, but were lost again in the darkness and smoke before they could hear the hails from the dinghies. Then an M. L., under Lieut. H. W. Adams, loomed up in the gloom and luckily heard the shouts.

"Lieut.-Commander Young died on the way across. He was conscious till the last, and wonderfully plucky over his wounds. His left arm and right leg were badly hurt, but it was a gash in his left lung which proved fatal. His death will be a great loss to the R. N. V. R. in general and in particular to the Dover base, where he had been for over two years. Young was a 'white man'; a mean or lying action was impossible to his nature, and no man ever set or kept a straighter course than he. A most efficient officer and a very hard worker, he expected others to be the same; but he would never ask a junior officer to do what he would not willingly do himself; in fact, he often did more work than he need have done in his position, a fact which all who served under him appreciated. I have often heard men say, 'You'll always get a straight deal from Young,' and it was true. He was the essence of fairness in all his dealings. What finer epitaph could he have had than this:—'We sincerely mourn the loss of a true friend and a very gallant comrade, who died as he would have wished, at his post of duty.'

"Lieut. Oswald Robinson was the second M. L. officer to be killed. The circumstances were unsimilar to those connected with the death of Lieut.-Commander Young. His boat was hit while off the Mole,

One of the most audacious adventures in Naval History; attack on Zeebrugge.

and again it was the bridge that was struck, the shell killing the C. O. and the Coxswain instantly. Lieut. Robinson's body was never recovered; it must have been blown away. Another incident that was almost the same as that experienced on the first boat to go: Number One, in this case Lieut. J. W. Robinson, was on the bridge at the time the M. L. was hit, but came off unscathed. The dinghy was launched, but before it could be manned, another M. L., under Lieut. R. Saunders, came up from out of the smoke and took them off. Lieut. Oswald Robinson will be missed by all and his cheery personality is a great loss to our little fleet. Only a few days before the action he was one of the principal performers in a concert we got up in the wardroom of *Arrogant*. He was a wonderfully clever mimic and actor, and his impersonations were the feature of the concert.

"Some of the M. L.'s had remarkable escapes. One of the narrowest was that of the boat under Lieut.-Commander L. S. Chappell, on which the Flag-Captain, Captain R. Collins, R. N., who was in command of the Motor Launch Flotilla, hoisted his flag. Through the hottest part of the action Lieut.-Commander Chappell kept his boat right off the Mole, on the beam of *Vindictive*, to screen, as much as possible, the latter vessel with his smoke. Every now and then when they came to the end of their short patrol the smoke blew away, exposing them to the full glare of the searchlights from the Mole. The only escape was to turn sixteen points into their own smoke and make their way back and renew the manoeuvre.

"This the M. L. kept up during the time that the storming party, from the *Vindictive* landed on the Mole, and it undoubtedly saved them from much of the fire from the western shore batteries. It was Captain Collins himself who hailed the blockships during the early part of the action and directed them to the entrance of the enemy harbour, after Lieut.-Commander Young's boat had been sunk, whose duty this was originally. It was during one of the exposed moments that I have mentioned that Lieut.-Commander Chappell's boat had its miraculous escape. A 6-inch shell landed on their magazine hatch, ricocheted on to a box of six-pounder ammunition and blew up the latter without, however, exploding every shell. The iron top of the hatch was blown clean away, but fortunately the explosion expended itself upwards instead of downwards, otherwise nothing could have saved the ship.

"Some of the cordite from the six-pounder shells exploded in mid-air after the shells had been blown to pieces in a very curious way, for the force of the explosion really burst the shells instead of detonating them in the usual way. The only real damage it did was to set the foredeck on fire, but once again the magazine was saved by the quick action of the Number One, Lieut. C. C. Calvin, who extinguished the flames very promptly with pyrene.

"There were other narrow escapes on M. L.'s that night; for instance, on one a shell fell into the engine room, but did not explode. But it is not possible to narrate every story, or to pretend that this account is that of an eye-witness, the dense artificial fog, or smoke, in which the action took place would render such impossible. As regards the eye-witness point of view, I can speak only of what happened on my own M. L. Perhaps I am justified in telling the story.

"We were the most westerly boat of unit 'G,' whose duty it was to find No. 4 buoy previously laid down by a Coastal Motor Boat. This in the darkness, we failed to pick up, so when we considered we were in the approximate position (fairly accurately, we subsequently discovered) we dropped our buoy, and stood by as the smoke patrol boats passed us, turned, and disappeared to the eastward. It was a signal for a fresh shower of shrapnel and pompom shells around us, a good deal closer than was pleasant. This gave us an idea. If the Germans liked to fire at us, why shouldn't they, as long as the position of those buoys was where *we* wanted them? Accordingly, under cover of the thick pungent smoke, we steamed northwards for a minute and then westward at full speed for two miles, and then, more cautiously, we made our way in-shore. We must have been about five hundred yards or so away, for by the light of the star shells over Zeebrugge we could see the beach and the sandhills plainly.

"All at once the beams of a powerful searchlight blazed out from the shore and swept about us. At first, we were not located, but after a moment they picked us up and then the batteries opened up. A buoy was dropped at once and managed to dodge the beams of the searchlight behind the thick smoke that poured oft. We drew off about a quarter of a mile, but the batteries still continued blazing away at the buoy and the searchlight was trying to pierce the smoke to discover what was behind the flare. We dropped a second buoy, and about a quarter of a mile further on let go to a third. All these sent up the same bright flare, and a perfect fusillade from the western shore batteries was poured forth at them.

"We were out to sea again, and as no shots came near us, we waited to note the effect of our little ruse. It certainly seemed to be answering, for we undoubtedly had the Hun guessing. Those lights so close to shore, away from the main operation, evidently puzzled him; possibly he imagined that something in the nature of a landing was being attempted, but whatever he thought, he certainly wasted a lot of ammunition on nothing, which meant the less for *Vindictive* alongside the Mole.

"It appealed to our sense of humour to think that one solitary little M. L., a couple of miles away from its friends and relations, could put the 'wind up' the Hun to that extent. Had we not been getting short of buoys and in need of what we had left for our correct position, we should have been tempted to repeat the experiment, but we steamed back to our original place in the line and carried on smoking till the time for the retirement. But we had nothing much nearer us, beyond stray shots. I think the western batteries were still waiting for the fictitious landing party somewhere Blankenberge way. Credit for the success of our run is very largely due to my Number One, Lieut. Gordon Ross, who carried on during the whole action with a broken finger, superintending and assisting in the dropping of the buoys, no light articles, and awkward to handle on the narrow gangways of an M. L.

"On our way to the rendezvous we waited for about half an hour off Zeebrugge in case we could be of assistance to any men or vessels in distress. *Vindictive, Iris* and *Daffodil* we knew had gone, for they were working to a schedule of time, but we saw nothing, though we kept a good look out for pursuing German craft. Apparently, none came out. I think they were too rattled, and too thankful that the British had done, to worry about pursuit.

"Then full speed for the rendezvous, but there were no ships there. And so on, still full speed, for Dover. I shall never forget that run, tearing through the blackness of night 'all out.' About half way we had a bit of excitement, a dark shape was sighted upon our port bow; it was a ship of sorts and looked very like a submarine. We challenged it at once, and by its reply we knew it to be a friend, so we closed it and discovered that it was an M. L., curiously enough one of our own unit. They also had seen no one since leaving Zeebrugge, so we sped on in the darkness together. When dawn broke, we were still out of sight of land and a slight haze on the water made visibility bad.

"The first thing we picked up was a wreck on the Goodwin Sands, which loomed up out of the mist rather nearer than we thought ourselves to be. Soon the white line of breakers warned us that we must alter our course to the northward. We reached Dover Harbour just as

Vindictive had entered. That entry will be in my mind for ever. About six M. L.'s were converging out of the fast clearing mist, and I am afraid we all raced for the western entrance. Our ship won; and had the honour of being the first M. L. to enter harbour from the Zeebrugge action.

"Then came what was to me the most stirring part of the whole affair. As the six M. L.'s passed *Vindictive*, battle-scarred and covered with the signs of her wonderful fight, all eyes were turned upon her and the men who thronged her deck. Then those men, remnants of the landing party and the ship's company, each of whom deserved the V. C, waved their caps and cheered again and again as the M. L.'s steamed slowly past. We could scarcely believe our ears that these men, whom we felt we ought to be cheering, actually got in first with a cheer for the M. L.'s who had helped them in their wonderful achievement.

"That cheer went home straight to the heart, and its echoes will sound there till my dying day. Our little ships' companies replied lustily and our sirens added their voices. But to be cheered first—well, I am not ashamed to own that a lump came into my throat. To lead the first M. L.'s into harbour from Zeebrugge and to be cheered by *Vindictive's* crew—it seems like a dream now that I look back upon it.

"During the next few hours, the M. L.'s returned to port in driblets, some bearing the marks of their narrow escapes from enemy gun fire or collision in the fog. These hours were anxious ones for us, waiting to learn who was safe and who had fallen. At length all had returned but two, and of these two we had received reports of their loss. Then we knew the fate of all who had gone into action with us. The feeling in our hearts was mixed; genuine sorrow for the good comrades who had made the Great Sacrifice and thankfulness at our own escapes, and, being human, a certain amount of pride that we had helped in an action that will live in History."

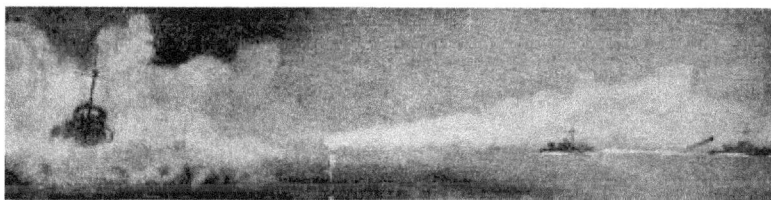

THE M. L.'s PLACING GUIDING FLARES AND SCREENING THE LARGER VESSELS WITH AN ARTIFICIAL FOG.

Simultaneously with the attack on Zeebrugge, there was launched a similar raid on Ostend, at which point the other end of the Bruges Canal furnished a second convenient haven for the German subs, and while this offensive was destined to meet with less success than that at Zeebrugge, the M. L.'s carried off their part of the program just as efficiently.

The block ships *Brilliant* and *Sirius* were unsuccessful in reaching the mouth of the canal, but the work of rescuing their crews was accomplished by the M. L.'s under conditions just as harrowing as those at Zeebrugge. To be sure there was no breakwater to negotiate, but. on the other hand, there was no landing party to divert the fire of the enemy, which was concentrated on the blockships and their tiny escort.

The motor launches were under the command of Commodore Herbert Lynes but the organisation of the flotilla at this engagement as well as Zeebrugge was the work of Capt. Hamilton Benn, D. S. O., R. N.V. R., who led them into action.

The failure of the blockships to find the narrow entrance to the canal on the night of April 22nd was due to the shifting by the Germans of the buoy oft' the entrance and to the fact that a last minute shift of wind carried the smoke screen landward across the mouth of the harbour, obscuring it from view. Both block ships were lost after a hot engagement during which they returned the enemy's fire until practically shot to pieces, but their crews were rescued and returned to Dunkirk in safety.

A second and more successful effort to block Ostend harbour was carried out on the night of May 9th. The story of this "*pukka* show" as the "limies" themselves would call it, has been told by S. M. R. in *The Yachting Monthly*, and is in part as follows:—

★★★★★★★★★★★★★★★★

"The first daring stroke failed to block the harbour and the *Sirius* lies in the surf some two thousand yards east of the entrance, which the old war ship gallantly failed to obstruct, and when in the early hours of morning the battle scarred *Vindictive* groped her way through the smoke screen and headed for the entrance it needed but little imagination to picture the old fighting ship awake and looking on. One of the M. L.'s had visited her and hung a flare in her slack and rusty rigging, and that eye of unsteady fire, paling in the blaze of the star shells or reddening through the drift of the smoke, watched the whole great enterprise from the moment when it hung in doubt to its ultimate triumphant success.

"The main problem now was to secure the effect of a surprise attack upon an enemy who was clearly from his ascertained dispositions, expecting him. The *Sirius* and the *Brilliant* had been baffled by the displacement of the Stroom Bank buoy, which marks the channel to the harbour entrance, but since then aerial reconnaissance had established that the Germans had removed the buoy altogether and that there were now no guiding marks of any kind. They had also cut gaps in the piers as a precaution against a landing, and further when toward midnight on Thursday the ships moved from their anchorage it was known that some nine German destroyers were out and at large on the coast.

"It was a night that promised well for the enterprise—nearly windless, and what little breeze stirred came from a point or so west of north; a sky of lead blue, faintly star dotted, and no moon; a still sea for the small craft, the motor launches and the coastal motor boats.

"From the destroyer which served the commodore for flagship the remainder of the force was visible only as swift silhouettes of blackness, destroyers bulking like cruisers in the darkness, motor launches like destroyers, and coastal motorboats showing themselves as racing hillocks of foam. From Dunkirk a sudden and brief flurry of gunfire announced that German airplanes were about—they were actually on their way to visit Calais—and over the invisible coast of Flanders the summer lightning of the restless artillery rose and fell monotonously.

"'There's the *Vindictive!*'"

"The muffled seamen and marines standing by the torpedo tubes and guns turned at that name to gaze at the great black ship, seen mistily through the streaming smoke from the destroyer's funnels, plodding silently to her goal and her end. Photographs have made familiar that high side profile and the tall funnels with their Zeebrugge scars, always with a background of the pier at Dover against which she lay to be fitted for her task. Now there was added to her the environment of the night and the sea and the greatness and tragedy of her mission.

"She receded into the night astern as the destroyer raced on to lay the light buoy that was to be her guide, and those on board saw her no more. She passed thence into the hands of the small craft, whose mission it was to guide her, light her and hide her in the clouds of the smoke screen.

"There was no preliminary bombardment of the harbour and the batteries as before the previous attempt; that was to be the first element in the surprise. A time table had been laid for every stage of the operation and the staff work beforehand had even included precise orders for the laying of the smoke barrage with plans calculated for every direction of wind. The monitors, anchored in their firing position far to seaward, awaited their signal: the great siege batteries of the Royal Marine Artillery in Flanders, among the largest guns that have ever been placed on land mountings, stood by likewise to neutralize the big German artillery along the coast and the airmen who were to collaborate with an aerial bombardment of the town waited somewhere in the darkness overhead. The destroyers patrolled to seaward of the small craft.

"The *Vindictive*, always at that solemn gait of hers, found the flagship's light buoy and bore up for where a coastal motor boat, commanded by Lieut. Slayter, R. N., was waiting by a calcium flare upon the old position of the Stroom Bank buoy. Four minutes before she arrived there and fifteen minutes only before she was due at the harbour mouth, the signal for the guns to open was given.

"Two motor boats under Lieut. Reid, R. N. R., and Lieut. Poland, R. N., dashed in toward the ends of the high wooden piers and torpedoed them. There was a machine gun on the end of the western pier and that vanished in the roar and the leap of flame and debris which called to the guns. Over the town a flame suddenly appeared high in air and sank slowly earthwards, the signal that the airplanes had seen and understood, and almost coincident with their first bombs came the first shells whooping up from the monitors at sea. The surprise part of the attack was sprung. The surprise, despite the German's watchfulness, seems to have been complete.

"Up to the moment when the torpedoes of the motor boats exploded there had not been a shot from the land—only occasional routine star shells. The motor launches were doing their work magnificently. These pocket warships, manned by officers and men of the Royal Naval Volunteer Reserve, are specialists at smoke production. They built to either hand of the *Vindictive's* course the likeness of a dense sea mist driving landward with the wind. The star shells paled and were lost as they sank in it; the beams of the searchlights seemed to break off short upon its front. It blinded the observers of the great batteries, when suddenly, upon the warning of the explosions, the guns roared into action.

"There was a while of tremendous uproar. The coast about Ostend is ponderously equipped with batteries, each with its name known and identified—Tirpitz, Hindenburg, Deutschland, Cecilia and the rest. They register from six inches up to monsters of fifteen-inch naval pieces in land turrets, and the Royal Marine Artillery fights a war long duel with them. These now opened fire into the smoke and over it at the monitors. The marines and the monitors replied. Meanwhile the airplanes were bombing methodically and the anti-aircraft guns were searching the skies for them. Star shells spouted up and floated down, lighting the smoke banks with spreading green fires, and these strings of luminous green balls, which airmen call "flaming onions," soared up to lose themselves in the clouds. Through all this stridency and blaze of conflict the old *Vindictive*, still unhurrying, was walking the lighted waters toward the entrance.

"It was then that those on the destroyers became aware that what had seemed to be merely smoke was wet and cold, that the rigging was beginning to drip, that there were no longer any stars—a sea fog had come on.

"The destroyers had to turn on their lights and use their sirens to keep in touch with each other. The air attack was suspended and the *Vindictive*, with some distance yet to go, found herself in gross darkness.

"There were motorboats to either side of her, escorting her to the entrance, and these were supplied with what are called Dover flares— enormous lights capable of illuminating square miles of sea at once. A Very pistol was fired as a signal to light these, but the fop and the smoke together were too dense for even the flares. The *Vindictive* put her helm over and started to cruise to find the entrance Twice in her wanderings she must have passed across it and at her third turn, upon reaching the position at which she had first lost her wav, there came a rift in the mist and she saw the entrance clear, the piers to either side and the opening dead ahead.

"The inevitable motor boat dashed up (No. 23, commanded by acting Lieut. Guy L. Cockburn, R. N.), raced on into the opening under a heavy and momentarily growing fire, and planted a flare on the water between the piers. The *Vindictive* steamed over it and on. She was in.

"The guns found her at once. She was hit every few seconds after she entered, her scarred hull broken afresh in a score of places and her decks and upper works swept.

"The machine gun on the end of the western pier had been put out of action by the motor boat's torpedo, but from other machine guns at the inshore ends of the pier, from a position on the front and from machine guns apparently firing over the eastern pier, there converged upon her a hail of lead. The after control was demolished by a shell which killed all its occupants, including Sub-Lieut. MacLachlan, who was in command of it. Upper and lower bridges and chart room were swept by bullets, and Commander Godsal, R. N., ordered his officers to go with him to the conning tower.

"There they observed that the eastern pier was breached some 200 yards from its seaward end, as though at some time a ship had been in collision with it. They saw the front of the town silhouetted again and again in the light of the guns that blazed at them; the night was a patchwork of fire and darkness.

"Immediately after passing the breach in the pier Commander Godsal left the conning tower and went out on deck, the better to watch the ship's movements. He chose his position and called in through the slit in the conning tower his order to starboard the helm. The *Vindictive* responded. He laid her battered nose to the eastern pier and prepared to swing her 320 feet of length across the channel.

"It was at that moment that a shell from the shore batteries struck the conning tower. Lieut. Sir John Alleyne and Lieut. V. A. C. Crutchley, R. N., were still within. Commander Godsal was close to the tower outside. Lieut. Alleyne was stunned by the shock. Lieut. Crutchley shouted through the slit to the commander, and receiving no answer rang the port engine full speed astern to help in swinging the ship.

"By this time, she was lying at an angle of about 40 degrees to the pier and seemed to be hard and fast, so it was impossible to bring her further round. After working the engines for some minutes to no effect Lieut. Crutchley gave the order to clear the engine room and abandon ship, according to the programme previously laid down.

"Engineer Lieutenant Commander Bury, who was the last to leave the engine room, blew the main charges by the switch installed aft. Lieut. Crutchley blew the auxiliary charges in the forward six-inch magazine from the conning tower. Those on board felt the old ship shrug as the explosive tore the bottom plates and the bulkheads from her. She sank about six feet and lay upon the bottom of the channel. Her work was done.

"Most of the casualties were incurred while the ship was being abandoned. The men behaved with just that cheery discipline and courage which distinguished them in the Zeebrugge raid. Petty Officer Reed found Lieut. Alleyne in the conning tower, still unconscious, and carried him aft under a storm of fire from the machine guns. Lieut. Alleyne was badly hit before he could be got over the side and fell into the water. Here he managed to catch hold of a boat fall, and a motor launch under Lieut. Bourke, R. N.V. R., succeeded in rescuing him and two other wounded men.

"The remainder of the crew were taken off by Motor Launch 254, under Lieut. Drummond, R. N.V. R., under a fierce fire. When finally, he reached the *Warwick* the launch was practically in a sinking condition. Her bows were shot to pieces. Lieut. Drummond was himself severely wounded. His second in command, Lieut. Ross, R. N.V. R., and one hand were killed. A number of others were wounded. The launch was found to be too damaged to tow and day was breaking.

"She and the *Warwick* were in easy range of the forts, so as soon as her crew and the *Vindictive's* survivors were transferred a demolition charge was placed in her engine room and she was sunk.

"Always according to programme, the recall rockets for the small craft were fired from the flagship at 2:30 a. m. The great red rockets whizzed up to lose themselves in the fog. They could not have been visible half a mile away, but the work was done and one by one the launches and motor boats commenced to appear from the fog, stopped their engines alongside the destroyers and exchanged news with them.

"There were wounded men to be transferred and dead men to be reported, their names called briefly across the water from the little swaying deck to the crowded rail above. But no one had seen a single enemy craft. The nine German destroyers who were out and free to fight had chosen the discreeter part."

THE M. L.'s IN TABULAR FORM

(Number Built for Allied Nations, 720)

DIMENSIONS

Length over all .... 79 ft. 7 in.
Length on the water line..............,.........78 ft. 9 in.
Extreme beam over guards ....12 ft. 5 in.
Beam on deck .... 12 ft. 1 in.
Draught to bottom of deadwood .... 3 ft. 1 in.
Full load displacement .... 78,000 lb.

CONSTRUCTION

Planking; yellow pine, $1\frac{1}{8}$ in. thick.

Frames; white oak, steam bent, $1\frac{3}{4}$ in. sided by $1\frac{3}{4}$ in. molded, spaced 12 in. center to center. Heavy frames at bulkheads, $2\frac{1}{4}$ in. by $2\frac{1}{4}$ in.

Deck planking; Oregon pine in strips, $2\frac{5}{8}$ in. wide by $1\frac{1}{8}$ in. thick.

Deck beams; white oak, sided $1\frac{3}{4}$ in., molded $2\frac{1}{2}$ in.

Keel; white oak, sided 4 in.

Keelson; yellow pine, 4 in. by 5 in.

Floors; galvanized wrought iron, $1\frac{1}{2}$ in. wide, $\frac{3}{4}$ in. thick at center, tapered to $\frac{3}{8}$ in. at ends.

Knees connecting frames to beams; wrought, 3 in. by $\frac{3}{8}$ in.

Upper clamp; yellow pine, $1\frac{3}{4}$ in. by $4\frac{1}{2}$ in.

Main clamp; yellow pine, $1\frac{1}{2}$ by $4\frac{1}{2}$ in.

Main clamp; yellow pine, $1\frac{1}{2}$ by $5\frac{1}{2}$ in.

Hogging clamp; yellow pine, $1\frac{1}{2}$ in. by $5\frac{1}{2}$ in.

Side keelson; yellow pine, $1\frac{3}{4}$ in. by $6\frac{1}{2}$ in.

Bilge stringer; yellow pine, $1\frac{1}{2}$ in. by $4\frac{1}{2}$ in.

Bulkheads; six steel, about $\frac{1}{8}$ in. thick, located at frames Nos. 6, 26, 40, 47, 52 and 71. The bulkheads at the ends of the gasoline compartment were made gasoline tight by the use of a special paint composed of litharge, glycerine and shellac.

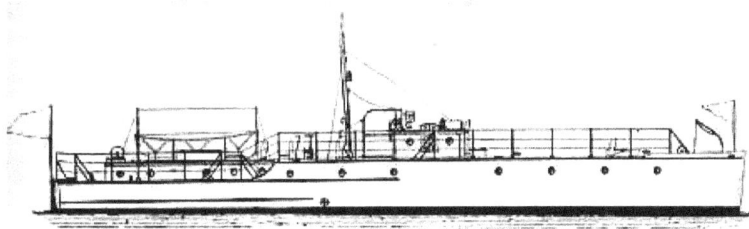

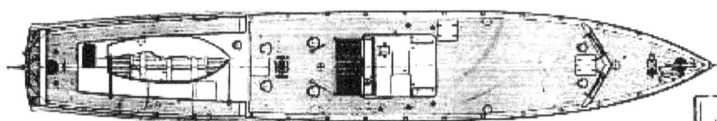

PLAN VIEW OF
CHART HOUSE

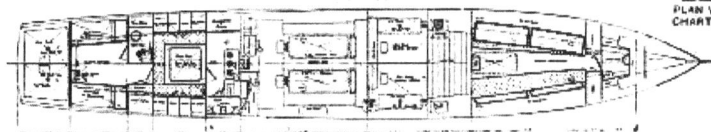

DECK PLAN

INTERIOR ARRANGEMENT

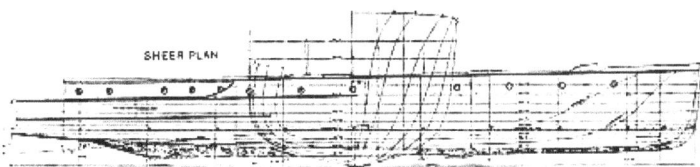

SHEER PLAN

BODY PLAN

HALF-BREADTH PLAN

The design of the British M. L.'s.

It will be noticed from the outboard profile and arrangement plans that the difference in appearance between one of these boats and a modern express cruiser of about the same size and power is slight, except for the long fore deck of the M. L., which is kept clear of all obstructions to give a wide angle of fire to the short-calibre 13-pounder mounted just forward of the low chart house, over the midship fuel tanks. The reader may have noticed that it was found necessary later to build up a permanent shelter for the helmsman just aft of the trunk.

In form these boats are nothing more than big runabouts. In fact, if the scale were changed to give a length of 35 ft., they would have not only the proper proportions but about the correct displacement for a high-speed runabout of that size.

Machinery

The power plant consists of a twin screw installation of two 6- cylinder, 4-cycle air-starting and reversing motors having cylinders 10 in. bore by 11 in. stroke, built by the Standard Motor Construction Co., of Jersey City, N. J. These motors, which are rated by the builder at 220 hp. at 400 r.p.m., are directly connected to the three-bladed propellers, 42-in. diameter by 63-in. pitch.

An auxiliary set, also made by the Standard Motor Construction Co., includes an air compressor, a 4½-kw. generator and a bilge and fire pump. The total capacity of the tanks is 2,100 gal., giving a radius of action of 750 nautical miles at 19 knots and 1,000 nautical miles at 15 knots.

The maximum speed obtained on trial varied on the different boats from about 19¼ knots to almost 21 knots.

The 720 M. L.'s were built for the allied nations by the Elco Co., at Bayonne, N. J., Montreal and Quebec.

LEONAUR

ALSO FROM LEONAUR

AVAILABLE IN SOFTCOVER OR HARDCOVER WITH DUST JACKET

ESCAPE FROM THE FRENCH *by Edward Boys*—A Young Royal Navy Midshipman's Adventures During the Napoleonic War.

THE VOYAGE OF H.M.S. PANDORA *by Edward Edwards R. N. & George Hamilton, edited by Basil Thomson*—In Pursuit of the Mutineers of the Bounty in the South Seas—1790-1791.

MEDUSA *by J. B. Henry Savigny and Alexander Correard and Charlotte-Adélaïde Dard* —Narrative of a Voyage to Senegal in 1816 & The Sufferings of the Picard Family After the Shipwreck of the Medusa.

THE SEA WAR OF 1812 VOLUME 1 *by A. T. Mahan*—A History of the Maritime Conflict.

THE SEA WAR OF 1812 VOLUME 2 *by A. T. Mahan*—A History of the Maritime Conflict.

WETHERELL OF H. M. S. HUSSAR *by John Wetherell*—The Recollections of an Ordinary Seaman of the Royal Navy During the Napoleonic Wars.

THE NAVAL BRIGADE IN NATAL *by C. R. N. Burne*—With the Guns of H. M. S. Terrible & H. M. S. Tartar during the Boer War 1899-1900.

THE VOYAGE OF H. M. S. BOUNTY *by William Bligh*—The True Story of an 18th Century Voyage of Exploration and Mutiny.

SHIPWRECK! *by William Gilly*—The Royal Navy's Disasters at Sea 1793-1849.

KING'S CUTTERS AND SMUGGLERS: 1700-1855 *by E. Keble Chatterton*—A unique period of maritime history-from the beginning of the eighteenth to the middle of the nineteenth century when British seamen risked all to smuggle valuable goods from wool to tea and spirits from and to the Continent.

CONFEDERATE BLOCKADE RUNNER *by John Wilkinson*—The Personal Recollections of an Officer of the Confederate Navy.

NAVAL BATTLES OF THE NAPOLEONIC WARS *by W. H. Fitchett*—Cape St. Vincent, the Nile, Cadiz, Copenhagen, Trafalgar & Others.

PRISONERS OF THE RED DESERT *by R. S. Gwatkin-Williams*—The Adventures of the Crew of the Tara During the First World War.

U-BOAT WAR 1914-1918 *by James B. Connolly/Karl von Schenk*—Two Contrasting Accounts from Both Sides of the Conflict at Sea D uring the Great War.

www.ingramcontent.com/pod-product-compliance
Lightning Source LLC
Chambersburg PA
CBHW032050080426
42733CB00006B/227